Abdelhak Lamiri, born in Algeria, holds an MBA and a PhD in Finance in addition to post-doctoral studies and research at LEREPS, University of Toulouse. Abdelhak has published six books on economics and management issues, the latest of which was *The Economics of the Future,* and several related articles. He is a specialist on macroeconomic issues and their interactions with corporate management themes. His long field experience enabled him to incorporate the use of inputs from many disciplines in solving concrete problems. Currently he is Head of Scientific Research at INSIM SUP, a private establishment accredited by the Ministry of Higher Education and Scientific Research.

To all my family members.

In memory of my former professor, Peter F. Drucker.

To Thomas D. Willett, who kindly supervised my PhD dissertation at Claremont University.

Abdelhak Lamiri

GLOBAL SCIENCE: THE LAST OPTION BEFORE COLLAPSE

AUSTIN MACAULEY PUBLISHERS™

LONDON • CAMBRIDGE • NEW YORK • SHARJAH

A CIP catalogue record for this title is available from the British Library.

ISBN 9781035851973 (Paperback)
ISBN 9781035851980 (Hardback)
ISBN 9781035852000 (ePub e-book)
ISBN 9781035851997 (Audiobook)

www.austinmacauley.com

First Published 2024
Austin Macauley Publishers Ltd®
1 Canada Square
Canary Wharf
London
E14 5AA

Table of Contents

Preface

This book is mainly an economics book, but a very specific one. It intends to anchor this discipline or science into Global Science, yet to be created in order to fill out a missing gap in our world of knowledge to overcome most of the deficiencies that plague our modern planet. We have shaped a dangerous world where future generations may well be condemned to live in hell on Earth. And we do not know how to fix the chaos we leave our children as a poisoned heritage. But Global Science blends many relevant disciplines and sciences whenever it would be useful to do so. The history of science and human behaviour is confusing. We have little adequate knowledge to be able to discern with satisfaction what might shape a Nazi or a Mother Teresa. We have some clues, but very few certainties. We do not know how to create nations and institutions that are equal to the ethics advocated by the majority of humans. Advocated, but not lived! The social formations that we build quickly become the masters and we humans the slaves subjected to their modes of operation. The room for manoeuvre that was thought to be sufficient to control social, economic, political and environmental systems is rapidly shrinking to imprison the average citizen. In modern Western countries, democracy is largely confiscated by visible and invisible lobbies, powerfully organised and endowed with colossal resources. In the formations of the former or still socialist countries, political monopoly will immediately create a powerful machinery to suppress all dissent and erect despotism as the ultimate dogma of 'social equality' and 'the fight against human exploitation.' Certainly, within these models, we have watered-down versions where a charismatic leader for a period, or a more peaceful nation, gives the illusion that the question of power and building social systems would be practically under control.

The greatest planetary danger lies at the level of human subjectivity. It is a pandemic that cannot be eradicated, but we can only maximise its control and reduce its harmful impacts. In semantics, one can defend everything. During the

COVID-19 crisis, left-wing economists analysed the phenomenon as a result of the advent of neoliberalism in China. The reckless risk-taking of developing viruses in laboratories that are not sufficiently controlled and the development of free markets for exotic animals were pointed out as new logic of the capitalist system. Right-wing economists recall that the development of exotic animal markets originated in the great famine in China between 1958 and 1961. Estimates of the disaster vary between 15 million (government) and 60 million (contemporary Chinese journalists and researchers) deaths. Natural events and catastrophic economic and scientific policies were the main culprits. It was the era of the famous leap forward. It was at this time that many Chinese began to eat animals that had previously been untouched (dogs, snakes, rats etc.). So how do we tell the difference? With the tools and methods we have at hand, it would be almost impossible to have even very approximate estimates of the degree of significance of the different causes that prevailed for the emergence of COVID-19. This is just one example. It is impossible to eliminate contrary opinions. But in social science, we have a problem of quantitative estimates of causes and consequences.

Introduction

Historically, nations have been shaped by a series of two types of decisions: opportunities or revolutions, some of which are modest in scope, while others are more rare and revolutionary. The first are sequences of decisions that partially change the social structure of a nation. For example, Bismarck's introduction of a social security system against illness and ageing. The opportunity was to avoid a communist revolution by the working class. But by socialising the risks, a significant breakthrough was introduced in the way modern nations operate. Dozens of such reforms will shape the architecture of many countries. But revolutions will introduce more systemic and profound upheavals that will modify all the achievements and modes of interaction of economic and political actors. The French Revolution in 1789 is the archetype of a profound overhaul of the economic, social and political architecture of a nation. However, it is the forces at work, the different active social components that will privilege their philosophies and their orientations in the modes of operation of the new structure. Even if the latter is inspired by a rigorously established doctrine, as the Bolshevik Revolution of 1917 is supposed to be, it is the most prominent political activists who lay the essential foundations of the future economic and social formation.

Modern nations have been shaped by one method or another. The current forms are the outcome of these modes of progression, sometimes simple reforms and occasionally large-scale revolutions. Even if the line between the two is sometimes blurred, we can retain that profound economic, social and political transformations have taken place, starting from these two types of configurations. But, there is a third that has never been tested for several reasons. When nations have not reached an exorbitant complexity, these forms of mutations can, under certain conditions, produce forms of human organisations that are 'tolerable,' in the sense that they do not appear to be going in the direction of a predictable self-destruction. Some even appear to many citizens as suitable, most would mention the Scandinavian countries for the many socio-economic achievements integrated into their ways of operating. It is quite holy to note that no system is unanimously agreed upon, which is quite reasonable. There will never be a creation of an ideal economic and social formation. But even the nations that have made the most spectacular progress are discovering with fright that what we considered colossal efforts in building advanced nations are in fact too little and in reality dangerous. During the thirty glorious years, we thought we had acquired a lot of knowledge about the dynamics of the evolution of our societies. And, if a social formation is lagging behind in the process of architecting efficient sets, it is simply due to the political will of its leaders. Today we come to the observation and conclusion that what we have built up, even the most accomplished forms, are insufficient, too approximate and even worse dangerous in the long run.

The various economic, health and environmental crises that we have experienced bring us back to our own deficiencies. But the most frightening thing is yet to come. The COVID-19 episode has revealed our deficiencies in terms of prevention and management of disasters. And, what we are doing in terms of prevention of economic, social and especially environmental crises is even more lamentable. The price that we risk making future generations pay could reach proportions that are unimaginable today. The two forms of social and economic formation structuring that had prevailed in the past are completely inoperative to face these new types of challenges. So, it remains for us to be more innovative in terms of building new and totally revolutionary social forms in order to have a chance to get out of it. The third method, theoretically much more rigorous and potentially more promising, has never been tested as such. It is the core of a discipline or science that has yet to be developed: 'Global Science.' This is the main purpose of this book. It is the beginning of a reflection on a theme that requires the involvement of a large number of experts and the mobilisation of all the intelligence of citizens in order to make a difference. We can no longer rely on only two past methods to create radically different societies capable of rising to the level of the planetary risks that weigh on our modern nations, but it is an enormous work that requires the collaboration of many people and multiple specialities. Just like a complex project such as landing a person on the moon, the international space station or any other, it requires the coordination of hundreds of people working towards the same goal. If in the hard sciences, we have learned a lot about these approaches, in social sciences we are still in our early stages. In this work, we expand our investigations on social, political and economic determinants of historical evolutions of nations to see if we could impact their trajectories. We evaluate the knowledge gap that prevents us from doing so and acting on the perils facing us. After a profound scientific diagnosis, we present the alternatives facing us in a crossroads full of dangers and opportunities for mankind.

Part I: An Unprecedented Area

World economic history has shown an incredible continuity in the process of near-universal stagnation until the beginning of the nineteenth century. This is not to say that there have not been episodically flourishing civilisations. The examples are too numerous to ignore. Historians and experts in the various social sciences have suggested the root causes of discontinuities (see Eric H Cline, 8) in the performance of civilisations. However, it must be said that, in general, all the world's nations were in a state of near stagnation. It would have been impossible for growth to have come close to 0.5% per year. An income of $100 per capita 2000 years ago would have yielded $2 148,400 of income per person, which is outside the prowess of the most powerful modern nation. Yet it is almost impossible to live decently on an income of one hundred dollars a year. Current statistics show that the poorest countries have an average income of $700 per year. Growth is a recent phenomenon. Like stagnation, inequalities have been present in a strong way throughout history. According to Piketty's (22) extensive work, which is a reference in the field, globally around 10% of the population took 90% of the wealth of the different countries. During the twentieth century, 70% of the world's wealth was distributed as wages and the rest as capital income, according to Piketty.

We therefore need to assess progress and compare it with past performance to support a balanced assessment. It is easy to demand the impossible or to evaluate a situation in relation to an idea, but a comparison with the past would be the first form of assessing progress. If we had objectives, the situation would only be better. The goal, however, of securing the continuity of life on Earth is not unknown to anyone. Improving living standards without further increasing inequality would also be a reasonable purpose, but both of these targets began to be problematic in the early 1980s. The economic, social and environmental damage caused is a strong challenge and leads us to conclude that we have unleashed deadly perils that we no longer control. The two forms of social structuring of the past are no longer able to manage the threats that we ourselves have created. Do we have alternatives? In the past, it was thought logical that social structuring was done through incremental reforms or political revolutions.

Marx considered that the process of evolution of social formations was independent of human consciousness. The evolution of material reality (structure) determined the superstructure (laws, arts, religion) outside of any human will: this is historical materialism. The transition from slavery to feudalism and then to capitalism was explained by the mutations that occurred in the economic sphere and their consequences on the dynamics of the class struggle. Human intervention can slightly accelerate or delay the process, but its course and destination (communism) are irreversible

We have been left with this for many decades. Nations were shaped by reforms, revolutions or minor, but astronomical decisions, and the result is technology and social upheaval on a scale we can hardly control. The outcome is increasingly difficult to predict. The reasons are multiple and some of them will be revealed. But others more abundant are already exposed to us or will be exposed by many researchers. We are left with the last chance formula, the mixed conceptualisation: a science animated by our best researchers and fuelled by the intelligence of all. The methodology requires long development. It is the fundamental purpose of this book. It requires the development of new paradigms. It allows us to devise new social forms more in line with a global equilibrium within modern societies that have lost their bearings and their priorities.

The stage is set. Having said that, we already have in the human, social and natural sciences the essential conceptualisations that we need to act. It is a question of harmonising and combining them with a minimum of new input. But in the new method of social conceptualisation, there is no hero or genius who would have produced alone or in a small group the whole or most of the fundamental schemes that allow this social architecture. It is especially the mobilisation of an impressive number of brains that would allow this feat. However, at a time when we need to better design our nations, a challenge of tremendous complexity is becoming an absolute priority: repairing the lack of equilibriums that we have created ourselves, through ignorance and/or greed, within the various ecosystems of our planet. It is necessary to act in both directions simultaneously in order to overcome these two deficits, from which the two deficiencies emanate and which are self-perpetuating and feed each other in a vicious circle. One problem cannot be solved without solving the second one. Two challenges are imposed on us at a time when we are beginning to doubt our ability to build ethical, fairer, freer and more environmentally friendly nations.

Immense Challenges Ahead

Within the two issues that are at the heart of our analysis, we are faced with numerous themes that are only very partially analysed and addressed. Social sciences have reached a large gap with hard sciences. The capacities of the latter to create products and services that affect community life are far from being domesticated by the former. Thus, it is about the polluting technologies for which the social, economic and political organisation has evolved very little to control their consequences. The gap is widening and seriously threatening the human systems created to collapse. It is largely the gap that has been created between the humanities and social sciences on the one hand, and the hard sciences on the other, that is responsible for the upheavals we have experienced in recent decades. The economic, social and political structures and mechanisms that we have put in place have been unable to cope with the onslaught of hard science innovations. The upheavals brought about by the scientific revolutions have created a serious gap between the human structuring modes and the perils induced by these revolutions.

Robotics, ICT, nanotechnologies, quantum products and others have brought human systems in need of innovation to their knees. There are no fundamental differences between the human organisation systems of the 1950s and those of the 1990s. We have remained static in the face of great technological changes. We will present some themes that seem relevant to our problematic. They concern for the most part the very slow evolution process of social sciences.

Intuitive and Analytical Minds

Human occupations have always been linked to executive or decision-making roles. These can be simple, repetitive or complex and have immense consequences. A car salesman might have a prior agreement to decide to give a 5% discount to customers he considers worthy of loyalty. His decision has a limited impact on the future of the company. But his CEO must fight back against aggressive competitors who have already taken 30% of the firm's market share. How should the former decide and how should the latter make his decision? A few mistakes by the salesman will have a small impact on the company's future. But a mistake by the CEO can be fatal. The decision-making process is then different. Even more important is the decision of a top policy maker to intervene or not in order to curb a recession that could be self-correcting or deepen and turn into a depression. Even worse, a country's top leaders are considering various options for mobilising and channelling resources to address global warming. They have relatively little time to finalise their decisions, but the consequences would be extremely far-reaching. The types of decisions are diverse and complex. They are summarised in a simple matrix such as that shown in Figure 1. It also shows the decision preparation typologies for each case.

But the case that interests us most would be the third one: we can have relatively mild weather (a few months) but an error of judgment would be devastating: this would be the case of the environmental problem or the choice of social formation typologies. Faced with problems of such magnitude, we have two types of decision-makers: the intuitive and the analytical actors (Frantz Rieger and Durhane Wong-Rieger, 10). An intuitive person is one who puts his or her own biases, viewpoints and subjectivities above all other considerations. In 2017, against the advice of the vast majority of scientists, the American president decided to withdraw from the Paris COP 21 Agreement, possibly putting the entire planet at risk. This is an intuitive choice given that the vast majority of scientists who specialise and study the issue have diametrically opposed points of view. There are always a few scientists who have doubts about the conclusions of the majority. We always have this phenomenon in science. However, models and an impressive number of specialists in the field alert us to the urgency and the profound reality of the phenomenon. In general, a human intuition, not subjected to scientific validation protocols, has a very high probability of being inaccurate. Many studies indicate that this is the case.

In a company, when you double the production and sales, you might think that you have to double the storage volume, but mathematically this would be a mistake. The storage volume varies according to the square root of the production (Wilson's formula). But the author who proved beyond a reasonable doubt the irrationality of pure intuition without analysis remains unquestionably Frederick Taylor. We remember him especially for his famous scientific organisation of work (SOW) which revolutionised the way of conceiving and executing work in workshops, factories and construction sites. It would be tedious to describe his analytical method, the benefits it has brought to humanity and its shortcomings. The result on productivity is impressive, but its impact on human motivation is very problematic.

However, our concern is quite different. Human beings have always worked in workshops and built buildings (administrations, housing). Why haven't they discovered Taylor's methodology? Simply because they worked more by intuition than by process analysis. Taylor, as a good engineer, did the opposite. He was one of the pioneer scientists in the field of analysis by scientific processes of the workplaces where people sweat, perform and produce the goods that have freed human societies from the burden of effort. Thus, it has permitted millions of people to become lawyers, doctors, and professors allowing few to produce for many. The fact that this explosion of productivity has allowed some people to become richer, faster and more intensely than others is a completely different reality from its goals. What challenges us is that analysis allows human beings to free themselves from the yoke of non-validated intuition. Taylor liberated himself and millions of humans from the slavery of pure intuition not tested by scientific logic.

When dealing with highly complex problems, an intuitive manager pretends to listen to the scientists, but draws his response from his subjectivity, his experience; in short, from his deep intuitions. Sometimes intuition can be good and even innovative. However, it should be analysed in order to distinguish between good and destructive intuition. The former is useful and can lead to

23

substantial progress in all areas. When confirmed, good intuition sometimes allows spectacular progress. But when applied without validation, without testing, it can lead to immeasurable debacles. According to numerous studies, most developing countries, specifically those that are struggling to make progress, have developed an overly intuitive culture (Frantz Rieger, 10). An alarming proportion of the decisions taken are based on mere invalidated intuition of decision-makers: from the top to the lowest level of the country, which may include the lowest hierarchical structures of local administration, the vast majority of important or unimportant decisions are taken solely based on the impression of the leaders.

In a country, there are millions of decisions made by thousands of persons at different levels. If 95% or a large number of the decisions reflect only the perceptions and often only the interests of the leaders, then we are bound to have a 'Brownian society,' a social formation torn on all sides by a multitude of contradictory decisions and is stagnating. Substantial improvement in economic and social performance would be impossible. One of the essential tasks of leaders would be to change the way the country operates, particularly its top leaders, from an intuitive mode to an analytical mode. However, changing the decision-making culture of a country is not easy. It is not impossible either. Even countries that have built up analytical cultures over many decades are not immune to a counter-revolution in this area. The United States reneging on its global warming commitments is tangible proof of this. It was decided on pure intuition, while the vast majority of scientists agree on the human responsibility for the origins of pollution. A tiny minority is sceptical, but the intuition of the president of the United States has prevailed over the rest. Our perception often plays tricks on us. President Trump's administration has tapped into a slogan that has hit home 'America First.' It challenges the fact that the United States has a large disequilibrium of the balance of payments deficits with the rest of the world and contributes more than other nations to the funding of international institutions such as the UN, WHO and others. Many Americans thought this was unfair. It also seems to be true.

President Trump had thought that he had found, by his own intuition, a gigantic flaw in the way the country was being run that no other leader or internal institution had discovered. Many citizens considered this situation untenable and did not understand why no other leader had corrected this gross injustice.

In fact, the United States has always known that it was generous in the eyes of the world and assumed this fact. This situation could continue indefinitely as long as the dollar remains a dominant currency in the international reserves of various countries. This allows them to finance huge deficits and manage a massive debt without having to worry too much about how to finance it. If all countries reduce their percentage of dollar holdings to 15% or 20%, the US economy would pay a terrible price and, in the future, would not be able to finance these deficits, fight severe economic crises as easily and attract as much world savings. The gains from these mechanisms are X times greater than the so-called excessive contributions to international institutions. A significant part of the economic growth comes from this unique phenomenon, but it is ignored by the advocates of 'America first' and 'excessive US generosity.' The danger of decisions by perception is that you always deal with a small part of reality, and what you leave out may be a thousand times what you consider. The same is true for extreme right-wing parties that are against immigration and blame it for all the problems of their own country, often for wrongs that originate elsewhere. But how to compensate these same immigrants for the severe droughts, destruction of their biodiversity, the shrinking of their living resources in their countries caused by global warming and pollution from developed countries? Not to mention the after-effects of colonialism, corruption of local politicians, over-exploitation of their resources, etc. Here again, we consider a part of reality as being the whole picture.

The Three Key Questions

However, when the vast majority of a country's decisions are of the analytical type, then we will have millions of relevant and coherent choices that will not fail to move the social formation in the desired direction. For the crucial decisions, it is vital to consider them after a rigorous methodology has been carried out. When designing a plan to respond to a severe economic or political crisis, when considering a serious fight against global warming or when wanting to drastically reduce social inequalities we find ourselves in the third square of our decision matrix.

Decision Matrix

Consequences
Huge Minimal

	Huge consequences	Minimal Consequences
Short time	Viruses Pandemics	Discounts on sale Years end gifts
Long time	Fight against global warming Reducing Inequalities	Improve confort of waiting rooms

The four decision types require different responses and action methodologies. The situation in square 1 requires preventive planning. Response plans are established in advance with specific preparations. Each time, we evaluate and improve the selected measures. Square 2 requires decentralisation with slight control devices. Section 4 involves a large degree of decentralisation with small-scale evaluations over long periods of time. Square number 3 is the one that particularly concerns us. We need at least a few months of preparation before we finalise a rigorous, comprehensive and concerted action plan. Misconceptions will lead to disastrous consequences for the future of the country and even of mankind. The long time does not mean very elastic. Sometimes we have serious limits. If we go beyond a few months or at most one or two years before acting quickly and vigorously, we risk terrible consequences. Long time only means that we have a period of time that allows the methodology of 'Global Science' to unfold. This is where the methodology presented in chapter three is applied, but the core of the resolution of the system formulation revolves around the answer to three key questions:

1. What does science know about the issue and what do we still need to know to make the best decisions?
2. What are the experiences already made in this field with the identified successes and failures?
3. What are the lessons learned?

Each of these three questions needs to be elaborated. For any vital decision, we must go through these three steps. The first is to summarise the most important knowledge in the field. Summaries are often carried out by the best specialists in the field. The answers are best used when they are categorised as safe or high, medium or low probability knowledge. It would also be wise to identify the understanding that we lack in order to increase our chances of success and to make sure that we budget for the necessary research projects. This is what we are trying to do with the global warming problem within different governmental commissions, NGOs or international institutions (UN). The second question is essential to identify the best practices and integrate them into the final plan. The last question allows us to summarise, simplify and provide the specialists from different disciplines with the essential contents to know and add to their own knowledge to improve the level of solution. The methodology will be detailed later in this book, but we can already see the usefulness of the approach on an individual and collective level. When we have a problem of vital importance, we do not have the right to make a decision if we do not have the answers to these famous questions, both at the overall and micro level. When managers or a team are asked to reorganise a company, if they have not grasped the requirements of the three questions, they can only produce incomplete options, which are sometimes purely intuitive and often far from the optimal alternatives. Sometimes we refer to these considerations without structuring them in this way. We have enough information about what is known, what is unknown and the best practices to make informed choices. This helps to embed an analytical culture in the country. Then the millions of decisions made by citizens in one year of activity will be more coherent, more coordinated and closer to achieving the optimum.

However, on many occasions, many countries have overly diffused cultures of intuitive and untested decisions. Thus, massive resources and human energies will be wasted because the options chosen are based on fragile foundations. Developing countries are the biggest victims. The percentage of intuitive decisions that are made with little thought is so high that the country is caught in a Brownian whirlpool from which it is impossible to escape. Too often, just remembering or asking ourselves these three questions would make us humble. We then measure our level of ignorance and the degrees of knowledge required to make informed choices. We become modest. We are urged to improve ourselves rather than play the scholar in all fields as many politicians do. We become aware of the complexity inherent in any option and we estimate the complications related to the decision-making process. Without asking these questions, we would think of ourselves as a super human who has all the answers. These questions should also be part of the journalistic lexicon when questioning senior officials. When you ask these questions, you do not always have a clear picture. Sometimes the subject is so controversial and confusing that we do not have a clear view of the situation, but at least we will know. There would be answers like 'among Ph.Ds in climatology, people who have done more than five years of research on global warming, more than 85% think that the main cause is human economic activities.'

Science Takes Revenge

Science takes revenge is a maxim that is voluntarily accepted for hard sciences. Some people die because of self-medication. A person who takes pain relief drugs to soothe meningitis for more than ten days can die because of his audacity to play the doctor when he is not. Many people died because they had built villas in earthquake zones without taking technical standards into consideration. Often it is simple bricklayers who construct the building. Obviously, there is often collusion with the specialised administrative departments. When the earthquake strikes, a large proportion of the people die, as a result of the collapse of their houses. Yet these misfortunes could have been avoided. When the laws of science are not respected, they will end up taking revenge. This sentence is readily accepted in natural sciences, physics, chemistry, mathematics and so on. But, we hesitate or ignore it too often when it comes to social and human sciences.

However, an in-depth analysis shows that the same phenomenon occurs in the soft sciences. When a country creates abundance and avoids creating a social parachute (buying and using the available working hours to allow citizens to make a healthy rebound) it exposes itself to crimes, thefts, social chaos, and lack of civic responsibilities and so on. The loss of financial resources, human lives and suffering is enormous but untold. This is what helps many officials to hide the countless harm they inflict on their citizens. The harm caused is imperceptible and can hardly be attributed to one person or group of citizens. If an unqualified person were to perform heart surgery, they would be quickly identified and incriminated. But the position of President of the Republic, especially in an underdeveloped country, allows one to get away with all sorts of mistakes with disastrous consequences.

Take a simple example. It is often rightly stated that a comparison is not good enough because there are so many factors that could differentiate two countries: resources, geostrategic aspects, political structure, and sociology of the countries and a whole host of other parameters. You can always find circumstances to justify any difference in performance, up to a certain reasonable point. But there are limits to any justification by third and fourth-degree mechanisms. Consider a staggering fact. In 1963, Venezuela's GDP was $9.8 billion; South Korea's was $3.9 billion. In 2018, the GDP of the first country was 173 billion while that of the Asian country reached 1619 billion dollars, more than eight times more. Much can be written about the reasons that contributed to this difference. We should not forget that South Korea is one of the poorest countries in the world and Venezuela is one of the richest with the largest oil reserves in the world. South Korea has benefited from very little international aid but has financed its development mainly through international bank credits, mainly from Germany. However, it was millions of decisions at all levels that helped shape the differences in performance. Science has taken its revenge on Venezuela. Its GDP in 2018 should have exceeded 3,200 billion dollars considering its potential, but the most important potential is science, human resources motivation and the political, administrative and social architecture of a country. With each passing year, Venezuela loses more than 3,000 billion dollars of wasted production: science takes revenge.

We could give many examples without ever providing an exhaustive picture. Often, thousands and millions of human lives, horrible distress and catastrophic threats are initiated by incomprehensible choices. It is very often the case that the categories of people who pay the heaviest price are not the decision-makers, as the saying goes: 'When the rich wage war it's the poor who die.' We do not have enough clarification on the performance discrepancies between countries. Surveys conducted are scattered and insufficient. They focus only on quantifiable variables, whereas qualitative data can provide more clarity on the reasons for successes and failures. We can learn valuable lessons from this by digging deeper into the variables that led to the performance patterns. Still, there are valuable insights to consider in this area. It is valid to look to international experiences to learn from what is replicable. For example, we might know that South Korea's extraordinary growth is mainly due to the channelling of resources to human development, quality industrial policies and the entrenchment of an analytical culture.

Millions of annual decisions are made by qualified people with an analytical culture and the information and vision to avoid the Brownian effect. We learn more from success stories than from failures. We often hear politicians say: 'We must learn from the mistakes of others.' This statement is partly correct. But there is something better. One is well advised and informed by the successes rather than by the blunders of others. It is not useless to be informed about the setbacks of our fellows. This could prevent us from doing the same, but the number of possible mistakes is almost unlimited. Avoiding some of them will not be of much help. What is the point of knowing 40 mistakes to avoid when there are tens of thousands of other possible ones? On the other hand, the causes of success are limited and often transferable. It is then necessary to focus on them. It is better to know the underlying reasons for the successes of South Korea and Malaysia than the origins of the setbacks in Venezuela. Time and other resources are scarce: it is better to focus on what is more promising. We learn best from the successes of others because the number of possible mistakes is almost unlimited.

Model Transfer Problems

Following the globalisation trend, social and human sciences are becoming more and more homogenised throughout the world. Various departments of economics, philosophy, sociology and others are delivering globally codified patterns of thought and models as acquired and universally recognised knowledge and know-how. At the most, a chapter on local specificities is added. Knowledge in social sciences and humanities is universalised just like hard sciences, and this has many advantages. When one examines the cultures and management practices of many companies and administrations around the world, one is surprised by the abundant similarities. There are no big differences between the management tools used in Europe and Malaysia or Korea. Accounting, inventory management and organisational systems show many similarities. There are some pronounced differences at the level of human resources management. This is where the different practices are most diverse. It is therefore easy to defend the standardisation of teaching to a certain extent. We cannot have an English sociology and another Senegalese one. We first try to identify what is universal in sociology and then identify local specificities. This complex theme requires many studies to be able to sort out what is universal and what is specific.

Fortunately, we have many universal models that need to be taught and that are valuable for almost all countries. Excessive money issuance in times of euphoric economic growth would cause multi-digit inflation in any country in the world. A project-based matrix organisation would be very useful for any infrastructure construction company in the world. High taxes on tobacco and alcohol discourage the production and consumption of these commodities. Examples of this type can be multiplied at will.

But we must be aware that this process of universalisation has its limits. It is fortunate that many—I would say most—of the lessons we have learned are useful all over the world. But we need to know how to draw the contours and limits of such openness. Sometimes, a theoretical scheme used out of its context can cause more damage, occasionally disasters, when one does not master its foundations. Is there a way to know what to transpose and in what circumstances? Despite the complexity of the problem, it would be possible to identify the parameters that explain and cause the damage. Let's first assume that this phenomenon can exist in the first place. We have examples of unfortunate transfers of inadequate patterns to contexts other than their own. In 1947, when Peter F Drucker introduced the first outline of what was to be called Management by Objectives (MBO) at General Electric, several variants were immediately reproduced by many other firms. Many of them benefited greatly from the practice. Those who used it as a tool for participation and integration of their human resources in the United States and Europe made significant progress in their companies, but when the scheme was introduced in many developing countries at the time, there was almost universal disappointment. The scheme had trouble operating. Why? The same is true for some macroeconomic schemes.

The Keynesian theory is one of the most famous and most adulated, and rightly so, in macroeconomics. It was used to curb the major crises of 1929, the subprime crisis and a significant part of the consequences of Covid-19. Neoliberalism makes this its critical target, but as soon as a severe crisis appears, the Keynesian therapeutic scheme is brought out to curb it. And we continue to live with this apparent contradiction: minor crises are ignored rather than treated; they tend to work themselves out, but major crises are relieved with the help of Keynesian therapy, which is disputed in the theoretical schemes taught. However, Keynesian theory has done very little to help developing countries during the major crises they have experienced. But why?

To the extent that the most French Keynesian economist François Perroux wrote in a famous article 'The Multiplier of Investments in the Third-World Countries' (22) that Keynesian theory has no validity in developing countries. Many exchanges came to the same conclusion in seminars on our central concern. We can give many other examples of transfers that have stumbled because of different contexts. But these few setbacks should not blind us to the fact that there are many more success stories. There have been many more efficacious transfers than setbacks. The number is incalculable. IBM was one of the very first companies in the 1930s and 1940s to practice lifetime employment and quality circles. These were transferred and perfected in Japan and became somewhat differentiated practices in many global institutions. The transfer of good practices and useful theoretical schemes should not be underestimated. We should not ignore these experiences when they are useful and relevant to the new environment that hosts them.

Now let us consider why in some cases these transfers of schemes turn out to be burdens rather than tools for improving performance. We need to develop expertise in this area or we will continue to make mistakes. This matter will be closely related to the 'Global Science' issue presented in this book. But there is a point on which we must focus our attention. We often do not pay enough awareness to the assumptions of the models or the good practices transferred. That said, let us remember once again that very often transpositions are successful, but when they are not, we need to examine the fundamental assumptions of the scheme or practice. For example, for the famous schema of proper functioning of a practice of management by objectives two assumptions are fundamental. One relates to the degree of integration and participation of human resources at all levels of the corporate hierarchy. In fact, some authors wanted to improve the scheme by talking about Participative Management by Objectives (PMBO), a useless concept because, although it was well understood, MBO already included it as an assumption of the appropriate functioning of the scheme.

But the most important thing is the second assumption. In the practice of MBO, each manager becomes the coach of his subordinates. Every month he reviews with them their achievements, helps them, coaches them and guides them to improve themselves and their performance before evaluating them much later. The underlying assumption is that the company's hierarchy is a pyramid shape where the higher up the ladder you go, the more skills, wisdom, experiences and willingness to help others improve. This would be true for some companies that have developed traditions and cultures of participation and promotion through skills. Businesses that do not have these characteristics must first acquire them before they can claim to work with the system at all. The vast majority of third-world businesses do not have these distinctive features. They therefore risk importing a scheme whose most fundamental assumptions are not met by their modes of operation. These businesses risk creating more conflicts than is necessary. Performance may even drop dramatically. A thorough examination of the models' assumptions is required before they can be transferred. Today, large companies and small and medium-sized enterprises practice some form of management by objectives but do not call it that. It is an inherent part of business management without being interested in its origin or its history. But maybe thousand-year-old civilisations have used it without characterising it as such. Hence, the complexity of looking for the historical origin of a concept or a practice.

The same is true of Keynesian theory. Aggregate demand management implies that the government regulates its expenditures according to the level of capacity utilisation by economic activity including the workforce. When unemployment is high and capacity utilisation is low, the government triggers a number of actions through its expenditures, credits, taxes, interest rates and the like to bring demand back to the level of full employment. We ignore the problems raised by the neoliberals and the famous natural rate of unemployment, which can be high despite government action and the coordination of fiscal and monetary policies. But, it is clear that when crises become severe, the dogma of non-interference by the government is abandoned in order to beg it to contain the crisis. The Great Depression, the Subprime Crunch and the COVID-19 crisis were largely curbed by Keynesian-type policies. Yet third-world countries have been underutilising resources for several decades. Countries that have pursued purely Keynesian policies have had very disappointing results.

From 2004 to 2014, taking advantage of an oil boom during the first years of this century, Algeria had injected into its economy more than 600 billion dollars in various economic recovery plans, more than 35% of GDP per year. The economic growth was a modest 2.5% on average per year over that period. After these different gigantic plans, the economy was more dependent on hydrocarbons and imports than before the recovery in the Keynesian style. It was not understood that the Keynesian doctrine helped to overcome cyclical problems and could not in any way emancipate a country from its structural constraints. Without explicitly stating it, Keynes was a market economy man. His hypotheses are related to the way the economy works: it has a good educational system; its microeconomic institutions are efficiently managed, entrepreneurship, innovation, research and development, and so on, function properly. Corruption does not reign supreme, and domestic supply is elastic to demand. The remaining problems would be broken confidence following a crisis, fear of the future, consumer worry and investor anxiety. All this can be remedied by a greater demand from the government, which will boost investments, purchases, employment and thus consumer confidence. However, aggregate demand does not correct deficient education, resource-destroying management, squandering, mismanagement, insufficient entrepreneurship, poor innovation, lack of research and development and so on. Keynesianism only works if its assumptions are fulfilled. So the country must have strong fundamentals to leverage Keynesian-style stimulus.

Before that, the country would be better off investing in education, management modernisation, research and development, rehabilitation of entrepreneurship, fighting corruption and a whole range of restructuring measures that will consolidate the country's fundamentals. So transferring Keynesian practices to a chaotic society is very often suicidal. This brings us back to the same conclusions. Before considering the transposition of a model, it is necessary to examine its assumptions and whether they are met within the new context of use. If the conditions for success are not met, then it is better to abstain.

Origins of Great Economic Ideas

It is scientifically very uncertain to trace the origin of an idea to any one personality, as many thinkers from different civilisations have dealt with various themes in countless degrees of detail. And researchers often do not go beyond the historical contours of their own civilisations. This is true for many sciences, but we will only consider the subject of our main inquiry: economics. We are not qualified to discuss other sciences. We will be concerned only with one of our most brilliant scholars and display his economic ideas that have been ignored for a long time by Western thinkers: Ibn Khaldoun, in particular his book the *Muqqadimah* (22). This work has been mainly analysed in terms of its historical and sociological contributions; but his economic ideas, although omnipresent in his chapters, were overlooked.

In this context, we will only mention a few of his great contributions to economics. It would be very wise to see our economists doing PhD dissertations and other academic research on this outstanding thinker. Ibn Khaldoun lived from 1332 to 1406. He travelled throughout the Maghreb and part of Egypt. When we go deeper into the economic readings of his works, we realise that a large part of the economic contributions attributed to Western economists were very intelligible in Ibn Khaldoun's analyses. The theory of supply, which states that supply creates its own demand (when one produces a good or service one also generates purchasing power to buy it) is attributed to the French economist Jean Baptiste Say (1767-1832), whereas it is more explicit in the writings of Ibn Khaldoun.

The Examples Abound

There are many more examples, but we will highlight a few significant contributions to situate the enormous contributions of this ignored thinker. Take a first case. The Scottish economist Adam Smith is credited with having devised the labour value of goods exchanged on the market. If it takes twice as much labour time to produce a pen as a pencil: the price of the pen will be twice as high as the price of the pencil. No need to go into details. Later, Karl Marx used this theory to show (according to his assumptions) that profit (surplus value) comes from human labour not paid by capitalists. Ibn Khaldoun said the same thing on many occasions and in particular: 'Now we should see that the capital earned and acquired through the exercise of a profession, is the price of the craftsman's work. There is nothing but work…So, we see that profits and gains are entirely or mainly the price of human labour…Power is the source of wealth. The influential person receives the labour and money of others.'

Indeed, Karl Marx elaborated more complex concepts and definitions to demonstrate this. But Ibn Khaldoun's ideas on labour value and products are exactly the same as those elaborated by Adam Smith and Karl Marx. Yet this thinker who developed them more than four centuries before the Western writer was not mentioned. We cannot affirm that there would not be a Chinese or Hindu or any other thinker who would have developed these same theories before. We have no information on this subject. But as far as we know, it is this illustrious thinker who produced the concepts of exploitation, surplus value and labour value. The fact that other economists have elaborated on the idea by introducing more details about costs, depreciation, etc. does not justify taking away from Ibn Khaldoun the primacy of the idea. In fact, Marx knew from his writings all the other details introduced by Ibn Khaldoun. The former simply formalised them with simple arithmetic.

Table 1

Over-taxation Leads to Laziness: Ibn Khaldoun the Misunderstood

His writings also contain the premises of the Quantity Theory of Money. But he is beginning to be credited with the so-called supply-side theory, which contains much of the 'too much tax kills the tax' mechanism. President Reagan quoted him specifically in one of his speeches. This is what Ibn Khaldoun said: When a dynasty remains faithful to the spirit of the body and superiority, it relies on Bedouinism, which means indulgence, generosity, humanity and respect for the property of others: at least in most cases. Also, individual taxes are low...later the tax exceeds the limits of fairness. The people lose all willingness for agricultural development. Many abandon the land. Sometimes tax authorities pretend to get out of trouble by increasing the tax rate. As a result, national income continues to decline and taxes to increase...Eventually, the fall of civilisation follows the disappearance of all agricultural possibilities. Ibn Khaldoun equates agriculture with national income because in his time it represented more than 90% of the GDP.

It is therefore Ibn Khaldoun who invented the theory of supply and not Arthur Laffer as some economists advocate. But Ibn Khaldoun's theory has been taken out of context and used for the wrong purpose. Neoclassical economists stipulated that taxation should be very minimal. For this reason, they often advocate tax reductions for businessmen so that they invest and create wealth for the whole society (trickle-down economics). However, recent experiences have mainly made employers richer and increased inequalities. Ibn Khaldoun spoke of taxing the working people, the peasants, the poor and not the rich businessmen. Moreover, in his time, taxes were mainly used to finance wars and opulence for the ruling class. Today, one can choose to improve education, the health system or infrastructure with a part of taxes. Ibn Khaldoun's contribution to the theory of supply is certain. But its interpretation and use by the modern political class is out of context with Ibn Khaldoun's original vision. We invite concerned researchers, especially those involved in doctoral dissertations, to examine the writings of Ibn Khaldoun on economic topics. There is a real untapped wealth in his books whose significance remains beneficial for contemporary problems.

Current Challenges and Tools of the Past

With the advent of a new millennium, the little-perceived messages of the last decades are becoming more and more palpable. New challenges appear to be inevitable and are putting human beings around the world at greater risk. First of all, classical fears are becoming more prevalent and more complex to identify. The problems of controlling economic crises, peace, pandemics and inequalities are classic concerns. They are regenerating under new characteristics but their essence has remained the same for many decades. In the past, the most feared threats were mainly in the economic field. We always had the perils of international or civil conflicts that could be exacerbated. The nuclear risk makes them more frightening. But all in all, what people are most concerned about is economic activity. Only activists and enlightened people would rank the environment as the dominant concern. It was the economic modes of operation that gave little comfort to individuals. A little bit of particular economic history would not hurt. The first economic theorists—Smith, Says, Ricardo—and others had begun to build it (the economy) by what we could call the descriptive-analytical method, like history, philosophy and a good dose of ethics. It was necessary to think about how to improve human welfare by creating conditions for improving productivity, especially since during almost all the previous centuries the economy was in a state of near stagnation. Several avenues were identified for this purpose, particularly the division of labour observed by Adam Smith in a pin factory. These early thinkers had finally identified labour as the source of all wealth. It is the volume of labour incorporated into a good that gives it its value.

Karl Marx took up the idea but elaborated it further. He developed concepts, definitions and mechanisms that showed that the profits made by businessmen came from the labour of workers. Ownership of the means of production by the capitalists allowed them to exploit the working masses. The latter therefore had to revolt to recover what had been expropriated from them. The 'science' developed by Marx reinforced his militancy.

Faced with such a serious turn of events, many analysts of the time either disagreed strongly with Marx or wanted to produce theoretical schemes that made a complete break with him. They came up with the marginal notion, which was one of the most powerful bases of neoliberal theory. The value of a good would not be the volume of work incorporated into it, but the satisfaction derived from the last unit of this good (marginal utility). Menger and Walras are credited with this approach which is strongly incorporated into neoclassical models. All the universities in the world still teach these schemes which have shown their usefulness and their limitations. These theoretical representations gave their followers two great satisfactions. The first was to eclipse the Marxist theory with its labour value which could eventually lead to serious social upheavals. The second was to give the illusion of bringing economics considerably closer to the natural sciences. In fact, the proposed schemes lend themselves considerably to the use of mathematics in their presentations. Walras did not hesitate to erect the equations of his famous general equilibrium which would be the apotheosis of the 'marginalist school.' The system would only hold under very restrictive assumptions: atomicity of economic agents, information, homogeneity, etc. The monument was superb but its usefulness was limited.

Fortunately, later on, many studies, particularly those of Marshall, made it possible to draw up partial equilibrium diagrams in which specific markets were analysed under particular conditions and from which economic policies could be implemented to improve the situation in a specific context. If we want to discourage tobacco, we tax it and we would obtain a better partial equilibrium without any strong intervention. The approach proved to be much more useful. When Keynes proposed a complementary scheme that showed that we can have a prolonged general disequilibrium, thanks to public intervention, we made a greater leap forward by seeing that we must help the system to get to equilibrium and not rely on automatic mechanisms that do not exist. But we have had a negative relic of these developments: the belief that economics is like a natural science and that it can be mathematised to the extreme, such as Newton's gravity equations.

The thirty glorious years had benefited from favourable conditions -the reconstruction after the Second World War; they had induced enviable performances in terms of growth, fight against unemployment and reduction of inequalities. An economic revolution was underway. But by the end of the 1970s, preparations for a counter-revolution were well prepared. The performances of the 1970s, with the resurgence of stagflation (joint inflationary pressures and recession), were interpreted as the beginning of a weakening, or worse, the inauguration of a failure of public interventionism. It was thought that the excessive involvement of the government in economic affairs had begun to derail the economic engine. Two shocks of unprecedented magnitude that had a severe impact on economic activity were ignored: the end of the fixed exchange rate and the oil price shocks.

The USA put an end to the fixed exchange rate system and started floating exchange rates. This led to enormous economic restructuring. Two oil shocks in 1873-74 and 1979-81 also caused major disturbances in economic activity and price levels. This decline in performance was simply interpreted as a failure of state intervention, and a theoretical blow was orchestrated to economics by the neoclassical school. Citizens panicked by a decade of repeated crises wanted to try something else. Politicians inspired by monetarist currents were brought to power and helped to strengthen international institutions with human resources dedicated to the neoclassical cause. The movement took root in the most powerful countries of the world. The changeover took place gradually and was established, consolidated and cemented by the domination of international institutions and, above all, by the control over the teaching of economics in the most prestigious institutions in the world. The collapse of the Berlin Wall gave an implicit and sometimes instinctive legitimacy to the neoliberal movement for a long period of time. It seemed as if we were heading towards a consensual continuity. An avalanche of Nobel Prizes conferred on the proponents of the neoliberal approach confirmed the relevance of monetarist narratives to the actors and spectators. However, the essence always ends up transcending propriety. Signals of various premonitions that had been imperceptible until then began to grow and become more and more noteworthy. Many developments convinced more and more citizens and economists that we were far from having found the path to sustainable development that had been thought possible with neoliberal policies.

At the beginning of the twenty-first century, mankind entered an era with very uncertain outcomes and the most treacherous challenges. Scientists warned us of the dangers of the future but these signals were largely ignored. In the economic sphere, the only satisfaction remained the control of inflation by most of the world's countries. It was one of the few variables that were under control, but perhaps at a major price.

Unemployment has become a major concern because of its volatility and resistance to traditional economic policies. The sector distribution of employment has changed considerably with the restructuring of the global economy. New jobs are being created mainly in ICT, robotics, nanotechnology, sophisticated services and therefore in professions that require high qualifications. Moreover, these jobs are not very sensitive to public programs, to the traditional government stimulus packages that target infrastructures and low-skilled labour-intensive sectors. The problem of unemployment is becoming less and less noticeable to the average person as many people discouraged by endless searches for work are withdrawing from the labour market. However, overall, this concern remains the most feared distress, especially for the most vulnerable and poorest segments of modern societies. A country without an adequate social safety net becomes a frightening menace for its fragile citizens.

The abrupt appearance of increasingly unexpected and more profound crises arouses the astonishment and then the indignation of citizens who are becoming more and more incapable of making sense of nonsense. And yet! They had been told about the gigantic steps taken by economics. Dozens of econometric models that mix thousands of equations should have alerted us to the possibility of the appearance of the terrible 2007-2009 Subprime Crisis. We had experienced the most severe crisis after that of 1929. However, these crises always appear in places where the market reigns. Where there is the least government, and the crisis appeared when market ultras removed most of the public controls on the financial sector. But we still have the Austrian interpretation of the crisis which points to low interest rates and abundant credit from the central bank as the source of these problems. But these same policies practised before had not induced such flagrant disequilibrium. The debate is long and tedious but the result is there: imbalances are bigger and more unpredictable. We are assured of the usefulness of some of these costly econometric models. We understand better the interactions between certain variables in a given context. However, with the numerous setbacks observed, their costs/benefits need to be reconsidered with greater scientific accuracy.

However, what emerges as more apparent and incomprehensible is the incompatibility of the types of growth promoted with the sustainability of the biosphere. Threats of a never-known kind are emerging. Messages from many rigorous scientists suggest that mortal dangers for mankind are looming in the medium and very long term. We have ignored such signals for COVID-19 and the world has paid a severe price. We are underestimating perils thousands of times riskier than COVID-19. And that is something humanity cannot afford. It is precisely economic activity that is taking too much of a toll on a biosphere that was never thought to be so fragile. Economic and political schemes did not integrate these data that are being confirmed every day with greater acuity and danger. The conceptual schemes we have in the humanities and social sciences should be rethought in the light of the new context. We cannot continue to teach and use models that are still useful but designed to function in a world that no longer exists.

In a previous book, I developed a representation of the major challenges we face, the most important tools we have to fight back and the avenues of innovation we need to pursue to increase our likelihood of responding correctly to these perils (A Lamiri: The Economics of the Future, 1). It should be pointed out that the proposed work requires colossal resources and new methodologies. It is no longer possible to deal with economic problems outside the interdisciplinary fields that need to be strengthened. The feeble attempts of the past can no longer contain the tsunami of perilous challenges that are looming on the horizon. We were so poorly prepared to deal with COVID-19 that the price paid was many times more than necessary. Our shortcomings in more perilous areas are worse. We have managed these vital fields more by relying on the intuitions of political leaders than by calling on researchers and scientists in all fields. When intuition prevails over analysis, all kinds of devastation are not far away.

In the previous book, we raised three types of major issues related to contemporary crises. The first aspect includes the classic types of challenges in addition to the contemporary perils that threaten global economic and geopolitical stability. The second aspect examines the analytical tools and models that we use to forecast and make recommendations. Finally, the third aspect concerns the options -old and new- to be explored in order to seize the slightest glimmer of hope to get out of this situation and to make the salutary choices quickly, considering the fields of possibilities that are shrinking day by day. A brief summary of the analyses presented would allow us to deepen some of them and complete the rest with new schemes that have not been mentioned at all in the previous presentations.

Economics has always followed many paths under the major constraint of resource scarcity. One of the definitions used by the profession remains that economics is a science whose ultimate goal is to channel scarce resources towards the satisfaction of unlimited needs. In heaven, where resources are infinite, there would be no need for this science. Everything exists and for free for all. The context where such a science exists would be that of a limit to the resources we use. Thus the quantities of wood, steel, energy, soil and others that we can dispose of are limited in size and sometimes even very rare. The goal would therefore be to channel these resources to the best possible uses. Historically, we have had two tools that are sometimes complementary and sometimes mutually exclusive: public planning and the market. Some combination of the two is possible to achieve this mission. It is very instructive to analyse the course of planning methods within two different systems: indicative planning in countries close to democratic systems and centralised planning within one-party regimes. The first type makes extensive use of the market, and the second tries to manage the economy mainly through the use of signals from the planning authority, whose preferences are mainly inspired by the choices of political leaders. It is time to ask some fundamental questions about the effectiveness of one or the other method. Has centralised planning helped to produce an overall equilibrium (a match between resources and the capacity of the biosphere) or has it exacerbated the disequilibrium? The same question applies to the near-exclusive use of the market or any equilibrium between the two. It also applies to all the classical and new challenges that we have developed.

Therefore, we have explored the nature of contemporary challenges facing the economy with an embryonic interdisciplinary collaboration. Established challenges have acquired new characteristics that make them more resistant to traditional treatment regimens, just as microbes are becoming more tenacious against old antibiotics. On the other hand, we are also much less sure that we have the appropriate tools to face the new threats. We have explored in the previously cited book the most important ones, namely:

-   The problem of the meaning: What kind of society do we want? Who defines the primary and secondary goals, the tools, and the adjustment mechanisms and so on? We will need to clarify the vision and the meaning. Any science or discipline needs this to build itself. Otherwise, we will create Brownian societies that will be tossed around and stagnate, while the present threats require the most innovative and efficient strategies;

- The method: there is no human or social science that is satisfied with a single method. It is wise to have several with some or one that would be dominant. But it is time to ask a question such as: are the available economic methods sufficient to contain the new kind of perils we are facing? We also need to explore the assumptions of the models and mechanisms that we have established as the ultimate tools of human activity: Can the quest to satisfy infinite material needs with limited resources, the maximisation of profits under constraints and the search for maximum growth still be postulates that can be kept at the same level of priority as in the past? Can we use these methods and hypotheses to bring economics to its peak in order to face the current dangers more realistically and effectively? We have proposed to enrich the range of methods with the 'cumulative' historical approach. It is part of historical positivism but can be associated with any form of 'collective creativity.' These concepts will be well developed later.

- Unemployment: Inactivity has always been the major priority of the working classes. In spite of the numerous advances in the fields of cyclical and structural policies to overcome this scourge, there is still a long way to go before we obtain satisfactory results. This is because the disease has become more virulent since the new nomenclature of jobs has completely mutated and made the usual policies obsolete. The new economy is recruiting mostly skilled jobs that are not very sensitive to economic stimulus measures. A new generation of public policies is needed to adapt them to the recent job structure.

- Inequalities: After thirty glorious years, when we witnessed strong growth coupled with a reduction in inequalities, the latter is on the rise again following the implementation of neoliberal policies. Whether it is wage inequalities or inequalities between labour and capital income, the result is the same: a big distancing has taken place after the 1970s. It verges on indecency. According to several sources (including the NGO OFFAM), the richest 1% of the planet have more resources than the poorest 90%. Differences between capital and labour incomes as well as the distribution of salaries have increased significantly in recent decades,

46

making the political sociology of modern nations and their capacity to manage the economic and social systems they are responsible for more complex.

- Inflation: It would be the only reason to be satisfied with the macroeconomic management of the last decades. Apart from a few exceptions such as Zimbabwe and Venezuela, which have caused hyperinflations, the vast majority of nations can boast of having relatively better control of this phenomenon than in the past. Central banks in developed countries consider—rightly—that a rate of 2% or less would be judged satisfactory. And generally speaking, this is achieved without much difficulty, and the countries that deviate from it show relatively modest differences. Monetarist theories and recommendations are not indifferent to these achievements. But, one may wonder whether this excessive neutralisation of the currency has not had a negative impact on the growth of economic sectors that are not yet profitable but socially desirable, such as environmental industries, renewable energies, health democratisation and others. We should then review what policy to adopt in order to reach an optimal monetary rule that builds a salutary equilibrium between price stability and the development of valuable businesses in order to reach a salutary global equilibrium.

- Debt: During the 1990s, economic analysts considered public borrowing to be the number one national peril that would overwhelm governments with the social upheaval that would ensue. Although this aspect of public finance must be managed rigorously, it has been found that this burden greatly limits the room for manoeuvre of public policies, but its threat remains somewhat exaggerated by the economic community. Nevertheless, we should delimit the contours of the debt problem: when can the government proceed with debt processes without great risk and when does public borrowing become an enemy of economic stability?

- Growth: The nineteenth and twentieth centuries were undoubtedly the two eras that brought mankind out of secular stagnation. Large-scale human development and technology have played a fundamental role. It was believed that humanity would be freed from misery and malaise. The economy has played a fundamental role but we are discovering with amazement that the type of growth being promoted is endangering the biosphere and future generations. For the moment we have not created the appropriate organisation, the necessary tools and mobilised the appropriate resources to hopefully control this danger.

- The financial sector is becoming increasingly disproportionate to the real economy and turned out to be more and more disconnected from it. In addition to reproducing more social inequalities, it deprives the productive economy of resources, which it directs towards more speculative activities. Furthermore, finance is one of the largest sectors, along with armament, fossil fuels and others, which has an intense lobbying that blocks the sectors of the future that offer solutions: green industry that fosters global equilibrium.

- Environment: the environmental threat is emerging as the most imposing challenge facing humanity. The economy would be a major actor but far from being unique. The growth model promoted and the national and international structures of states are largely powerless to face this inextricable situation. Existing sciences were capable of boosting growth and the well-being of an impressive number of individuals, but in periods of high resource availability. However, these sciences, especially the human and social sciences, are not designed to invent solutions to threats of this dimension and other equally complicated issues such as peace, equity and so on. They were thought to be conceived outside of ethics and of an overall coherence that would avoid the Brownian functioning of nations. How should the social sciences, especially economics, evolve in order to vigorously contribute to unravelling this complex dynamic that risks devastating planetary socio-technical systems? The causal factor being the financing of political campaigns by private funds, political sciences are called upon more than any other discipline to shed light on the possible solutions.

- World overpopulation: In a few years, mankind will consume in three months what the planet earth can only reproduce in one year. We are devouring the seeds (capital) of future generations. The way of life is the main incriminating factor, but it is aggravated by the rapid growth of the world population and the expansion of the Western consumption model. What has been tried so far does not seem to work. Two tsunamis seem to be breaking over our boat at the same time: the environmental crisis and overpopulation. Two extremely serious threats of a new dimension are dealt with by tools, models and action paths that are proving to be more and more ineffective every day. So in the context of a new approach, questions arise. Do we still have a chance to get by? Under what conditions?

These are not the only challenges we face. We cannot be exhaustive in listing all kinds of problems, but only in identifying the major perils, which could lead to devastating consequences. But in our context, we are manipulating only one lever: the economy. We must therefore be very modest. However, we review the tools we have at our disposal and try to adapt them to the new conditions created by these growing threats that are not well integrated into the dominant economic models. Among the variables considered we can mention:

- Consumption: This theme was analysed mainly in terms of the quantifiable economic factors that determine it. The intention was to smooth out the amount of consumption so as to avoid variations in income and therefore in employment. The main objective was macroeconomic stabilisation. It was necessary to reorient the angles of analysis in order to manage it differently: to establish a quantitative and qualitative level of consumption in order to get closer to an overall equilibrium. The latter is reached when human expectations are not very far from material reality and when the latter is compatible with the reproduction capacities of the biosphere;
- Investment: Until today, it has been considered mainly from the point of view of profit maximisation. The techniques developed, such as the CAPM, the NPV, the IRR and others, all contribute to this end. Engineering firms, equipped with these methods, have practically replaced businessmen in order to strip them of their right to decide and to integrate other values in the decision-making process such as the ethics of more social equality, environmental protection and others. The investment must reintegrate other values in its matrix of decision parameters;
- Equilibrium: Economics has always idealised the notion of equilibrium. It is a very useful concept. Partial equilibrium, primarily developed by Marshall, has been a valuable tool for designing microeconomic or sector-economic policies. Taxation, subsidy or competition policies are

largely inspired by it. Walras' general equilibrium is an equilibrium of exchange among a multitude of interconnected markets. The author shows that it is possible, under certain conditions, to have a simultaneous general equilibrium of all markets. The beauty of the structure contrasts with the operational utility of the model, which is far from being unanimously accepted, but the global equilibrium concept is more relevant to the current challenges. It has two levels: the first concerns the matching between human expectations and the volumes of goods and services provided by the economy; and the second between the national product and the overall capacity of the biosphere to reproduce itself without endangering future generations.

- Fiscal policies operate mainly through the budgetary mechanism. In the past, many rebalancing operations were carried out through budgetary management. However, we have not exploited the full potential in this area. Budgetary re-engineering could bring the expectations closer to the economic potential compatible with the overall equilibrium. Moreover, budgetary re-engineering could revolutionise the ways in which resources are channelled.

- Expectation management: Balancing the potential of the biosphere and the volume of world output has been strongly elaborated by talented researchers who have made us make huge leaps. Wakernagel (53), and others were among them. But other social sciences have the responsibility to build coherence between the expectations of economic actors and planetary possibilities under the constraint of global equilibrium.

- Monetary policy: This is where we need to make significant progress. Within a properly structured economic system, money is not neutral; it is often neutralised by economic decision-makers. An optimal monetary rule could free it and allow it to whip up whole sections of the economy that will enable us to rise to the challenges of our time.

- Development policies: The economic development policies advocated by social sciences are so complex and sometimes so contradictory that economic decision-makers are sometimes perplexed and hesitant to favour one strategy over another. Yet there are successful experiences but they are interpreted differently. Refocusing our thinking on the key success factors of development would allow us to make significant leaps forward.

The assessment of the overall situation enabled us to glimpse the immensity of the task and the need for much greater collaboration between institutions, countries and researchers from different sciences. Analyses developed in a later work (A Lamiri op cited) allowed identifying some lines of thought and the priority to undertake the following actions:

1. Economic models and theories seemed to minimise the problems of modern societies before the resurgence of large-scale perils: global warming, global overpopulation, excessive unbridled Financialisaton and the beginning of the destruction of planetary ecosystems.
2. Economics, like any other science, does not have a solution to these interdisciplinary problems. The most important economic proposals on the table are the carbon tax and the pollution rights market. Both proposals are very useful but too insufficient.
3. Traditional economic problems such as unemployment, inequality, healthy and hopeful growth, excessive Financialisaton and abrupt variations in activity remain far from being controlled. And now, more urgent and potentially devastating challenges are emerging.
4. We need new concepts and methods in economics for two reasons. First, there is a need to link our discipline to other sciences in order to create interdisciplinary models useful for a better understanding of new challenges. Second, integrating the new threats into the fields of economic analysis by updating existing models and theories.
5. We need a new discipline that could be called 'Global Science' to create the tools and multidisciplinary concepts necessary for two things: to generate the schemes and practices necessary to control the new perils and to devise new economic and social formations other than those of the two great variants proposed to us: typologies of market economy or forms of non-democratic socialist nations.
6. Walras's general equilibrium is an equilibrium of economic exchanges. We need another type: The global equilibrium. The latter is established in two stages. The first is to establish harmony between human expectations (economic, psychological, etc.) and the realities of a nation.

The second phase coordinates the level of production (output) required by the first concordance and the renewable capacities of the biosphere: to deliver what is expected by the first equilibrium without damaging the capacity of nature to safeguard its intact potential for future generations. It is this global equilibrium that must guide the economic and social policies of nations.

7. Economic growth would be useful and desirable if it contributes to harmonising human expectations with the output and expansion of the biosphere's potential to match the desired level of production.

8. Managing expectations becomes the key element of global equilibrium management. The role of 'Global Science' would be to shape them in such a way as to achieve an equilibrium between human expectations and natural possibilities.

9. Traditional structural and cyclical policies remain useful and valuable. They will be refined and pursued vigorously while recognising that they are not sufficient. Fiscal re-engineering should allow the government to buy the labour hours that are not being taken up by the market, to use them, to keep them employable, and to create a social safety net that will give citizens a sense of security about their future and put an end to the growing fears of the future as societies prosper.

10. The monetary rules to which the current central banks refer have proved their worth in the fight against inflation. Their performance was mixed in the past. But when facing new challenges, they become totally inoperative. The optimal monetary rule should accommodate past growth, finance unemployment reduction and direct part of the resources to research and development that equilibriums the output of the biosphere with managed human expectations. However, it would have to be carefully formulated to avoid any slippage. Its mission will be to create an output gap, to make the Phillips Curve non-vertical and thus to contribute to full employment without triggering inflation. The notion of laser money (targeting activities) will be preferred over helicopter money.

11. A thorough study of the global environmental situation shows that even if global warming is naturally reversible, humanity has an interest in acting vigorously on the phenomenon. A simple game theory analysis proves this.

12. Underdevelopment theories have always minimised the most important key variable in the process: managerial effectiveness. Its introduction too little too late (good governance) has not had the desired effect on the understanding and conduct of development policies. We need to include it in a visible way in the production functions used to analyse the phenomenon. For the time being, the notion of the economic pyramid (see Lamiri op cited) may be far more useful than the schemes we currently have;

13. Marxian economics contains schemes and mechanisms that could prove salutary with revisions and improvements required by recent developments. Until now, Marxism has had an appreciable explanatory power for past historical events, but it fails miserably to predict the future. A renewed analysis, free of outrageous definitions, would allow to keep the past explanatory power and to obtain forecasts more in conformity with the real developments.

14. Environmental economics produces very useful but insufficient recommendations: carbon tax and the pollution rights market. It is almost exclusively confined to the fields of economic analysis, whereas very valid avenues could be found mainly in psychology and political science.

15. A tiny fraction of the world's military spending (40% minimum) could help us achieve global equilibrium and almost eliminate the terrible threats to humanity. But this option is politically impossible.

16. Re-engineering budgets would create a social safety net that would relieve citizens of the fear of unemployment and social decline. The dread of tomorrow sharply contrasts with the levels of development and the technological and economic capacities of modern nations. The government could buy a large part or all of the available manpower that cannot be bought on the market and use it and keep it in an employable state.

17. In response to the increasing number of disasters—hurricanes, viruses, droughts, etc.—it is in the interest of governments to develop skills to manage these emergencies, if possible jointly if not in isolation. Planning and preparation must regain their nobility.

18. NGOs and various research centres have already produced schemes and even prototypes of works that would allow us to make considerable leaps

in the fight against threats of all kinds. These innovations are most often profitable. But the national and international structuring of nations would be incompatible with the production of salutary human solutions.

19. Economics would play a central role in finding solutions to these new and dangerous challenges, but collaboration would have multiplier effects within 'Global Science' by integrating with other sciences. By mobilising the brains of the vast majority of humans (if possible all of them), we will be able to invent the social forms, the goods and services and mechanisms that will bring these perils under control.

These themes have been widely commented on in a previous book entitled *The Economics of the Future* (1). These representations have been extensively discussed, situating their potential contributions and their limitations. The objective was to initiate debates and research that would produce the most appropriate schemes to define and act upon the new perils that were barely considered in the past.

At the beginning of the 1980s, the worst nightmares of decision-makers and citizens were unemployment, inflation, debt, equilibrium of payment deficits, crime, potential wars, etc. Countries had developed a whole arsenal of tools to contain them: structural and cyclical policies, social programs of all kinds, arms control treaties, political alliances to create an equilibrium of terror, etc. Despite the remaining risks, these threats looked manageable and the tools put in place seemed to allow humanity to continue developing its technologies and productive capacities. After the fall of the Berlin Wall and the considerable decline of socialism, many analysts believed that history was beginning to come to an end (Francis Fukuyama wrote *The End of History* (14).

However, the mapping of global risks, instead of becoming clearer, would quickly become darker and broader. The risks of large-scale conflicts were replaced by endless struggles with limited geographical contours that had produced multitudes of microstates and 'chaos states.' Economic crises have become more unpredictable, deeper, costlier and more complex to resolve. However, the perils that became increasingly urgent, acute and potentially devastating were not, for most citizens, expected. Global warming, deteriorating ecosystems and disasters of unprecedented magnitude in the past have emerged as the ultimate threats facing mankind. We will then have one of two directions to take in a distant horizon: a true end of history, but not the one envisaged by inadequate analyses of the last decades, or a true rescue of our human societies conditioned by the invention of appropriate solutions. We would then be in the evening of history. The world boat is sailing through the decades of the last chance.

However, faced with these dangers with completely new characteristics and immeasurable dimensions, we always referred to our old good tools of the human and social sciences, often compartmentalised, to guide us whereas they were designed for past threats with relatively limited consequences. The capitalist system that created scientific, technological and managerial innovations to extricate humanity from stagnation, then revolutionised all sectors of social life from transportation to telecommunications to medicine etc. to improve, facilitate and embellish human life seems today incapable of creating the solutions to the upheavals it has initiated in the past and this time to correct its own excesses and preserve its own actors and clients from extinction. Not because it cannot produce the technologies and logistics to do so, but only because the national and international institutional organisation locks it into the logic of actions and incentives contrary to what it would be desirable to accomplish.

Modernisation of the tools of response to these new fatal risks would be done in other directions:

1. Interdisciplinary knowledge;
2. Mobilisation of the maximum number of brains;
3. Integration of these risks as one of the priority objectives of these instruments;
4. Mobilisation of significant resources, most probably the design of an inclusive discipline—or science(Global Science) whose purpose would be to mobilise all human potentials to overcome major threats and/or allow humans to design and operate social formations with other alternatives than the only ones available: uncontrollable capitalism or dictatorial socialism. Today we do not have the laws, the principles and the mechanisms necessary to make other types of social formations work with different objectives and tools. The essential reason lies in the fact that we humans have abdicated and allowed mainly politicians to shape our human societies through a series of incremental decisions that do not always make sense. Social sciences and humanities are not sufficiently equipped to have a huge impact on the evolutionary dynamics of nations.

We only have to consider the withdrawal of the USA from the Paris Agreement on Climate Change against the advice of the vast majority of scientists to be convinced of this.

These themes will be developed in the following chapters. We have created neither the tools nor the structural conditions to weigh heavily on the course of serious events that are shaping the social and natural landscapes of modern nations. It is easy to be dissatisfied with a good or service. The existing human and social sciences have greatly helped humans to advance the dynamics of history. They have enabled humanity to move out of the secular era of stagnation that lasted for thousands of years into an era rich in technological advances and improvements in living standards. We could always have done better, but what has been achieved is impressive. It is easy to overwhelm an analytical apparatus with today's information that was unavailable at the time of its conceptualisation. As a Chinese proverb says: *we should not cry over a broken jar or over spilled water*. There is no point in lamenting our past shortcomings. However, a meticulous review of our experiences is necessary only to locate our deficiencies, avoid repeating our mistakes and, most importantly, to identify our errors and successes that can be expanded upon.

It is always within the fields of analysis of other disciplines that one generally locates the obstacles to the implementation of salutary solutions. The carbon tax would be the beginning of the process of completing the reform package, but many citizens reject it. It would be interesting to understand why and what alternative actions are available by using psychology, communication, sociology and anthropology. On the other hand, politicians, inspired by powerful lobbyists, also resist such an endeavour. Do we have any political science schemes to counteract this strong opposition? Economics alone will not be able to produce a solution. It would even be very likely that all the sciences together do not have the solution to implement these reforms, but at least we can identify the fields of research, the experimentations and the necessary investments to be mobilised in order to have a high probability of acting effectively on these denials.

Scientific evolution, the dynamics of new technologies and the new products and services that will be derived from them and will shape our world are not neutral. Today, the vast majority of resources are directed towards the destruction and pollution industries. The proportion of resources channelled into repairing ecosystems and building a sustainable future is comparatively paltry.

Economic and social evolution leads more and more to untenable social forms. And this evolution is getting stronger with time! Hard sciences (physics, chemistry, sciences etc.) and the products and services derived from them, as well as their socio-economic and political consequences, are progressing much faster than the social and human sciences, which are supposed to channel them towards salutary situations. This double unequal and parallel evolution is the most devastating cause of the dynamics of the Mutations of our modern social formations. This disconnects between hard and soft sciences creates multitudes of dysfunctions with often minor consequences and sometimes deadly repercussions for the way our modern societies function.

We must close this evolutionary gap. This is easier said than done, as with any attempt to revolutionise our morals! But in this context, if we abstain or fail to do so, the consequences would be devastating. So, we would be condemned to try to accelerate the level of our knowledge in human and social sciences and by questioning them better and by establishing a new science that combines them: 'Global Science.'

End of History or Prehistory of a New Era?

Economics does not deserve its nickname of pessimistic science because of Malthus' predictions. The big names in contemporary economics have mostly produced enchanting predictions. Milton Friedman thought that with the expansion of the market, the shrinking of the state and his famous monetary formula, nations would live happily ever after. Keynes imagined that with the public policies of aggregate demand management, most of the citizens' free time would be spent on developing the arts, sports and other desired activities. Mankind would be freed from unemployment, inflation and the abrupt variability of economic cycles. Marx speculated about the inevitable proletarian revolution that would take us to the edge of the communist society where we would write on our flags 'From each according to his abilities, to each according to his needs.' Promises to free human beings from their economic shackles abound in the schemes of great thinkers. It was enough to follow their recommendations. For Marx, the wheel of history is in motion independently of human will and 'historical materialism helps' the emergence of communism is inexorable. But this idealisation of the future was to prove much more problematic than the great economists of the past thought. It is easy to judge others with today's knowledge and information and to locate the failures of their models. Nevertheless, these thinkers had made extraordinary leaps forward that had allowed a growing number of countries to do better. But the context has been greatly disturbed by new and unpredictable developments, by the famous 'Black Swans.'

There have always been economists who have warned about the externalities of economic development, but no one foresaw that our global ecosystems were so fragile and that the long-term consequences of poorly controlled development could be fatal. It is the beginning of an interaction between climatology, biology, economics, political science and the rest that allowed us to place global risks at a frightening level. We will have to readjust our forecasts. We can no longer be satisfied with the scenarios of Marx, Friedman, Keynes and the rest: for a simple reason. They produced their forecasting schemes with information and knowledge far below what we know today. The first observation we can make is that there is no inexorable evolution. There is no mechanism in operation that would lead humans or the world economy towards one alternative rather than another. The dynamics of evolution will depend on a host of factors, the most important of which will be: structuring social and political movements, fiscal and monetary policies and their consequences on the channelling of resources, evolution and application of new hard and especially soft sciences (human and social) to shape social expectations and priorities. We can go in any direction: a long-term destruction of human societies or a salutary leap forward that would put us on a global recovery path. It would be one of these two scenarios or a very close one that is looming on the horizon. At this point, we do not know which future we are headed for. We can only envision that one of the two possibilities would occur. We do not know an intermediate scenario except that timing could well be longer or shorter depending on many conceivable developments. We will elaborate on each of the two possibilities briefly. We take up the essential of the almost foreseeable developments of one or the other hypothesis.

The Continuity Scenario

Today, most of the social and economic changes come from the initiatives of the political class. Scientists have a minor role in the consciously planned evolutionary dynamics of modern nations. The political class is supposed to have an offer that responds to the aspirations of citizens. The latter would be the customers to whom the political offer would be addressed. Within their systems of priorities and values, access to and retention of power for as long as possible would be the main goal of the political class. Agendas will reflect the revealed preferences of active supporters (those who vote). But these voters are divided and have rather short-term orientations that do not take into account the very long-term consequences of their current actions. Only a minority is aware of this and acts on this basis.

On the other hand, given the fragmentation of customers, a more organised fringe, endowed with substantial resources and adequate strategies, is polarised on a single commodity: to produce more and preserve the status quo. As a result, politicians are trapped by these structured consumers: the negative lobbyists. Powerful proponents of the status quo, they can influence continuity (Business as Usual) as long as a sense of urgency and the devastating level of risk do not seize the vast mass of consumers of political agendas. But by the time this sense of urgency becomes widespread, it will probably be too late and humanity will enter a very dangerous phase of droughts, coastal flooding, hurricanes, dislocation of many ecological systems, pollution and a whole host of horrors described by the simulation activities we have now. The few innovations of the scientific elite that are integrated into the political culture remain at very insufficient levels compared to the new requirements of modern societies. Even if the developed nations integrate more scientific contributions, this is still far below the requirements of the current challenges.

Citizen actors have systems of rationality that cover mainly their life horizons and institutions want to think over a longer period (up to fifty years or more) but are constrained by the political class in order to privilege electoral calendars that are shorter term. Major risks have longer timeframes than human or institutional logic; this is the major risk. For the moment we are imprisoned in the logic of status quo with a whole series of actions and agendas close to too little too late. Subject matter specialists are making a series of very worrying predictions on this topic. The most alarming aspect of this situation is the fact that the problem is becoming irreversible and the outburst of natural phenomena is likely to be fatal to the human race. We have a potentially infinitely devastating cost here, and yet the vast majority of humans treat it with disconcerting nonchalance. But to convince the poor Indian farmer to refrain from producing and selling coal when his day-to-day life depends on it is an arduous task. Just as the Wall Street financier who should channel more resources into the research and development of recyclable products; renewable energies etc. instead of the research of ever more sophisticated derivatives that are always far from the real economy would be more than painful. It would be the same to convince a professional lobbyist to stop defending the sole interest of the oil industry, armament or anything polluting when the greatest cataclysms will occur when even his children cannot be there is the most difficult thing. Thus, the dice are loaded. Moreover, the strategies and interests of actors as well as the global engineering of the system show fatal deficiencies. For the moment we do not know how to build typologies of nations that have the potential to face modern challenges with brilliance.

Consumer/actor citizens are strongly trapped by their own conditions. They feel that there is a deep contradiction between their immediate interests and their deep long-term desires. In such circumstances, they privilege their short-term situation. This of course applies to the average citizen and not to each specific person. Social science and humanities laws are probabilistic so is the political class, trapped by unfavourable time frames. Politicians also behave like normal average individuals. Whenever there is a contradiction between their interests and those of the nation they will also benefit themselves. They will make a series of decisions that will boost their chances of being elected or re-elected. This explains why nonconformists are mainly recruited among young people and scientists, without forgetting a minority who have become aware of the drama that could shake our planet. More and more the youth and the scientists enter into the game the more chances we will get out of it. In the future, the scientific power will surpass the traditional, the legislative and the judicial ones all taken together; but in a democratic setting.

Scenario II: Conditions for Renewal

The objective of decision-makers and citizens would be to halt the dynamics of the deterioration that has taken place in recent decades. Still, we have to appreciate that the average world growth rate is around 3% and that inflation is below 2% in developed and emerging countries. Overall, the picture is negative especially, when it comes to the deterioration of the planet's ecosystems. We are very far from a healthy global equilibrium. We have privileged the equilibrium between expectations and output without acting on people's behaviours to bring them back to the level of the potential equilibrium between human production and the renewable capacities of the biosphere. We are still consuming the seeds of future generations. The global disequilibrium is glaring and intolerable, and the potential long-term consequences continue to be debated more and more fiercely, but it is increasingly clear that the perils will be devastating.

The passions that are driving more and more responsible citizens would be to stop these deteriorations as quickly as possible but at a lower cost. The vast majority would not accept paying exorbitant prices now to achieve a global equilibrium restoring the world's fragile ecosystems and consistent with sustainable development. This extremely complex and hardly conceivable possibility is only credible if four conditions are met, all of which are problematic:

1. A federation of harmful capacities of transmutation forces: youth, relevant NGOs, a majority of intellectuals and an increasingly broad swath of the middle class and committed citizens. Structured national and international federations and a global confederation (or two or three) with the key success factors would give the movement a higher probability of putting in place the mechanisms that will accelerate the global equilibrium.

2. An inclusive doctrine: It contains the strategic configurations at the global, national and regional levels as well as the values and tactical plans. A titanic organisational work is necessary to weigh heavily on the political decision and the channelling of resources. The rightness and nobility of the cause do not exempt an organisation from a structuring

which, although democratic, needs to be scientifically conceived and implemented.

3. Adequate resources: The cause is disproportionate to the resources mobilised, even if the level of commitment and sacrifices made compensate somewhat for the lack of resources. However, strategies and operational plans can largely influence the budgetary resources that would help these movements work better.

4. Scientific methodologies and tools: Currently, most of the scientific knowledge and research is directed towards obtaining more growth, goods and services and few resources are devoted to the problem of restoring the equilibrium of planetary ecosystems. Human and social sciences have not yet produced the knowledge and mechanisms needed to build social formations that can promote and preserve sustainable global equilibriums.

No human being, no matter how intelligent, and no NGO alone would be able to meet these four essential conditions. Yet a common approach is slow to materialise on the ground. We certainly have encouraging operational actions and remarkable commitments of heroic activists as well as remarkable sacrifices. These energies can be the basis for more structuring actions in the future. We need more synergies to channel these resources and energies, to increase the mobilisation capacities of the movement and to strategically influence the conscience of citizens who are still reluctant to make the necessary efforts to weigh in on these major planetary events. Today, the average citizen is wholeheartedly in support of the objectives of the alter-globalists, but they vote for their opponents. Can we implement these conditions, in time, to favourably influence future events and contain the peril or the 'dynamics of inertia' that still prevail? In other words, are we on the eve of the end of history (fatal scenario) or in the prehistory of history (survival scenario)? For the moment, no one can tell with certainty, even if more and more analysts are beginning to predict the worst scenario.

Humans and Institutions

Human economic development has been achieved in parallel with the resurgence and multiplication of institutions. It would be possible to show that there is a good correlation between the proliferation of institutions and the degree of development and flourishing of civilisations. If there would be no relation -which would be surprising- it would seem inevitable that the quality on the other hand would be a preponderant factor in the promotion of the economic and social formations in great civilisations of their times. However, it would be tedious to measure with acceptable accuracy the institutional merits with the knowledge we have today. This hardly implies that we cannot build indicators to monitor and improve them. In fact, we absolutely need them for the future. Audits will be revolutionised by more efficient tools. We have not invested enough to create these devices and those we have are still rudimentary to manage the future challenges. Institutions have mainly been human creations in order to pool efforts and resources to create the best possible living together. Through institutional modes of operation, we are supposed to secure quality education and health, to ensure our security, to live together with civic-mindedness and mutual aid, and to prevent and avoid major disasters. Modern life is structured by an abundance of institutions. In the end, the quality of their governance is what gives us a high degree of economic, political and social efficiency.

Often, the malfunctions lie either in their mode of operation or in their interactions. Management specialists, as experts in institutions, have always been concerned with coordinating the anticipations and actions of their members and the various internal entities in order to avoid their worst nightmare: the Brownian effect. The Brownian effect occurs when elements internalise cultures, behaviours and objectives that are different from those of other members and from the ultimate goals of the entity's purpose. For example, a company's production department might be focused on cutting costs to get more bonuses. The sales department might want to improve quality to boost sales. The management of the company with its policies, rules and communication plan should not waste the opportunity it has to coordinate the expectations and actions of its members. Otherwise, it would be a Brownian system with difficulties in moving towards a certain trajectory. The situation is highly complex for a country or a group of countries that coordinate their activities in order to achieve a huge objective such as the fight against global warming, building a sustainable universal peace, the fight against famine etc. In fact, the last three missions have failed miserably and the first one is in the process of achieving the same result. The complexity of creating institutional arrangements is such that instead of facing it with vigour, determination and method, we prefer to create easy alternatives with even less chance of success. The UN does not work, so we do not capitulate, we create an array of other arrangements: the G7, the G20, and the COPs etc. But within these new institutions, we find the same shortcomings, and worse: the lack of authority, responsibility, contradictions between actors' interests, the lack of resources, the motivations for deviant actions and so on. Everything contributes to creating situations where easy victories are achieved on problems that are relatively simple to deal with (recessions), but where human challenges of great magnitude, such as climate, peace, development, etc., remain at a standstill.

We have been acting like this for many decades. Despite the many wars, famines, and increasingly virulent economic and health crises, we have been able to survive and maintain the hope of improving on the challenges we face. Moreover, in most countries, living standards have improved. Certainly, not in the same way for all, generally inequalities have increased everywhere. Even the poorest got some improvements. Access to education and health care also improved. Science and technology have grown at an unprecedented rate. But the obvious observation is chilling. Traditional challenges such as wars, famine and economic crises cause great human and material damage. Yet, our repeated failures and successes can be a source of inspiration for improvement, although it would be doubtful to conclude that we have really made progress in all kinds of challenges. However, the ultimate new reality is the degree of uncertainty and the level of risk involved in the new threats to humans.

The Core Thesis

Every rigorous work develops a core thesis supported by many conceptual developments and diagrams. Sometimes it is proposed for improvement, for debate and often for experimentation. In hard sciences, it would be rather a hypothesis, preferably testable, that is put forward to explain, predict and possibly act on a phenomenon. But in social sciences, it is rare to experiment so we have a multitude of situations to try to prove and we often resort to historical information. The situation becomes complicated when the interconnected parameters do not lend themselves to quantification. Historical materialism is a central conceptualisation in Marxist doctrine. It seems to explain well past socio-economic upheavals but struggles to predict correctly the future or to become a tool of preponderant actions in order to usefully change our contemporary societies have still to wait. The core thesis presented in this context is that human socio-economic and historical evolution has passed through two important and distinct effective stages and we are on the verge of making a third choice a choice for the creation of new economic, political and social forms. These distinct phases are:

1. Classical 'Natural' evolution;
2. Partially oriented transmutation;
3. Choice between mutation by Global Science or continuity.

Classical 'Natural' Evolution

Historical events such as battles, rise to power and conquests can be dated with much more precision than historical mutations such as the development of agriculture, the expansion of trade or others. The same is true for the events to which we are referring. We can only situate these historical episodes very approximately. We can roughly estimate the phase of natural classical evolution from the beginning of history until the second half of the seventeenth century, which coincided with the beginning of the industrial revolution in Great Britain. It was the era when technological and social innovations were minor, slow and had little impact on the future of humanity. There were many wars and conquests, but the consequences were much more limited. The economic necessities, intuitions and personalities of the leaders were the essential causes of the social developments of the time. For this reason, historical materialism had a great power of explanation for the great social developments of that time. The historical movement developed outside the consciousness and good will of humans. Economic transformations had a great explanatory power for the political, social and cultural mutations that were taking place. Human decisions are driven by many requirements, but economic mechanisms seem fundamental.

There are several reasons why the impact of human actions was so limited that they had little consequence on the fundamental structure of societies at the time. We can cite some truisms. During these periods, the economic sizes of states were very limited compared to the rest of the social body. The most important public institutions of the state in contact with the civil society were mainly the army and the tax collection entities. Any public action had a limited impact on the way nations functioned. According to the little information available, public authorities weighed less than 5% of the GDP of the nations of the time. Second, technologies had limited impacts. They can neither enormously improve the situation of the planet nor jeopardise it. Incremental improvements were very limited and could not disrupt lifestyles or impact large segments of society. Thirdly, revolutionary ideas or hints contrary to official dogmas and practices were generally repressed and could not spread to create large social movements. Societies were therefore very slow to change. Finally, the biosphere's reproductive capacities were much higher than the economic and social demands of those times. In such a context, Karl Marx's historical materialism offered a generally accurate explanation of the course of economic and social developments. It did not explain everything, but it clarified the deeper reasons for the most important historical changes. We will need a lot of work by sociologists and historians to complete it, but we already have a very valuable basis for work. But things were about to change.

Partially Oriented Transmutations

From the beginning of the industrial revolution until now, the economic and social evolutions of nations and large regions around the world have undergone progressive and increasingly profound changes. The constraints that limited social evolutions and allowed historical materialism to play out gradually dissipated. If during the first period, social evolutions globally transcended human consciousness, it would be difficult to defend such a thesis in its extreme version. The latter could be defended somewhat during the first phase but not during the second.

Economic and social characteristics have changed dramatically. The weight of the government was becoming increasingly heavy on the course of economic and social developments. In some democracies, public expenditure exceeded 40% of GDP. This would have little consequence in the context of the Marxist vision. The government would be only the expression of the ruling classes to soften, support and ultimately implement their visions and programs. However, for those who believe that the government tries to balance the demands of many stakeholders, its impact would be appreciable. Despite this debate, something has changed and governments now have the capacity to greatly influence social change. The Keynesian consensus has weighed heavily on the historical development of nations. Government spending had prevented unemployment from becoming a threat of social unrest. It had thwarted the mechanism of the industrial reserve army advocated by Karl Marx. Even though the state is largely controlled by powerful groups, it took economic and social measures in favour of the majority when the threat became imminent. Precisely the corollary of a powerful state is its ability to steer the system and not just let it go in a 'historically determined' direction. Historical fatality fades away and leaves a preponderant place for human designs. The (partial) democratisation of developed nations has given reformers more opportunities to speak out and influence the perceptions and actions of decision-makers. The struggle of women and the support they have found among men of culture, literature and science have allowed them to be partially integrated into political life. The progress made should not hide the substantial reforms that remain pending.

Undoubtedly, however, the substantial change lies in technological evolutions. They have brought to light many developments, sometimes positive and often destructive, but which have not failed to put a stop to the irreversibility of social and economic developments. Modern technologies have begun to have a major impact on economic and social formations. Atomic energy has radically created another geostrategic world, modes of production and energy use have revolutionised the modern world; ICTs have disrupted our communication traditions and a whole flowering of technologies has enabled a per capita income that is disproportionate to ancient history in the developed countries. Providing an affluent society for the vast majority of citizens allows the 'class consciousness' to be acted upon to blur the citizens' demands for social change. Technology has also created a 'class' or sub-classes that hardly claim to be proletarian. Engineers, doctors, teachers, administrators outnumber blue-collar workers in most modern nations. Instead of having two distinct antagonistic classes, modern societies have crumbled into a multitude of distinct sub-classes that are difficult to separate. Pension funds owned by workers possess more shares (and therefore more tools of production) than the highly publicised capitalists. Of course, the fact remains that managers are sometimes beyond the control of the majority of workers/owners. But still, the crumbling of the underclass is largely due to technological developments over the last two centuries.

This dissemination of multiple sub-classes with different characteristics and aspirations from the classical proletariat has had two major effects on social structures. The first is that groups of citizens, States and ideas can now have more influence on the forms of society we create. They are no longer totally independent of human will. The rise in productivity assisted by technologymeans that more can be given to the most vulnerable although the most affluent get more. Nations become a positive sum game. The different strata play a win/win game even if some gain more than others. The Marxist analysis of historical materialism assumes a win/lose game. No one can argue that improving living standards is surely more important than increasing inequality, but it can only be stated that this offers an additional possibility for decision-makers to structure economic nations and not only be dictated by historical materialism. The problem of sharing and the ethics of more equality still exist, especially after the 1980s, but social developments have been much more complex than Karl Marx had envisaged. Marx apparently did not learn all the lessons from the concepts he himself had developed. Simple labour (muscular work) and compound work (especially mental work) have become distorted. It is rather compound work that produces more value in modern societies. The demand for this kind of work is growing for a simple reason: it induces families of products or services impossible to obtain by simple work. Infinity of simple (muscular) work cannot crack an atom or make a quantum computer.

Comparing the values of goods produced mainly with simple labour power and those obtained mostly with compound labour power can no longer be obtained as easily as the Marxist theory of value advocates. This is a long and complex debate beyond the scope of the problematic addressed here. However, what interests us in our discussion is the capacity of humans and institutions to create social structures that are consistent with human aspirations.

Historical materialism stipulates the existence of a historical determinism independent of human will. Attempts to influence the march of history can only result in accelerating or delaying it by numerous subterfuges. This is strangely similar to the law of gravity: it can be defeated for a period of time (aeroplane) in order to solve a problem, but it cannot be stopped indefinitely. But modern States, technology, ideas and societal innovations seem to prevent historical materialism from operating at all. It also appears that it has been very poorly understood. Society was about to fragment into several social layers, sometimes rival and often united to demand social transformations consistent with a society based on human intelligence and mental work. The economic problem that was to arise was much less a class contradiction, which faded without disappearing, than an antagonism between social evolution and technological evolution. The latter is developing at a pace that undermines social innovations that are too slow and too minimal compared to the challenges created by scientific and technological innovations. The latter are often salutary and contribute to improving the well-being of more and more people, even if inequalities remain problematic. But the most important lesson that can be drawn from this period is that human beings have created for themselves, through ideas, technology and innovations, the possibility of influencing the structuring of the social and economic forms of nations, and not just being subject to some sort of determinism. The question of the degree of freedom that the decision-makers of modern nations have created for themselves remains a subtle research problem, but this freedom exists.

However, being able to act on social formations does not mean that we have succeeded in generating the best possible forms. It even seems that we have put ourselves in great uncertainty, or even in danger, because of our ignorance of how to mutate social formations. We have a much better command of the atom and of genetic manipulations than of the construction of modern, egalitarian nations, respectful of ecosystems and compatible with the biosphere's equilibrium. Until now, we have created capacities for social mutations but without much control of the consequences. We have operated with a mixture of knowledge, intuition and, mainly, convictions. We have abandoned our role as builders of socio-economic models to politicians who do an amateur job in this field. We have built societies that are more and more unjust and that endanger the planet, and having become aware of the deficiencies created, we cannot implement corrective mechanisms. This is the central thesis of this contribution. We have created for ourselves capacities to design social formations but we do not know how to shape them efficiently; therefore our intervention in modern nations creates more dangerous problems than those we have. There are three main reasons why we are creating nations incapable of meeting human ethical and ecological challenges. When it comes to working together to create the conditions to work for peace, social justice, and the sustainability of global ecosystems, we are failing miserably and we know why. We have trapped ourselves. The three causal factors explaining why we are failing to build successful nations are:

1. Contradictions between the interests of nations, especially the superpowers, and particularly the organisation of the international decision-making process, do not allow us to deal with large-scale dangerous perils. The common system is based on the incentives of the political class which exists mainly for itself and therefore it privileges its own nation (Me First) and in the short term. Even if it is the global synergy which allows the viability of the 'world nation' in the long term there is a remote possibility that will take place.

2. Civil societies have largely abandoned their power to the political class in fundamentally unstructured political systems. Politicians, tied hand and foot to various interest groups, make decisions with little knowledge

71

or room to manoeuvre about the tragic consequences of their choices. Scientific input is marginal in political decision-making. This allows short-term political interests to take precedence over long-term ethical and survival requirements. The 'confiscated democracy' characterises modern societies more than the simple term democracy. This explains why we have structured ourselves to self-destruct at the expense of ethics and sustainability.

3. The absence of a knowledge body that draws from all human sciences in addition to developing others specific to the creation of nations and international organisations capable of meeting the challenges of current perils. 'Global Science' or any other name that we would like to give it would allow us to build viable nations and international structures. But for the moment we do not have such a discipline or science.

With this in mind, we are entering the twenty-first century with a major challenge. Are we going to continue to operate globally with the same mechanisms of partial incremental mutations or are we going to revolutionise our ways of operating by relying more and more on 'Global Sience?' We can already start working with the few principles we have—for example, hyper-transparency and zero dependence on private funding—to avoid the worst. But, there are other reorientations to be made as well. We are on the verge of making a complicated choice: to continue to grope or to move quickly and inexorably towards salutary mutations

Continuity or Revolution by 'Global Science'

With an insufficient development of social technologies and an unprecedented boom of hard innovations, historical materialism is far from functioning as Karl Marx predicted. It is irreparably neutralised. Its effects are becoming more and more inoperative. The social mutations created by the incremental choices of politicians are not inspired by the different scientific developments but mostly initiated by their short-term interests. But still, they have had some successes. They have created deadly challenges for humanity that the current world structure is unable to correct. Now, are we going to continue on this path or are we about to question it thoroughly in order to bring out of nothing a saving spurt that can only come from our common thoughts and actions? For the moment, the probability of self-destruction in the long term is higher than the possibility of recovery for several reasons that we will explain.

We have a long experience with partial and incremental mutations. We have experienced this since the beginning of the industrial revolution. Sometimes a highly significant development (passage from dictatorship to democracy) is always followed by a multitude of partial social and economic reforms whose consequences, somewhat positive in the short term, often have disastrous impacts in the long term because they are not well integrated in the costs/benefits of the different choices. Ecosystem destruction is one of them. We can always continue to do the same thing and hope that the same socio-political systems that have entrenched the perils, by changing their objectives, would be able to eradicate the threats they have created. The gamble is too risky. The main fear is that with all the good will that can be generated, we would be unable to do so. The matrix below explains the available alternatives.

Actions or Inactions on the World System

	Potentially effective system	Inefficient background system
Keep it	Time savings Resource savings 1	Collapse of the world system and nations Very low probability of successful rescue 3
Change it	Loss of time Loss of resources High probability of success but with possible unnecessary costs 2	Rescue of the world system Low probability of failure But with inevitable costs 4

Available options

The table above illustrates the dilemmas we face. Since the beginning of the industrial revolution, social changes have come from profound upheavals (revolutions) or from a multitude of incremental changes. The nation systems created had allowed for many beneficial technological and social leaps but also created potential threats that were unwise and too risky. National and global structures have a low probability of overcoming the threats created. So we are put in a situation where we have to make a substantial choice between continuing to attempt with the same methods and the same structuring or trying something else.

The dilemma that confronts us is seemingly very complicated. It may be within our reach scientifically but not politically. Consider the possible choices related to contemporary challenges. The existing world and nation systems can be made to work with minor modifications and good will on the part of all (a rigorous debate can be conducted on the causes of the resurgence of good will). If this is the case, we run the risk of trying to change it profoundly when it is viable. This is the scenario we are currently dealing with. It is believed that with the United Nations, mobilising our best scientists and closer collaboration among nations, we can overcome the serious threats we face. Second, current structures may not be able to cope with contemporary challenges. Preserving them would be a fatal mistake. And changing them deeply would provide us with a high probability of coming out unscathed and stronger. Therefore, we can find ourselves falling into one of the four squares of the matrix above:

1. Keep the system as it is, because, with a few minor modifications, it could work well and take away the threats it has created through ignorance or carelessness. This is the current choice. We also count on the reversibility of perils: global warming, destruction of ecosystems, wars etc. This option allows us to save a lot of time and resources. We postulate that what we have already built is not bad. The equilibrium of terror (fear of an atomic conflict) will limit and circumscribe conflicts. The reversibility of the processes can receive a push from the current system of nations and the old equilibrium will gradually be put in place. We do not need to panic or risk upsetting a national and global order that has worked much better than the critics advocate. Neoclassical schools of economics are not too far from this position.

2. This is the situation materialised by the box 1 of the matrix. It implies disproportionate risks. If the hypotheses formulated by the followers of this position (especially the climate sceptics and the followers of the status quo) have drawn wrong recommendations, following them and persisting in the error would be suicidal. We risk ending up with increasingly serious disturbances that may even lead to our annihilation in the very long run (a few centuries). Saving resources, time and trial and error are the main potential advantages of this option. Current sciences are unable to provide us with the probability of such an outcome. However, we find that the more we learn about the fragility of global natural systems, the more we realise that the probability of such an alternative is low. Then the consequences would be so disastrous that the current processes of a 'Confiscated Democracy' cannot lead to healthy choices.

3. The square 2 is relevant to the situation where the system is potentially efficient but we will mutate it in depth by the implementation of national or international structures more rigorous, fairer and built primarily by sciences and not a trial and error of history. Global Science will allow us to mobilise all the citizen intelligence and the appropriate methods to build this network of institutions. These creations will produce the incentives, the organisations and the human behaviours to circumscribe

and then progressively control the risks. These perils are currently terrible threats to us, but there may be a small probability that we would have succeeded in doing all of this without mobilising so many resources and human energies. We would then have wasted a lot of resources for nothing. We would have banned or restricted certain activities and invested more than necessary in fields such as renewable energies, reconstruction of ecosystems, etc. when nature knows much better than we do how to regenerate itself. We would have allowed ourselves super reforms while the current modes of operation better suited the economic superpowers. We are committing a crime of lese-majesty that would have been useless.

In order for this scenario to be verified, we need to make assumptions that are dubious, to say the least. The reversibility of natural processes is the most important one. However, only a minority of scientists believe in it and the number of followers is getting smaller every day. We need a joint meeting of two highly improbable events to be serene: efficiency of the nation systems of the present world and reversibility of the natural processes of the biosphere to correct all the dysfunctions that have appeared. If we leave the system without deep mutations, we gain some resources but we inflict on ourselves an inordinate risk if our assumptions are not verified. It is better to risk losing some resources than to try to do nothing and expose oneself to severe punishment by natural processes.

4. Square 3 shows a situation where it is recognised that the nation and world systems are fundamentally inefficient. They are not equipped to deal with problems of this magnitude. Moreover, the most serious threats (global warming and ecosystem destruction) risk reaching a certain point of irreversibility. We have very little time left to get to this point of no return. Most scientists believe that we are in such a scenario. The proof is the way the pandemic was managed. The USA claimed that the disease was temporary and did not require a strong intervention from the government. The price paid for this misjudgement was hundreds of thousands of deaths and untold damage to the American and world economy. Is a world that fails to address a COVID-19 pandemic capable of successfully containing threats as dire as those awaiting us? Hence, the alternative of relying on existing nation and world systems would be

a dangerous choice. To continue doing the same thing will be fatal in the long run. We have been in this scenario for a few decades. And at the moment we have no indication that we will get out of it. The probability of failing and paying exorbitant human and material costs is very high;

5. Square 4 is where we recognise that world and nation systems as currently structured are fundamentally ineffective in combating challenges as complex as those we face. We have not produced the kinds of institutions, nations and human incentives to mobilise and overcome these perils that are considered distant, but on a 'biospheric' time scale are too soon. So, if we do not manage to mutate them very quickly, we are going to cause ourselves calamities whose consequences will be disastrous and possibly more horrific than we think. We would have an appreciable probability of getting out of it and correcting the serious disequilibrium caused by chaotic economic and ecological policies if we change our strategy and management practices.

The most rational conclusion is that we must act with more vigour and rationality. But when it comes to changing world and nation systems, where do we start and what do we do? When we have a problem in social sciences, we rarely have a single alternative to solve it. There are always many options, each with its strengths and weaknesses. We almost never have 'The One Best Way.'

Dealing with a problem of such severity, we must try to make the best use of our methodological scheme and ask ourselves the three famous questions. What do we know scientifically about the structuring of nation and world systems? It is tempting to try to continue doing the same thing with marginal improvements and hope to contain perils of a never-known magnitude. But most specialists continue to claim the inefficiency of the current nation and world systems to curb challenges of a never-known magnitude. We absolutely need a model for transforming the world and nation systems that prioritise social and natural rescue actions. Today, every NGO is doing some work to make our world a little better. This ranges from volunteers who help old people to live better to anti-pollution activists. These multitudes of institutions can do a wonderful job at their level and according to their goals. Their dedication and sacrifices are remarkable. Some NGOs have grown to impressive sizes and have considerable influence on public policy. They have developed networks of researchers, run simulations of various kinds, and incorporate the research parameters of national government agencies or international bodies into their databases and action plans. They have an influential weight in the international arena. At the end of the day, there are millions of women and men who are active, self-sacrificing and giving their best to their noble causes. However, there is a danger that they may be under the illusion that they are close to success. Most of them believe that the election of a new candidate, the success of a COP such as the one in Paris, or a better mobilisation of the main States would be signs of the beginning of a mutation of the powers that be in order to create a better future for the coming generations. Some see in the changing values of young people future solutions to our enormous problems. But we had exactly the same thoughts in France in May 1968; afterwards, these generous values began to fade gradually until they barely left a trace.

A careful analysis of the way current world and nation systems work would reveal that these possibilities for change are too slow, too costly and too uncertain to bring about the necessary results in due time. The equilibrium of powers, even if it evolves slightly, is not capable of vigorously reforming the system to reach a point of no return in due time. We can therefore continue to act with the present world and nation system and hope to perfect it to the point where it would be able to spare us most of the expected calamities. But the gamble is too risky. The likelihood of failure would, in the opinion of the vast majority of sceptics, be too high. Then it would be necessary to choose a completely different option. But there are many possible alternatives. We have to try to choose the best (or the one we think is the best) possible option among several available. We must therefore:

1. Clarify the doctrine necessary for the recovery process;
2. Propose a decision-making methodology;
3. Come up with a structuring of the world and nation system compatible with the operational solutions.

Part II: Global Science Concepts and Principles

The Doctrine

A doctrine is always multidimensional and when we propose to devise one for a scientific phenomenon it would cover both the necessary conceptualisations and the alternatives of actions to be carried out. Karl Marx had brilliantly produced a doctrine for the proletarian cause and the transformation of the capitalist system. Theories of surplus value, tendency of the rate of profit to fall and patterns of reproduction constituted the essential parts of the conceptual economic arsenal. Historical materialism and dialectics completed the Marxist edifice while integrating many other analyses. Fortunately or unfortunately, the socio-economic evolution has not conformed much to the predictions of the global scheme. Those who have tried to construct schemes to situate the socio-historical evolutions of nations have had more setbacks than successes. Schumpeter predicted that the educated and increasingly numerous middle class would establish democratic socialism (Schumpeter. 42). This expectation is far removed from the scope of societal evolution possibilities that we are experiencing today.

John Maynard Keynes considered that the conduct of macroeconomic policies would be sufficient to create a better world, without any major crisis and which, moreover, would free human beings from their most enslaving economic and social constraints. Thus they will create more space-time for the advancement of arts, entertainment and sciences. None of the liberating prophecies has materialised and on the contrary, the recent historical evolution produces more terrible threats than those we had known in the past. We have neither the tools nor the principles, let alone the mechanisms, to conceptualise social change, and even less to bring it about. These brilliant thinkers have tackled problems of staggering complexity and have tried to design tools to fill in our lack of knowledge. They faced a problem of unprecedented complexity: building from a few theoretical materials an extraordinarily challenging structure. They have tried to do without these tools that we lack until now. But this titanic work is not within the reach of a human being, however brilliant he may be. It is the construction of a whole science that is at stake. It would be like asking Einstein to conceive 10% of the laws of physics and chemistry. In spite of his immense contributions, it will be impossible for him to complete such a task.

Marx, Schumpeter and others took economics as a basis for integrating it into a larger system of social sciences and building mechanisms for societal evolution. But, what remains to be produced is much more significant than all the past attempts. It would be the work of a whole science to build. It could be called Global Science, social engineering, social construction or other. And we would need large numbers of people and research laboratories in innumerable countries to create all the concepts and tools we would need. Today, citizens or especially decision-makers who want to build a 'bio nation,' carbon neutral and with zero or positive impact on the biosphere, and who also want to reduce inequalities and create an environment of ethics, peace and social tranquillity, are facing an impossible task. The goals of those who must build nations of peace, progress and prosperity are frustrating. These decision-makers have many shortcomings compared to other professions and other projects. A surgeon who diagnoses the need to perform a triple coronary bypass has scientific references (established knowledge) and experiences that will guide the design and implementation of his surgical plan. A civil engineer whose mission is to design an anti-seismic building has sufficient theoretical and practical knowledge to carry out this construction. A consultant in a business organisation also has the knowledge and experience to guide him and to set up a matrix organisation by projects for a public works company. However, our decision-makers, who are called upon to design social formations compatible with a global equilibrium (between economic activities and the biosphere), more social justice and universal peace, do not have all the knowledge necessary to succeed. The scientific profession has little knowledge to help them achieve these enormous transformations.

We need a detailed doctrine to guide the actions of various social components, future research, and social modes of operation that would allow us to develop completely different kinds of social formations. This would include:

1. A theory of historical and social evolution;
2. A global equilibrium;
3. A system for managing expectations;

4. A Global Science presentation scheme;
5. A Basic Model (s);
6. The Global Science Paradigm Manifesto.

Producing a Theory of Societal Evolutions

We will try to summarise where we are in terms of historical and social evolutions. We have just come out of a historically very long era -from prehistory to the beginning of the industrial revolution—where world-nation structuring was too often done outside human consciousness. They were mostly 'laws' that transcended the goodwill of human beings. Historical materialism had an appreciable power of explanation, while other socio-political mechanisms were also in operation, but without much scope. It would be rare for a large-scale decision (such as introducing a universal health care system) to originate from anyone other than the sovereign or his very close circle. Afterwards, we gradually entered an era in which states and individuals began to weigh more and more heavily in the process of directing the world-nation system. The impacts of public decisions and opinions of elites began to steer the system in more desirable paths (less crisis, democracies, more equality, more science and technology etc.) and sometimes very inappropriate directions (wars, racism of all kinds, destruction of ecosystems, colonialism etc.). The size of states and emerging democracies began to allow elites and politicians of many hierarchical ranks to steer the world-nation systems.

In Marxist theory, this would make no difference because human beings will shape systems according to their own economic interests. Widening the circle of decision-makers would in no way be a revolution in ideas and practices. But in these new social formations, even minorities of people who were somewhat distant from any economic interest (researchers, artists, philosophers, etc.) would begin to impact the historical development of nations partly out of interest and partly out of pure deontology and ethics. Jean-Paul Sartre and the movement of May 1968 partially influenced French politics for a long period towards a better redistribution of income. After having dreamed that this capacity to direct the nation-world system would allow us to design a better global institutional architecture, we realise once again that we are beginning to create perils that we are unable to control. The technologies invented and the ways in which nations operate have far exceeded the potential of social science knowledge and know-how. We are now at a crossroads and we have two and only two possible alternatives: the first is to try to do the same thing as in the last two centuries with minor adjustments and hope to overcome very serious threats that are becoming more and clearer. We hope that the same parameters, very partially modified, will produce salutary consequences. We have briefly analysed this situation and concluded that the probability of failure is close to certain. The second alternative is to act, to mobilise all the intelligence of humanity, to create a 'science' or a discipline that is lacking and to improve our chances of getting out of this situation. In a way, instead of having a nation-world system that imposes itself on us through various mechanisms that paralyse us, we are taking control for a more judicious piloting and design of a trajectory approved by the vast majority of humans. For the moment, our destiny escapes us. We lack the doctrine, the methodology of implementation and a set of recommendations in order to build a viable and sustainable nation-world system.

Theories of the historical evolution of nations are in their infancy. In the field of hard sciences (biology), which have made gigantic leaps; however, it is sometimes more difficult to reach a consensus on complex themes. We rely more on Darwin's theory to try to explain evolution. Yet we can explain the modifications of adaptations to the context more than the mutations from one species to another. We have developed a consensus around the first phenomenon but not the second. This explains in part the fierce debates between 'Darwinists and opponents.' But, this topic is left to its specialists. In social sciences, the only systemic and complete theory that comes closest to a rigorous scientific formulation remains the historical materialism of Karl Marx. Although many grey areas still persist, the scheme seems to clarify a significant proportion of the historical developments of nations. However, the contributions of phenomena other than economic ones are difficult to clarify. The roles of elites, psychological dimension, arts, religions and other sciences may not be as neutral as that. Marxist theory, however, has neutralised them by stuffing them into the concept of superstructure, which serves only to validate the requirements of economic structuring. In other words, laws, religions, arts etc. only serve the interests of the ruling classes and if these benefits evolve then these elements mutate to fit them.

We have proposed the three phases of the social transmutation dynamics (STD): the supremacy of ultimate social or political near natural laws (where historical materialism had a strong explanatory power); the period of partial mutation (PPM)—since the industrial revolution—and the one we are facing now: the choice between continuing with the previous period or introducing a new phase that we can call 'societal engineering' or GSD (Global Science Design). In order to move on to this third generation of reforms, we would have profound methodological requirements. We can only hope for a holistic approach. Presently we are contemplating a stage of transmutations by successive approximations to another one more systemic and more multidisciplinary. During the second phase, which we had lived through, even the revolutions that brought about multiple upheavals were partial in nature, dominated by 'economism' in Marxism, the exclusion of ethics and the scientific principles of institutional transformations with a view to a global equilibrium and not a simple equilibrium of exchanges (Walras). During this second phase, growth, economic equilibrium (employment, prices, equilibrium of payments, etc.) and a slight improvement in the distribution of income were the main objectives.

The Continuity Process

The current alternative is what all nations have been doing since the beginning of the industrial revolution, with a remarkable acceleration since the end of the Second World War. We have reached dead ends of very large proportions and we have put ourselves in danger and above all we have greatly mortgaged the future of younger generations. The objective of sustainable development, to provide future generations with the same resources and the same chances of survival as ourselves, is becoming a notorious illusion. Our great-grandchildren will curse us for our cruelty, our selfishness and our incompetence. From our point of view, this assertion is to be moderated. We would have our own contexts, constraints and limits. But we are faced with an inescapable reality. Our alternative of persisting in operating in the scenario of continuity with sketchy alterations has a strong potential to lead to destructive consequences in the long run. A vast field of investigation awaits our researchers in order to locate the similarities and differences between the first two historical phases: the pre-eminence of ultimate social laws and that of partial mutations.

The first would be characterised by the fact that very few people or institutions of influence produce significant effects on the ways in which social formations function. Sometimes only the ultimate leader shapes the political and social culture of nations at will. Sometimes he or she shares the decision-making process with a small group of individuals. In the absence of a coordination and even consultative body at the 'world' level, conquests become a form of self-defence. This line of thinking remains alive in contemporary national political cultures. Many non-democratic third-world countries are still trapped in this first preliminary phase of economic and social evolution, characterised by the very small number of individuals capable of profoundly changing the national system.

However, the second phase allowed extraordinary developments in all fields of human life but also produced disasters of great magnitude. Perils that arise from all sides urge us to act quickly while the present structuring of the nation-world system can only procrastinate, accomplish too little too late and run the risk of sinking under huge risks. We know very little about the consequences of our current position of accepting a nation-world system driven mostly by a series of fragmented choices. We are certainly subject to multitudes of 'Butterfly Effects' whose consequences we underestimate. The butterfly effect states that the flapping of a butterfly's wing in the Amazon can trigger a storm in Texas. However, Lorenz, who proposed the idea, also had to integrate all the complexities linked to these meteorological phenomena. In social sciences, the situation is even more confusing, because it is impossible with today's knowledge to model very complex social and political systems. However, folk wisdom holds that the butterfly effect means that very minor events can have far-reaching social and political consequences. We need to analyse historical experiences with new tools and new methods that would allow us to better design new economic, social and political formations. We must learn to detect within the waves of chaos the elements that will contribute to re-establishing new equilibriums. We are not very capable of doing this today. However, we still dare to continue a process of trial and error in order to build sustainable equilibrium in the style of Walras's auctioneer to stabilise highly complex systems to some extent.

Today we cannot make sense of the multiple interactions that come together to form complex nation-world systems either in terms of simple principles or in terms of quantification in the context of chaos theory. But we see a simple result: failure of our approach to contain the system in a trajectory that allows us to ensure its sustainability. The tools, methods and practices that we have been trying since the early 1970s are risky and are bogging down the social fabric every day in worrying uncertainties. It is tempting to keep doing the same thing, hoping for changes in the results and not in the approach. The comfort of inertia has long been identified as a dangerous human predisposition. In the present circumstances, it would be similar to a process of self-destruction that is certain but slow, unspeakable, imperceptible and ultimately terribly deadly for future generations. We can no longer afford to continue in this way.

Nevertheless, an ill-considered evolution carries potential risks that are sometimes more perilous. We have explained that in social sciences we rarely, if ever, have a single alternative solution. We always have a series of possibilities with their strengths and weaknesses. The human quest in social sciences would be mainly to find the optimal combination of choices that could direct the system towards an optimal (not maximal) situation. It is in this sense that we must mobilise all the resources and all the intelligence of all to exploit the smallest possibility that we have to get out of the situation. The scientific community has long known and warned that we can no longer afford the luxury of procrastination. A broad consensus is emerging on the issue despite some marginal challenges. Yet the nation-world system is structured to fight back vaguely and belatedly. While a tiny possibility of exploitation persists, collective paralysis grips consciences and institutions to block out any attempt at vigorous actions. All that remains are desperate cries from stakeholders with little chance of being heard.

In Search of Global Equilibrium

The current period, marked by approximate partial increments, is far from being the best possible option for containing contemporary challenges. Social sciences are dominated without sharing by economics while political mechanisms transcend the rest even if interrelations are undeniable. It is easy to criticise this second phase by ignoring all its technological, scientific, political and social advancements. We were allowed to make progress unparalleled in the history of mankind. The widening of access to knowledge and the integration of contributions from a greater number of contributors allowed for advances of great magnitude. This is the great difference, the most important one compared with the first phase. It is difficult to say whether we could have done better and more without the knowledge of the time without altering our potential to ensure the biosphere's sustainability. 'Economism' has characterised the approach of this second phase for most decades. We operated theoretically under the search for a general equilibrium in the style of Walras and practically with the simulations of partial equilibriums in the style of Marshall.

During this second phase, humanity has made great leaps in all fields and false leaps in certain directions that have proved more fatal than we had imagined. Science and technology have made meteoric advances. Experts in the knowledge economy estimate roughly that our knowledge doubles every nine years, but most of this knowledge resides in hard science and material technology. The progress of social sciences and satisfactory societal experiences are far too slow to direct knowledge and know-how towards salutary horizons. Our capacities to create peace, social justice and global equilibrium (between economy and biosphere) have progressed very insufficiently. Here we have the

Gordian knot of contemporary perils. We have two parallel dynamics that endanger the future of our human societies:

1. Developments in hard sciences create a large gap between the potential for destruction and the capacity for repair: it is much easier to create and release a virus capable of wiping out humanity than to design a therapy to overcome it, to provoke a nuclear explosion than to repair the consequences, to degrade the biosphere than to restore the natural equilibriums within it.
2. The progress of social sciences is not capable, at the moment, of creating a nation-world structuring with mechanisms that prevent the gaps between the potential for destruction and the capacity for reconstruction from forming and threatening the system's structural sustainability.

No matter how much we analyse the problem from all angles and by broadening the variables considered as much as possible, we cannot avoid the conclusion that remaining attached to the incremental approach brings us closer every day to the destructive irreversibility of our current nation-world system.

Table 2. The Global Equilibrium Solution

We need to change the paradigm and open the door at least for a new alternative. We have no more time to procrastinate as in the past. One of the most serious avenues is to think, plan and implement not in terms of general equilibrium but to understand the nation-world system in relation to global equilibrium. The latter is designed to create a social fabric, within nations, and in turn a two-stage global equilibrium:

First, a matching between citizen expectations created by various societal operating mechanisms and the economic (demand), social and political apparatus. The pivotal point in current structuring lies in the economic and social expectations and what is provided by the economic and social formation (supply).

Second, synchrony between inputs derived socially from the biosphere and its capacity to reproduce without altering its fragile equilibrium and its capacity to provide the same inputs for future generations. We have developed the main lines of this approach (Lamiri, 12). The origins of the pressures on the biosphere's resources come from the structuring of our economic and social formations. We have created a nation-world system whose expectations of ever more materials generated by our social, political, economic and cultural (SPEC) arrangements far exceed our ability to extract resources from the biosphere without causing threatening alterations. It is this differential of dynamics that would be the origin of all our concerns. For the moment we do not know how to create societies that restore these harmonies. We have shaped our modern societies in such a way that people's consciences always demand from their leaders a continuous proliferation of goods and services that are assimilated to more well-being and elevated to the rank of 'reason for living.' A politician running for office always assures potential voters of an improvement in their material situation in the same way a child is promised a very comfortable material situation in relation to his or her seriousness and dedication to school. Material remuneration is the most used in business management. The whole life culture of a human being convinces him of a close correlation between his happiness and the amount of resources at his disposal.

The task of achieving a global equilibrium in the world system is imposed upon us by the nature of the threats that arise when we fail in this mission. To stop the threat requires that we operate on the foundations of our failures. And quickly! Any delay is very costly. Unfortunately, we are not acting on the deep roots of our past failures. As always, economists have provided us with realistic economic solutions that are useful but too insufficient. The carbon tax and the market of pollution rights are the essential mechanisms. While hoping for a broad awareness of the population, we believe we have what is necessary to build a sustainable global equilibrium. Consumers are starting to behave in a positive way overall, towards change. The vast majority of studies show that consumers are becoming increasingly aware of the attractions of green marketing. When a company's information system emphasises the efforts undertaken to protect the biosphere and health are credible, customers even make financial efforts (buy a little more) to contribute to the process of restoring the equilibrium. To give oneself a good conscience or to commit oneself to restorative actions!

Sometimes the price difference or the perceived quality tempers the prospects' commitments. But a general dynamic seems to be taking hold to put a little more influence on the economic system in order to make useful restorative investments. At present, this positive turnaround is still in its early stages. It would be necessary to develop it further in order to have a greater impact on the course of businesses. There are many opportunities for public policy support that are essential. But these efforts deserve to be given more resources and recognition while identifying their limits. Currently, we are operating under an ultimatum from the scientific community that gives us a respite of one to two decades before the devastating processes become irreversible. We also have a citizen's movement around the world that is gaining momentum as the perils gradually unfold and manifest themselves in unspeakable ways. The masses that are mobilising increase every day the number of citizens committed to revolutionising the system, especially certain categories such as young people, artists, scientists and all those who have the capacity to see into the very long term.

All these psychological and sociological changes are likely to have a very heavy impact on the dynamics of social evolution. But in the long term! Perhaps not quickly enough to avoid irreversible devastating processes. We must meditate on the COVID-19 pandemic. Acting too late at all levels allowed the epidemic to spread rapidly and cause more harm than necessary. When human intelligence was mobilised and focused on the search for alternatives (vaccines or cures) we were relatively successful in reducing the timing of solution protocols by at least a factor of five. We also failed to stop the destruction of the biosphere's ecosystems. The genie has come out of the bottle. The peril is real but unlike COVID-19 it is hardly noticeable. It is highly probable and more devastating, but much less obvious now.

At the same time, the number of human challenges continues to grow, which narrows our capacity to act to contain the risks. We are facing at the same time dangerous challenges such as pandemics, financial crises, social inequalities, risks of serious international conflicts and the distressing deterioration of the biosphere's equilibrium. We have difficulties in integrating all these elements, systematising them, apprehending them and acting with full knowledge of the facts. Global equilibrium, which we propose to analyse, criticise, amend and operationalise, remains a preliminary tool to apprehend the complexity of interrelations and to act more efficiently than we currently do. It is a rigorous alternative to consider. It is not a mirage, an unattainable dream or an improvised choice, but a rigorous option that draws its methodology from the emerging principles of 'Global Science.' Among the multitudes of complex interrelations, it is judicious to distinguish the most significant ones. Every science has to make use of all knowledge and experiences of humanity to capture the essence of the most significant variables, mechanisms and impacts.

The origin of any human action or attempt to act comes necessarily from the expectations engraved in his conscious and unconscious by a web of institutions that make up modern societies: the family, school, informational environment and others. This justifies that before thinking in economic terms, the contribution of our psychologists, sociologists and anthropologists would be invaluable. Basically, it is the expectations of citizens—an intangible reality—that shape our actions and ultimately our material life. The origin of their modes of appearance would be the first major field of inquiry for Global Science. We already have a few leads on this phenomenon, but they are not well coordinated between the different branches of social sciences. Psychology's contributions are very little integrated into economics. For a long time, economics assumed that the individuals investigated were endowed with a basic psychology. They were presented in the form of automatons equipped with algorithms for mathematical maximisation of their social choices. In the early 1970s, when the mode of emergence of expectations began to be formalised, the 'robotisation' of human consciousness was reinforced by more 'universal and automatic' schematisations of human thoughts. The rise of rational expectations during this period, a theory that had been put on the back burner for many years after its presentation by its creator John Muth (25), had completed the few efforts to incorporate more human analysis into economics. Even the adaptive expectations theory, although very basic for understanding a highly human phenomenon, was called into question by the then-current trend.

The new path of 'Global Science' begins its analytical journey by analysing the phenomenon in terms of global equilibrium and not general or partial equilibriums. The first part of this equilibrium consists of managing a societal equilibrium between expectations and the present and future potential of the economic apparatus to deliver goods and services. In the absence of equilibrium, the social consensus built by nations leads us to deploy a wealth of imagination to fill this gap. The second equilibrium to be constructed would be a harmonisation between resources derived from the biosphere and its alignment with the expectations created. Otherwise, the social consensus would be to draw non-renewable resources from the biosphere, alter its fragile equilibrium and wish to re-establish it through hypothetical future technological advances, while continuing to finance research and development that would aggravate this disequilibrium (armaments, fossil fuels, gadgets, etc.).

Currently, researchers have already created rigorous, useful and perfectible methods and tools to estimate the differential between the resources drawn by a region, a country or the world and the biosphere's renewable capacities (see Wakernagel. 52). Today, we consume twice as many resources as the renewable capacities of the biosphere in one year and in a few years we will use twice as much. We can no longer afford to extract so much without endangering the biosphere and ultimately ourselves.

The efforts we will make will go in these directions:

1. A better quantification of citizens' expectations and their implications on the output of the economic apparatus.
2. Estimation of the volume of resources to be mobilised and the biosphere's capacity to satisfy them without altering its potential.
3. Matching expectations with the capacities of the biosphere.
4. Act on expectations through various mechanisms and on the biosphere through significant resources in research and development and through the mobilisation of human intelligence in order to achieve a harmony that preserves the fragile equilibrium of ecosystems.

Global equilibrium gives us an insight into how irresponsible our economic policies are with regard to the instability of our situation. First, we completely fail to manage expectations in order to bring them to the level of the potential of available resources without altering the great equilibrium of the biosphere. On the contrary, expectations are boosted beyond the necessary level by many mechanisms, the most visible of which is the deepening of economic inequalities. Moreover, research and development resources are directed mainly towards sectors that increase the need for resources derived from the biosphere (armaments, gadgets, etc.), much more than towards activities or processes that save resources or boost the capacities of the biosphere without altering its long-term potential. Global equilibrium allows us to put our finger on the problem. We then identify expectations and their impacts as the source of all the destructive threats we have created in our modern nations. We have also designed great tools of amnesia: the increasingly sophisticated ways of modern distractions. Between the working hours and the potential of distraction (social networks, TV, tourism…) and the satisfaction of our biological needs, there would be little time left for reflection, reconsideration, questioning and especially little time to act.

The approach to global equilibrium is certainly multidisciplinary, especially when it comes to the formation of expectations. We would need to integrate the knowledge already produced by sciences such as psychology and sociology as well as to clarify future avenues of research in order to specify their origins and to manage them instead of undergoing them. Research and development programs are being called upon everywhere to advance our capacities for discernment and action related to the formation of expectations and their immense consequences on human destiny. Until now, they have been an exogenous variable, a datum outside the control of public decisions and practically a constraint to be fulfilled without questioning them or elaborating any strategy to keep them in a socially and politically acceptable zone. There are several avenues to explore in this area, such as:

1. Exemplarity: through their lifestyles, remunerations and honest and skilful communication the political class and elites can gradually influence the priorities and attitudes of the masses.
2. Educational systems are called upon to produce the best methods to instil in our citizens the happiness derived from wonder, nature, mutual aid, peace and love of others and not only from the ownership of more material things. It is legitimate to want to improve our material well-being as well. But we will need to acquire it by stimulating the biosphere to provide us with more without deteriorating its capacities and while also improving the situation of others.
3. Public institutions and NGOs would have the task of matching citizens' expectations with existing material potential in a context of global equilibrium.
4. Public policies can rely on judicious measures, other than the carbon tax and the market of pollution rights, such as imposing a high tax on products and services of second necessity and directing resources towards research and development of the great equilibriums sought. It makes sense, at a time when the biosphere is threatened, to act to limit

our human choices to those that are the least perilous and thus to direct expectations towards more beneficial alternatives.

5. To make useful use of the mobilised human genius (Global Science methodology) to develop possibilities that we have not thought of at the moment.

The Global Science Way

The number of disciplines or 'sciences' that are being created at the level of hard knowledge is constantly increasing. Nano sciences, quantum computing and others will not be our latest science inventions in a very short time. And rightly so! The frontiers of knowledge are always expanding. Interfaces between past knowledge are established as a necessity to understand the world around us as well as the appearance of new phenomena little known until recently. Sometimes a new discipline is developed to deal with these manifestations and sometimes multidisciplinary teams are formed to apprehend these new facts. Necessity knows no law! The new disciplines are created and spread, especially in the world of hard sciences. Within the humanities and social sciences, they are mainly disciplines created around epiphenomena such as calligraphy and others.

But here we feel the vital necessity to create a new discipline or science that would allow us to integrate all human knowledge with specific methods and tools in order to achieve the desired goals. We could not build such a 'discipline or science' without specific methodology and without mobilising permanently some of our best brains.

A Word About the Goals

Every science has one or more explicit and implicit goals that constitute its rationale. The ultimate goal of economics is to direct scarce resources to the most efficient uses possible. This is its ultimate purpose. We are not sure that it has done so successfully. But we have many intermediate steps before we reach that final outcome. It would then be necessary to avoid or temper crises, to achieve much equilibrium: growth, employment, prices, budgets, equilibrium of payments, etc. These intermediate objectives are supposed to contribute to the achievement of the final goal, but one is entitled to ask: efficient in what way? Is phenomenal growth that achieves the various equilibriums but increases social inequalities and endangers the human race acceptable? We can always say that these are constraints within which we can optimise the system. We are far from having dominated our subject. This has not prevented economics from performing real miracles in a large part of the world, but it has also laid the foundations for our euthanasia.

The ultimate goal of Global Science would be to synthesise all the multidisciplinary knowledge that we know and to identify those that must be produced to address the major perils that threaten us (destruction of ecosystems) and to be able to create nations with the ethics, human ideals and great equilibriums that we want to build. Today we believe that we are capable of managing a mixed economy, with a dominant private sector, in a democratic context. Of course, there are other possible typologies: such as public economies within dictatorships, or mixed economies with a single-party regime, etc. Societal typologies have been the result of sometimes happy and sometimes horrible historical paths by events and political classes that direct them mainly based on their own interests, which sometimes conflict with ethics and the global equilibrium. For example, we do not know how to build a democratic, hyper-transparent, very fair society, respectful of social ethics and which at the same time would be equipped with mechanisms to establish a permanent global equilibrium. This would be a fundamental purpose of Global Science.

On the other hand, our nation-world system has caused potentially alarming disequilibrium and perils. This is the number one challenge for national and global authorities. Global Science is called upon to help us set up the architecture and processes that would allow us to restore the great equilibriums with minimum costs. Sometimes the mission would be beyond the current reach of humans and any science. It would then be appropriate to explain the causes, identify the constraints and clarify the alternatives of action to accomplish it when possible. For example, the impact mechanism of financial lobbies on the political classes of the most industrialised countries considerably hinders the 'decarbonisation' of the world economy. An alternative of public funding of election campaigns through appropriate mechanisms (some of which already exist) would substantially reduce the power of this mechanism. But today humans cannot accomplish this.

Nowadays, apart from the economic systems that have been imposed on us by political decisions which are mostly incremental, we do not know how to produce nations based on peace, respect for global equilibrium, great social justice combined with green productivity that protects the biosphere from the consequences of our actions. Ideally, future nations should be designed as extremely complex systems (much more intricate than the latest aeroplane prototypes) by scientists from all backgrounds, after having received directives from the leaders and, in particular, from citizens on the expected performance of the new 'products.' Modern innovations are rarely made by an isolated individual or group backed only by their personal knowledge and brilliant insights. It is often extensive marketing research that determines the characteristics of the product desired by the consumer, the quality and particularly the ethics advocated by senior management which inspire the mobilisation of knowledge and creation of new collaborations to engineer the product. A successful innovation integrates and involves all stakeholders: intermediate and final consumers, suppliers, company members, public decision-makers, NGOs, citizens (noise tolerance level, for example). The key success factor of modern innovations lies in the structured mobilisation of everyone's intelligence within a virtuous division of tasks.

But in the context of Global Science, we are mostly talking about social sciences, human and institutional behaviours, methodologies, probabilistic laws and imprecisions. We will probably grope for a long time before we can correctly understand past experiences, codify them and deploy them to correct our past mistakes or consider architecting new forms of social formations. We can only be at the dawn of a new era if, by happy historical circumstances, we would be ready to shape our nation-world system with Global Science instead of the random increments we have become accustomed to.

A more structured conceptualisation, more connected to scientific principles and mechanisms, allows for better ensuring internal coherence and final outcome. Certainly, perhaps we would never have nations totally quantitatively reproduced and designed by large social laboratories equipped with the best simulators, but we would at least have nations consciously and intelligently built to achieve legitimate human ambitions.

The needs for social justice, peace, preservation of the biosphere and strong human collaboration are possible and desirable. The desire to make the world's population live with a level of comfort reached by the wealthiest 1% of the planet would be a utopia with the current scientific knowledge we have. No matter how effective Global Science is, it cannot produce miracles, especially in the short and medium terms. It is likely to set up a global equilibrium that would protect better, more and would allow a beginning of reversibility of the phenomena by acting on expectations, productive potential and new technologies to substitute a new type of real output. For the moment, we lack the real willingness, the structure, the knowledge and the implementation methods. But we are still at the beginning. Objectives and ethics intimately appropriate within the social conceptions must come from a process of citizen democracy. It will not be up to the experts of Global Science to set the ultimate goals to be reached nor the ethics that should accompany the process. People cannot abdicate their sovereignty over their ambitions and ethics to the ingenious scientists of Global Science; otherwise, the current political-financial tyranny will be replaced by the most totalitarian authoritarianism.

Political monopoly is always the gateway to dictatorship. This is the ultimate error committed by the Marxist doctrine. To believe that a single communist party with class consciousness and monopoly powers over the army, the institutions and the people would result in privileging the interests of revolution over self is the fatal delusion of Marxist theory. All revolutions fail in the long run if they are confiscated by a single person, institution or organisation. We can have in the short term a leader, a party or a single enlightened entity that will stay the course, but in the long term, mistakes, misuse and serious dysfunctions are inevitable. Temporary enlightened dictatorships are ephemeral signs of enlightenment in history that prelude the continuous barbarities of human destiny. This would explain that the objectives and ethical aspects of the nations established are not a monopoly of Global Science experts, but democratic issues decided by popular will by removing the financial and informational power over the current citizen choices. These aspects will be further elaborated later. In their essence, sciences, both social and natural, are not neutral. They can promote peace, global equilibrium, and social justice and ensure the sustainability of life on Earth and human flourishing, or they can promote wars, racism, biosphere destruction, social injustices and ultimately accelerate the destruction of living species, including ourselves.

Citizens can entrust Global Science with a multitude of functions except two that are non-transferable: defining the ultimate goals and control. So what would be the difference between a society that uses Global Science and one that does not? Today, any institution that has to deliver results, be it a school, a company, a hospital or an NGO dedicated to animal protection, would need a minimum of management in order to achieve its objectives at the lowest cost. This is what has made management the resource of resources, the one that enables resources to produce acceptable results. Without effective management in modern institutions, there can be no macroeconomic performance, no development and no rigorous protection of the biosphere. However, when you have institutions that are supposed to use all the sciences of humanity, you will need other things. A city council manages education, social problems, environment, recreation, political events, economy, scientific development, etc. It would need Global Science at its level. A region would do the same. A political party, a global foresight entity, a national planning body, governments, research entities on social developments, international institutions, climate investigation entities; in short, all institutions that will need to integrate the knowledge and programs of several scientific disciplines will be concerned. For example, political parties will have to develop multidisciplinary and multi-year programs designed by Global Science experts and audited, criticised and improved by scientists from other parties.

Nowadays, it is enough to take the preferences of the first leader and a small team of economists or, rarely, sociologists, summarise them and, in particular, build around the choices of the leader's arguments to adorn the program presented. These bodies shape education, health, communication, the environment, research and development and complex interconnections of knowledge and sectors, not just the economic aspects. A political party that wishes to 're-found' a country needs to carry out a holistic re-engineering of all sectors in a systemic way. The approach is necessarily multidisciplinary and interconnected. It must review education, family policy, the health system, environmental policies, taxation, etc. In fact, by redesigning one element of the system, it is practically all the elements of the scheme that need to be made coherent again. For example, in order to establish a global equilibrium and not just a general equilibrium, we must act primarily on expectations. The education sector is strongly called upon to create more symbiosis between human needs and nature as well as to anchor the idea of well-being derived from satisfactions other than material assets. In this context, psychology and sociology will be of greater help than economic models. However, it is rare that a party proposes a program of action designed by a multidisciplinary team (in the way of Global Science) and according to the qualitative and quantitative elements developed specifically to reform a whole social complexity.

We already have a basis formed by existing disciplines that has produced a lot of concepts on the mechanisms of human and institutional mutations. But they need to be developed further. We will try to propose some ideas on qualitative themes for debate, improvement and use. For quantitative patterns only a summary presentation will be considered. There are much better mathematicians and statisticians than me who can help us make impressive leaps forward in order to obtain more precise simulations than those of our current econometric models which contain hundreds of equations. In addition to clarifying the theoretical relations between the different disciplines, we must know how to create quantitative interfaces between the different sciences. Making different disciplines discuss and collaborate together in order to produce the best possible nations would be the ultimate goal of 'Global Science.'

Today, we sometimes rightly speak of the need for slowing down growth or initiating recessions. In fact, the latter would be the only alternative if the restructuring of research and development and the efforts to control the world's population were too insignificant to have a strong impact on the process of restoring the biosphere. Only a thorough analysis based on 'Global Science' would allow us to detect this. However, suppose that a slight economic recession would be necessary to restore the global equilibrium before starting to grow again without negative impact. But a negative growth policy requires profound changes in all sectors: education, communication, political regulations, new rules of income distribution and so on. We do not have the tools to do this now. We do not have the equivalent of 'Global Science' to allow us to consider such an option. We can cobble together an attempt, but we will probably create overwhelming problems that will turn public opinion against this option. We do not yet have the social technology to do it properly. We know how to partially adapt in the medium term when it is undergoing (crises), but we do not know how to provoke it, maintain it and take advantage of it. No modern nation knows how to deal with a provoked long-term decline and the state of our knowledge is so rudimentary that we can cause more harm than good. There are many options that we are not allowed to take. Today we do not know how to create human societies, more egalitarian, more efficient and, most importantly, more respectful of the global equilibrium. Not that we cannot manage in the future to build these kinds of social formations, but because of a lack of focus on the resources to be engaged and the political mobilisation necessary for their engineering.

It is important to remember that we are at a crossroads. The methodology of architecting entire nations through partial choices and piecemeal incremental decisions has reached its limits. It can no longer allow us to achieve global engineering equal to the challenges we are facing. Either we commit ourselves to creating nations or nation-world systems by mobilising the intelligence of all or the vast majority through a complex but effective scientific methodology or the partial incremental approach will lead us to a collective dead end signalling a gradual suicide. Social scientists compare our situation to what is called the 'boiling frog effect.' If you put a frog in boiling water it would jump out and save its life. But if you put it in cool water that was gradually heated up, it would die by gradual habituation when the water became boiling. Mankind is somewhat in this situation with a slight difference. We still make some mediocre attempts to get out of it. But caught up in the comfort of inertia, we pray and hope that the feeble efforts we are making in the fight against global warming, racism and conflicts will allow us to curb these perils.

Global Science's goal is to develop nation and world systems capable of overcoming the ever-increasing and fatal challenges we have brought upon ourselves. A judicious restructuring of modern systems would allow us to multiply our capacities to master our problems and radically change our own 'nature.' We have a pure example. Chemistry teaches us that coal and diamond are composed of practically the same chemical components (carbon) but organised in a completely different way. We would therefore have coal nations and diamond systems. Moving from one to the other would be complex but possible for social organisations. However, we would need a completely different approach. One of the ultimate goals of 'Global Science' would be to enable our human societies to make appreciable qualitative leaps in terms of modes of operation that would allow us to rise to the level of contemporary challenges; otherwise, we would be condemned to risk our survival. No single person, institution or country can formulate the methods of such a process alone. A synergy between the vast majority of stakeholders would make it possible to tackle an increasingly perilous challenge, but we must structure this collaboration and also produce the preliminary method(s).

About the Methodological Issue

Global Science is mainly part of the social sciences family. Even if it draws a large part of its knowledge from hard sciences, to integrate them in its process of social transformations, it remains in its essence a human and social science among many others. When referring to these, we find that each of these disciplines or sciences, (we will use these two terms interchangeably even if they cover distinct notions) uses diverse methods and tools. For example, we cannot say that economics has one method. It uses a diversity of methods such as modelling, mathematical optimisation, comparison, descriptive-analytical analysis, simulation, experimentation (rare) with multiple tools: econometrics, national accounting, etc. The same goes for sociology, psychology and others. Admittedly, some methods are more widely used than others. Yet, it is always a variety, a bouquet rather than a single process reproduced ad infinitum. Global Science would employ all of these methods. Samuelson (39) found in these methods a common point for the economic approach: the optimisation process. He explained that, overall, economics uses the principles of maximisation through processes of models and finding a sustainable equilibrium. The situation depended on a host of variables. Changing one parameter (e.g., price) would change the nature of the equilibrium (Samuelson: Foundations of Economic Analysis).

Economics as a whole is based on models, a scientific activity that consists of choosing the most significant variables and interactions to analyse, explain and predict economic phenomena. Often this would allow correcting undesired trajectories by a host of possible interventions on the chosen variables. All other human and social sciences use them; it cannot be any different for Global Science. However, among the bunch of methods used would be the essential one which could be called incremental accumulation. Since Global Science takes from all scientific disciplines to shape nations or nation-world systems, its approach can only be holistic, cumulative, dynamic and systemic. It lends itself to partial analyses that can be integrated into global dynamics.

Let us take the example of a developing country that mobilises financial resources (through debts, or an increase in its export prices or other). The country wants to make optimal use of the channelling of its resources to the most optimal uses. It is its socio-economic and political characteristics that should guide decisions. If a country has an acceptable degree of managerial efficiency (non-profit companies and institutions), at least average human skills, etc., it would be eligible for a Keynesian type of stimulus (boosting demand). On the contrary, a country with poor managerial efficiency, low human resources, etc. would do better to improve its supply-side policies. It would direct the maximum amount of resources towards improving its fundamentals, which would lead to a better use of these resources.

Third-world countries have suffered from the lack of discernment of economics, which wanted to create a rather universal science, just like physics. The pre-eminence of the neoclassical model, adulated by the Washington consensus and international bodies, has brought some benefits but caused a lot of damage. Developing countries were the main victims. Conceptual schemes that had some positive connotations in developed countries were imposed on them and it was considered that third-world countries were all in a position to adopt them. The least developed countries would do better to think in terms of the 'Economic Pyramid' (Lamiri (22)). This simple concept is descriptive, but it allows us to locate the essential differences between the fundamental characteristics of an underdeveloped economy and that of an industrialised nation. Any economy is distinguished by three levels and three different tiers regarding its economic particularities and policies. These levels include:

1. The basic fundamentals: this is what really makes a nation strong. It is the quality of the educational system, the degree of entrepreneurship, the efficiency of management (businesses and non-profit institutions), research and development and its use, the strategy and organisation of the government. In short, these are the microeconomic foundations that give a country significant or modest economic and political potential. They are the foundation on which a nation's strength or weakness is built.

2. Sector policies: These are industrial, agricultural, housing, tourism, transport and other policies. They are supposed to give particular sectors efficient ways of operating. They also have the task of supporting the basic fundamentals to raise them to appreciable levels.
3. Macroeconomic policies: These are global, cross-sector policies such as budgetary, monetary, exchange rate and trade policies. Their impact is strongly manifested across all economic sectors of the country.

These three levels characterise mainly the economic aspect of nations. This is a summary description that aims to identify the essential problems of countries. These three levels are in constant interaction and obviously depend on a host of psychological, cultural and socio-political factors of the country. This is a purely economic description and therefore very incomplete from a Global Science perspective. However, for our economic analysis alone, which disregards a whole host of considerations, it is sufficient for us to differentiate certain economic policies that relate mainly to the conduct of macroeconomic affairs. The three-tiered architecture allows us to make the leaders of underdeveloped countries aware that they should not blindly ape the decisions taken by major economic powers. Indeed, there would be significant differences between the ways in which these two types of economic and social formations operate.

Moreover, the two types of economies function in very different ways. A deep analysis and the history of countries confirms that the problems of developed countries are mainly located at the macroeconomic level and those of underdeveloped countries are mostly located at the level of basic fundamentals. The major world crises, especially in the 1930s (29-39) and the subprime crisis, are mainly due to a series of macroeconomic errors such as allowing stock market speculation on credit, not ensuring a minimum amount of bank deposits (1929) and encouraging bank loans to insolvent people (subprime). Major economic disruptions are at the global level. The fundamentals are strong and rarely cause problems, but these difficulties come from the top of the pyramid. On the other hand, the key problems come from the bottom of the pyramid for developing countries. Dysfunctions at the bottom prevent macroeconomic policies from producing beneficial effects, even if they were the most effectively designed. Constructing a public building (such as a school) would be a feat for the local or regional authority. The project would cost three to four times as much as necessary, take years to complete, be riddled with defects, give rise to a series of corruptions and foster a culture of irresponsibility. There is no point in making Keynesian-type policies in such an environment. We need to change the basic fundamentals first to make the economy work normally and then inject public funds for development.

We have an excellent metaphor for this theme. If a billionaire father (or mother) has a child who is an alcoholic and a drug addict, he (or she) could offer him/her a large sum of money to build his/her future. But he/she would be likely to use it in the wrong way: drinking and drug abuse. But if his parents help him get clean, seek the services of a psychologist, support him in his recovery, and then give him a large sum of money after his recovery, he would have a good chance to make profitable investments and build a good future. There is a step to take before spending money to build a solid future. Third-world countries are spending unnecessarily by relying on alcoholic and drug-addicted institutions to build a future. Instead of Keynesian spending, we should be improving everything that contributes to a high level of institutional performance: anti-corruption mechanisms, human development, NPA (New Public Administration), promoting entrepreneurship, etc. Problems are mostly in the basic fundamentals. Therefore, development policies need to be fundamentally different in terms of priorities and channelling of resources.

Yet many developing countries blindly copy the policies of developed countries which will not be of much help to them. Even within the economic dimension, we cannot allow ourselves to put all the countries in a single block, otherwise, we will make serious mistakes, such as that of the European Union, which confused the Greek and German situations during the crisis that shook the old continent and began in 2008. When the international institutions somewhat understood the disasters, they produced they tried to promote the concept of good governance too little too late. Management was too far ahead of economics which clumsily tried to correct its mistakes. The founding father of modern management, Peter Drucker, kept repeating 'There are no underdeveloped countries, there are undermanaged countries.' However, economics wanted to promote a concept (good governance) without knowing how to root a culture to adopt it. It was enough to decree it. It is not established through processes that ensure its implementation. And here economists are not equipped for such a mission.

Too often during international crises, the concerned institutions had only one antidote for the whole planet: the contraction expansion model. At the beginning of the process, austerity policies (reduction of public spending) are implemented, and when the economy stabilises, growth is created. No one has asked why this approach produced satisfactory results for Germany in the early 2000s and why it produced disappointing results in Greece during the major crisis that the country experienced in the mid-2020s. If we were to follow the Global Science methodology, we would have dissected a set of parameters and established a monograph based on historical facts that would identify the types of countries for which contraction/expansion policies would work better and others for which there would be more appropriate measures. A table similar to the one below would be used to identify the distinctive characteristics of a country and to classify it according to an appropriate statistical methodology (e.g., factor analysis or other). There are many statistical innovations that could underpin the scheme. We can refine decision typologies based on common characteristics of groups of countries. Monographs can be drawn from historical analyses of different countries. A colossal task awaits our researchers in economic history in order to establish the typologies of countries in addition to the dynamics of their evolution. What is crucial here are the responses of social formations, by groups of countries, to the different manipulations of economic, educational, cultural and other policies.

The economic pyramid would be useful if one considers economics as a somewhat closed science, often isolated from the rest of knowledge. This is largely what is currently practised. However, in the context of Global Science, things would change completely. The main characteristic of the latter is the interaction of all significant variables relevant to a process. Parameters can be psychological, sociological or biological as long as they impact the same phenomenon. We will then have a schematisation close to the table below.

Consider the same problem: Keynesian recovery. Instead of taking only the economic characteristics, we will consider a host of psychological, sociological and environmental parameters in order to create monographs of countries and identify those that respond to or can benefit from a Keynesian-style recovery or, on the contrary, cause a serious loss of resources if the choice is to opt for such a policy. We will then have a more complete picture of the characteristics of countries and thus make fewer economic policy errors. We will therefore use a model close to the table below which is only a brief summary of parameters and sciences to consider. Probably new statistical methodologies are to be considered and the modes of simulations will greatly evolve towards a greater 'interdisciplinarity' and a better rebalancing of the sciences to be considered. At that point, it will become much clearer that developing countries will benefit much less from Keynesian policies—which are much needed in developed countries. It would then be much more obvious that the socio-technical parameters of Greece are so different from those of Germany that a contraction/expansion policy would cause more harm than good, even if the country will ultimately be fine. We would have caused human and material damage that would in fact be useless. We will also interconnect social sciences with hard sciences. We would then have minimised many social scourges. Digital fingerprinting software that makes double voting impossible will minimise ballot box stuffing so frequent in totalitarian countries, research bans on deadly viruses whose technology would be within the reach of mafia groups would be reassuring, polluting technologies would be better controlled, technological innovations would be better analysed under the scrutiny of their socio-economic impacts (by scientific committees) that adopt the methodology of Global Science

Country Characteristics and Decision Typology

(Global Science Methodology)

Count	Sociology	Psychology	....	Economics	Decisions
Country A	1.Discipline at work: good; 2.Ability to work in a group: good; 3.Expectations from the government: low...	1.Risk-taking: good; 2.Level of self-confidence: good; 3.Participation in decision-making: average...		1.Degree of managerial effectiveness: acceptable; 2.Entrepreneurship: acceptable; 3.Human qualifications: acceptable...	Keynesian Recovery
Country B	1.Discipline at work: unsatisfactory; 2.Ability to work in a group: poor 3.Expectations from the government: high;...	1. Risk-taking: weak; 2. Level of self-confidence: weak; 3. Participation in decision-makings: low...		1.Degree of managerial effectiveness: low; 2.Entrepreneurship: low 3.Human qualifications: low; ...	Stimulate supply and structural policies instead;

The Global Science methodology is not exclusive. Current modelling, optimisation, econometrics and others will always be used. It remains an additional tool to understand and act on complex interrelations. It would be a huge leap forward for our social sciences. We must then innovate at the level of all the human and social sciences and produce more precise and appropriate metrics. For example, in sociology, we would work to identify more precisely family influences compared to those of a home group. We already have a significant start, but Global Science would require more precision, more feedback and more improvements on what we already have. One reason for the backlog in humanities and social sciences is the lack of resources allocated to them. One could wrongly believe that this is a luxury that we cannot afford. However, a thorough diagnosis would make it possible to point out this flaw as one of the essential reasons for all the troubles threatening us and for the gap between the accumulation of knowledge among hard sciences, the humanities and social sciences that is getting wider. This dynamic will produce more and more perils in the future, and we cannot even imagine their magnitudes. We need a catch-up period where the humanities and social sciences would have more resources to rise to the challenges facing us. We will need to accelerate social innovations, not just the small incremental advances that current politicians are making. All disciplines (such as literature) as well as Global Science will leap forward as never before. They will have colossal challenges and cannot afford to evolve at the current pace. They will build, in addition to the mutations by the existing methods, more useful monographs by the methodology of Global Science.

The management of companies and non-profit institutions would be among the first to benefit. It would integrate more detailed and better-quantified parameters into a broader horizon and would integrate knowledge from other sciences more deeply. Assume that in comparative management one would try to better fit managerial typologies to the context of the countries. Then, in addition to the comparative management methodologies, we can use the Global Science methodology to enrich and better target the types of decisions to be taken. The table below is presented for illustrative purposes only. It takes into consideration some of the results of past research but makes assumptions that should be verified in the future. It is proposed as an explanation of the approach and does not pretend to be the reality. It aims to expose and explain the future method that will enrich the managerial approach. On the other hand, we have tried to take into account various researches in comparative management and used their conclusions. However, we do not claim that this table can contain exactly the desired information. Again, it is presented for illustrative purposes only.

Global Science Methodology: Applied to Management

country	Sociology	Psychology	...	Economics	Decisions
USA	PD: Good GI: Medium ----------	IA: A RT: Good ------------	-----	DoP: Good HQ: Good R et D: Good Orientation: LT ----------	MB0
Japan	PD: Good GI: Good ----------	IA: A RT: Medium ------------	-----	DoP: Good HQ : Good R & D : Bonne Orientation : LT -----------	Decision by Consensus
Europe	PD: Good GI: Acceptable -------	IA: A RT: Acceptable --------	------	DoP: acceptable QH: Good Orientation: LT -------------	Participating management
Developing countries	PD: Low GI: High	IA: I RT: Low	-------	DoP: Low HQ: Low Orientation: ST	Weberian first than participation later

PD: Power Distance. It is the degree of approval and adherence to the participative management process

GI: Group Influence. This is the degree of influence of the group on personal decisions

RT: Risk-taking. It is also the degree of entrepreneurship and personal commitment to non-conventional activities

IA: Intuitive or analytical

Orientation: Decision is made on the basis of long-term or short-term considerations only

DoP: Degree of individual and group performance measurement

HQ: Human qualifications (degree). The degree of human qualifications and resources devoted to this purpose

R&D: Research and Development. Quantitative measure of resources allocated to research and development

The parameters are classified into five categories: High, acceptable, medium, moderate and low

Thus, all disciplines would benefit from integrating other sciences in their fields of analysis. We would benefit from existing and future contributions to better define the problems that constitute their rationale. Each theme would be enriched a thousand times by the integration of all the scattered and little-used knowledge of the past. Nowadays, it is mainly through the intuition of ingenious researchers that we draw from various disciplines to complement the different social and human sciences in order to analyse, predict and act on the phenomena that interest us. Tomorrow, it would be through a rigorous methodological approach clearly established that we would make use of all or most of the knowledge at our disposal and especially identify those that remain to be discovered in order to combat modern scourges. For example, we would learn that in corporate strategy, the key variable for success is the mobilisation of global intelligence: qualifying all human resources to participate in the overall construction of the strategic plan. Each person is trained, mobilised and contributes according to his potential, not his position. Managing companies and institutions will be revolutionised by Global Science.

On the Structuring of Nation and Nation-World Systems

The current structuring of the nation and nation-world systems has unfolded in a heterogeneous way. Pressing historical contexts had mostly prevailed in their design. Immediate imperatives prevailed over a very long-term vision. The founding of the United Nations in October 1945, recognised the victors of the time as the ultimate decision-makers of human destiny. Among others, the Western countries, the IMF, the World Bank and the Bank for International Settlements expressed the desire to preserve American supremacy in the economic and political fields. It was necessary to have an instrument to reduce the tensions of the Cold War, but at the same time to preserve the pre-eminence of the victors' interests, and especially that of the United States. The vision of a club, an elite or a cartel with special privileges prevailed over an image of united humanity with a grand common project. The creation of a myriad of organisations (health, education, environment, etc.) under the authority of the UN has not been able to eradicate from the world's political subconscious the fact that the structuring of a world, regional or national organisation cannot be done without narrow interests for the most powerful and minor commitments in favour of the most precarious. All signs announcing a world structured destined to self-destruct by preserving the interests of the powerful rather than prospering together were widely noted. The current system of reforms through insignificant increments is an on-going arrangement to preserve the essence of the present structure and interests and to face with this outdated device new and complex challenges beyond the possibilities of the current certainties.

History has played a large role in structuring the current nation-world system. Powerful empires, kingdoms and republics with substantial armies have too often enslaved the vulnerable, except that this time the UN version is rather watered down. Neither its charter nor its organisational mode could raise our world to the rank of a civilisation that endures and guarantees the future of generations to come.

For lack of being able to achieve this ambition, two additional illusions are created; the first of which is a myth called sustainable development, as if the current world structure could allow us to achieve it. We only retain the attractive definition of the concept: the capacity to satisfy current needs without harming future generations. Except that nobody knows how to do it and we are not organised to know it or practice it. We have a few attempts but they are too insignificant to make any difference. Second, in order to convince ourselves that we have other potentials, we reproduce a proliferation of institutions and forums to multiply our chances of success: the G7, the G20, the IPCC, the COPs, etc. In doing so, we drown out the responsibilities and give the impression that we are untangling ourselves, that we are doing the maximum and that it is impossible to accomplish more or better. The number of summits that have mobilised the world's most powerful decision-makers and expert forums is impressive. The world is buzzing with excitement and activity, but in the end, the expert reports always bring us back to a sad reality: for decades we have been falling behind in tackling the crucial challenges facing humanity. The future structuring of the nation-world system, in order to be effective, should articulate and value four fundamental principles: the first would be to mobilise the maximum human intelligence around the issue to extract from our brains all the ideas that contribute to boost the system towards the peaks of better ecological performance. The second would be to bring together all existing human knowledge relevant to our objectives in an integrated and coherent way. The third would be to identify the most urgent ones to be developed (R&D) in order to have the tools to cope with the challenges. The fourth would be to structure the nation systems first and then the nation-world system so as to benefit from the synergies at all levels of the selected scheme.

At the level of the nation system, each country would have a hierarchical structure that derives from its originality and history, its culture and the managerial knowledge we have. The only change that needs to be made is to have a specialised Global Science entity within each country: municipal, regional or national entities. Political parties, NGOs and others should not be left out. Its role would be to mobilise all the intelligence of its community and to coordinate its activities with the national strategy which itself is derived from the jointly agreed global scheme. The cell of an entity at the local level can include one or two people, at the regional level it could be four or five with more consequent tools and at the national level it could be a structure (such as a super ministry, a specialised institute or others) which would have hundreds of people equipped with the most sophisticated means of simulation and which would integrate together all the elements to build the necessary coherences in time and space. There would be room for all the disciplines that must work in harmony to move the global system towards harmonious solutions.

At the global level, the structure would be many times more sophisticated. It would allow global simulations by integrating present and future (to be developed) knowledge from all disciplines in all countries as well as best practices and ideas proposed at different hierarchical levels and selected by a committee to incorporate the most beneficial options.

Global Scheme of the Nation-World System

The salutary scheme for dealing quickly and effectively with global challenges is scientifically plausible but politically impossible. It is technically possible to create a global structuring that would propel humanity to the peak of its performance with a considerable reduction in the major risk mapping. We would then be among the humanities whose propensity to prosper is immense, but the political challenges facing such a feat are simply phenomenal. It is not clear that the current structure and mechanisms are conducive to success. Now we know that historical materialism has been inoperative since the beginning of the twentieth century. Instead of having a predetermined 'natural' historical path, we actually have alternatives. We have choices that we can make according to the level of awareness and maturity of us humans. Currently, we can see that we are making much more scientific and technological progress than ethical and humanitarian ones. This is a widening gap that has disastrous consequences. We can produce plenty of scenarios, but we can stick to the basics. We have at least three:

1. Continuity
2. Accelerating attempts with the same methods
3. Global Science

First of all, the continuity scenario has been mentioned many times. It is the 'Business as Usual' scenario with its potential risks, which are enormous. There is a high probability that we will get bogged down in this uncertain and perilous situation. We cling to a model that has proven ineffective in dealing with such challenges. For too long, we have considered that a politically democratic system was sufficient to structure nations capable of realising human aspirations of prosperity, social justice, harmony with ecosystems and the perpetuation of the human adventure on Earth. We feel that we lack at least four other complementary dimensions: hyper-transparency, a code of ethics, a vector of objectives and a science of human and social systems (how to build complex human systems other than capitalism with confiscated democracy or a dictatorship). At the moment, the arsenal of models and theories at our disposal does not allow us to devise scientific schemes that would allow us to conceive economic, political and social formations that function differently from capitalism with confiscated democracy or tyrannical nations. The existing system is too risky for human goodwill to let it try to solve vital human problems. The failure likelihood is so high that it terrifies human beings who are properly informed about the situation.

The second scenario is the one to which we will transition very quickly. It consists of leaving the global institutional and political architecture as it is, mobilising more resources, and exponentially increasing the number of meetings, organisations in charge of the issue, and resource mobilisation. Efforts to allocate resources and institutions of all kinds will not be entirely futile. We will probably ease the heavy burdens on the shoulders of nations, but it would be pretentious for the rest of us to claim victory after a few marginal battles won in a Pyrrhic fashion. We are already seeing the beginnings of this scheme coming true. The issue of global warming is at the level of the UN, the IPCC, the G7, the G20, and the various COPs etc. Even a consensual decision, such as the one taken at COP21 in Paris, will quickly be challenged during the implementation processes. Another COP or another G7 is then needed to try to plug the gaps. While the ship Earth is taking on water everywhere, initiatives will multiply and promises will be amplified to encourage certain circles to a temporary and presumptuous optimism. Just enough time to realise that the approach is incoherent and that we do not have the structure, priorities and mechanisms to control the threats of such a dimension. So, we do the same thing again: more meetings, new forums, and promises of action and mobilisation of more resources. There is no way out of this vicious circle. We have put the great potential of the human race on hold by an inoperative or even defective organisation. It is very likely that this scenario will be our next and perhaps last step because the output will always be too little and late.

Theoretically, the number of possible scenarios is much bigger than the two we have presented. But what we have described are the possibilities that have the highest likelihood of becoming reality. Of course, goodwill must join forces to prevent our past mistakes from condemning entire generations to the hell of future catastrophes! We can hope that a third salutary scenario will emerge. There may be several. We will outline a credible and scientifically salutary alternative, but one that is very difficult to implement politically unless there is an extraordinary surge from a large number of people, institutions, NGOs and others. We call this scenario the adoption of Global Science. The third scenario is not a panacea, a perfection of the human spirit or a utopia derived from an absolutist doctrine. It is only one possibility among many others to control one's destiny instead of undergoing it. We are entering a phase where a merciless struggle, barely concealed, is taking place between the forces of survival and those of unconscious annihilation. This separation transcends the class struggle between the owners of capital and the owners of labour power, although there are interfaces between the two phenomena. The alternative of a single party with a monopoly of power over society, which would structure it towards a salutary path, is more naive and dangerous than the present situation. A promising alternative would always take place within:

1. A liberated democratic process;
2. A hyper-transparency;
3. A most rigorous structuring; and
4. A decision-making process that mobilises all human intelligence.

And finally, a Global Science that allows for the creation of political, economic and social formations as alternatives to capitalism with confiscated democracy and tyrannical socialism.

Fifty years ago, it was hardly conceivable that an ultraconservative communist party could create a flourishing market economy, with its strengths and failures. Today, China has demonstrated the possibility of such a system. No one has tried a socialist system with a democratic process, a multi-party system and the freedoms enjoyed by some advanced capitalist countries. However, social sciences have made advances that would most likely allow such a system to come into being. We will elaborate on each of these elements and draw the consequences for action.

Democratic and Motivational Deficiencies

Two huge deficiencies immensely undermine the potential for ingenuity in the nation-world system: the direction of global resource flows and the way the democratic process works.

Consider the first point. Economic literature is replete with analyses of all kinds of options for the allocation of a nation's resources. Public institutional choices (planning) are contrasted with solutions derived by independent economic agents according to market signals revealed by the price vectors of products and services. This often leads to claims of greater efficiency in the use of resources through market mechanisms and even to a superior system of human and institutional incentives. Under certain conditions, the statement is not unfounded. But to generalise it at all costs would be very problematic. During times of military conflicts, most market mechanisms are already put on hold, even if people believe in their superiority in normal times. It is considered that the average consumer is neither super-rational nor fully informed so that he can make the best possible decision in the short and long term. He has limited information and limited rationality. To suggest that he/she has all the data in hand to decide implies that a buyer of a cell phone knows its ecological footprint, the impacts on all social and environmental dynamics as well as the very long-term consequences on thousands of variables to compare them to the human, material and institutional benefits created by the acquisition and to conclude that there is an advantage for the short, medium and very long term.

Yet a very limited and temporary degree of rationality is always possible. In an 'abnormal' situation such as an armed conflict, we would need a high authority that has more information and that sets priorities according to the data in its possession. We are in a similar situation but with a more consequent potential of danger. Deciding on a carbon tax and therefore on signals to be introduced at the level of price vectors and creating a market of pollution rights may not be enough to reverse the process of environmental degradation. If a shortage of corn occurs, prices will rise and many farmers will dedicate more land for the next year and the crops will restore prices within a year or so. This is a simple situation where market mechanisms have few institutional barriers to produce desirable effects in an acceptable time frame. But when the delays can be immense, procrastination can render the effects produced obsolete. Take the example of the carbon tax. The example of the pollution rights market is even worse. We have at least four major types of delays that vary greatly:

1. Agreement delay: It takes multiple consultations and negotiations to reach an international agreement on the issue. Historical and geostrategic interests and situations will weigh heavily on the degree of cooperation of the actors and this delay can be abnormally long.
2. Institutional delay: For many countries, agreement of parliaments is required and internal political situations may delay the formalisation of an international consensus.
3. Organisational delay: Authority, resources and responsibilities must be allocated internally for each country between different administrations and the new package must be made to work coherently.
4. Impact delay: Time is needed for research and development to produce new products and services that are in line with the global equilibrium between economic needs and the equilibrium of ecosystems.

When the length of these delays is greater than the irreversibility of processes, a conciliator with more information, knowledge and power will be needed to advance solutions faster. In case of armed conflict, the state plays this role. In the case of global warming, we are deprived of such a judge. So, we multiply the responsible institutions: G7, G20, IPCC, COP etc. In doing so, we make it more difficult to solve the problem. And we are back to square one. The diagnosis could not be clearer: we have produced promising but still insufficient knowledge and too little social and human science to enable us to overcome such perils. And directing resource flows is the cornerstone of this. The latter is achieved through market mechanisms and leads to a limited rationality of economic agents with a short-term perspective and can only be appropriate in very specific situations: lulls and global equilibrium achieved. At the slightest turbulence, the system becomes incapable of delivering rescue bursts in and by itself. We would need an arbitration state to extend the duration and improve somewhat the degree of rationality of the system when facing major disturbances.

However, the rationality of a public institution is baffled when a nation-world system is insufficiently structured, when we do not have a Global Science that allows us to manage major risks and when the direction of resources is therefore problematic. Today it is the logic of conflict that still directs the world's resources. We will soon exceed 2000 billion in military expenditure to 'protect' ourselves from each other and let the most dangerous threats threaten us: destruction of ecosystems, meteorites, pandemics etc. Suppose that at the world level, we would have allocated less than half of this amount for research such as: using the solar energy or energy of planetary movements (like turbo) to provide us with renewable energy. We do not know how to do that. But, we would have tried. If we succeeded, we would have made a giant step towards restoring the equilibrium of our ecosystems. It would be a success story. But, what is success if every year we create faster supersonic missiles to carry more nuclear payloads and next year we invest even more money to improve the speed and the payload? What is the ultimate goal? There is no equilibrium horizon to such a process. Today, the process of channelling resources lacks an overall logic. We have neither a global political willingness, nor a science to analyse it, and even less an efficient structuring of human goodwill to overcome these messes.

The second area concerns human freedoms within societies that want to be havens of law and freedom of choice. The march of history is towards more freedoms, democracies and choices for the people. However, anti-freedom forces are leading and will lead hostile actions, too often with the support of the democracies of the developed countries, against the liberation of oppressed peoples and to postpone the coming of a more rational nation-world system. Strategic myopia has taken hold of the developed nations that make symbolic actions for the benefit of huge world populations in search of freedom and provide major financial, military and strategic support to the main leaders who oppress their peoples. In doing so, far too many resources are devoted to bullying populations than to creating a fair and sustainable nation-world system.

Short-term calculations take precedence over humanism, justice and the creation of a reliable international system that is suitable for its survival. It is enough for a country to be endowed with resources such as fossil energy, uranium, gold, lower production costs (China) or to be in an enviable geostrategic position to make the principles of human rights, justice and freedom of the people the nth concern of the ruling political classes. Countries with confiscated democracy have consciously or unconsciously played a major role in spreading despotic systems in the world, making them the norm and democracy, even a confiscated one, becomes the exception. In fact, we have the two biggest dramas of modern 'democracy' which are: Democratic high treason at the international level and negative lobbying at the national level. Confronted with this blockage of a global solution, many groups are seriously contemplating acts of violence. The system seems to them strangely flexible on the surface within the 'advanced democracies,' but terribly locked to seriously address the real threats.

The high democratic treason has emptied the rigour of international relations of its meaning. It is enough to possess coveted resources, to be capable of operating negative lobbying or to possess geostrategic assets in order to attract the favours of prosperous nations, even if you are a dictatorship. One can even claim to be a democratic example simply by manipulating elections through a complicit administrative process. In most developing countries, the falsification of elections has become the centre of gravity of political activity. Electoral fraud has become a global political issue encouraged by the barely concealed complicity of advanced countries. Yet, there are many alternatives to drastically reduce the phenomenon. We could assign the process of management and certification of results to a UN body and the developed countries would be the first to submit themselves to the process. They lose nothing because they already have a credible process in this area. This is to prevent other nations from using national sovereignty to oppress their citizens.

Political science is called upon to propose other alternatives. Researchers in this field are not short of imagination to enlighten us on the best possible choices. Of course, the countries concerned, national and international NGOs will also play observer roles. Hyper-transparency would then reign during the course of these elections. A small sacrifice by democratic countries (respecting the process of international election certification) would have a huge impact on international relations. It is this process that must be the basis for global cohesion. There would be two groups: those who respect the process and those who reject it. Politicians who deny the process will already be questioned by their own populations and will appear to all as tyrants and defenders of an order destined to be thrown into the dustbin of history. But continuing to protect despots because of their resources, their geopolitical positions or their negative lobbying potentials contribute to the spread of global chaos.

High democratic treason: The denial of one's own values, of human rights ethics and the perfidy of the current 'democratic' powers in exchange for material resources (oil) or geostrategic support (military bases), backing for the re-election projects of many complicit politicians, are rooting numerous fascist projects and the despoiling of the masses and the biosphere: the nation-world system is increasingly resembling global chaos. With the fall of the Berlin Wall, the concept of 'the end of history' appeared. In fact, we are rather close to the death of history. The choice practices of channelling vital resources to clearly sub-optimal activities; high democratic treason, negative lobbying and particularly the structuring of the nation-world system are the foundations of the undermining of our ability to ensure our well-being and sustainability.

The operating mechanisms are neither so simple nor impossible to undo, but the degree of urgency is agonising. In a few short decades, many of the processes that destroy ecosystems would become irreversible. The only relevant question that remains is: will we be able to take the right actions in time? More and more evidence is accumulating against the climate sceptics. The likelihood that the mechanisms they describe will bring about beneficial changes is diminishing by the day. We would have been delighted if they were right. Unfortunately, our aspiration to benefit from their assurance is getting worse every day! So, it was necessary to dare to make combinations of attempts. There is no single alternative that would be the best way to work. If it existed, we don't know it. But we must produce one as soon as possible. The one that we think is the closest to the optimum. It would be proposed to us by the 'Global Science' methodology, which has yet to be elaborated and validated by many scientists.

The central idea of Global Science is that by mobilising all available relevant knowledge, a maximum of human brains, and by channelling research and development where it is vital we could create the potential to reverse the degradation process that is sometimes voluntarily but often unconsciously initiated. We have briefly formulated some aspects of Global Design. This part will be devoted entirely to its development. We would then have revealed a little more about some of its contents.

Science, Ethics and Global Science

Ethics is a topic that is widely covered by a variety of disciplines. Its ramifications are many and varied. Specialists in epistemology deploy them, especially in the field of sciences. The latter extend themselves for the most part without sufficient regard for a certain ethics that should guide them. Only medicine adopts a coherent minimalist basis of deontology (the Hippocratic Oath or its derivatives) as a prelude to a more sound practice of the profession. It is not enough to have a code of ethics or deontology to safeguard against behavioural abuses. Many Nazi physicians practised the opposite of the Hippocratic Oath. A nation's system that is flawed at its core traps average citizens in a logic of power. This hardly implies that an ethics of science would be useless. If physics had a universally adopted code of ethics, perhaps more research and effort would have gone into developing clean energy than into the continuous, unrestricted effort to perfect weapons of mass destruction.

However, the philosophy and operating mechanisms of the nation system often take precedence over any contrary ethics or deontology. Past nation systems have been built through a multitude of minor choices and major upheavals. These mutations obey the historical logic of the moment. We have seen that historical materialism is made obsolete by human intervention in the process of social evolution. We do not have a single possible historical dynamic but several possible alternatives. We could continue to create natural cataclysms and destroy our social structures or we could build societies capable of meeting the challenges we have brought upon ourselves. We will need Global Science to guide us in building more responsible systems and more determined to avoid the mistakes of the past. It is becoming increasingly clear that the alternative of communism as advocated by Karl Marx is neither possible nor desirable. A monopoly of power can never bring about human freedoms and the economic and social equality that human beings want.

Global Science will need a code of ethics more than any other discipline. It should use existing knowledge; generate new understandings and mobilise the maximum number of human brains to build responsible national systems and to address current challenges. At present, such an approach is lacking. Of course, the code of ethics must be discussed and adopted. We will never be able to create an ideal code or one that would be unanimous. Its main lines should be integrated and respected by the followers and specialists of 'Global Science.' Practitioners would not commit themselves to projects and would not use their knowledge if the visions did not respect the ethical guidelines which could be:

1. Strict respect, without exception, of the principles contained in the Declaration of Human Rights;
2. Endangering the biosphere;
3. Degrading the productive potential and well-being of future generations;
4. Differentiate between peoples of different nations;
5. Specify the rights of animals; and
6. Avoid creating social formations for despotic regimes.

A code of ethics is essential. It guides thinking and action. We have many talented authors who can put the above and other principles into simple, appealing and engaging language. However, the content is also critical. It serves at least to clarify the priorities and basic precepts of the discipline. There will always be idiosyncrasies, singularities and anomalies. But with an explicit ethical code, it would be easier to detect them. Ethics should be the prerogative of the vast majority and not the monopoly of scientists, politicians or any community.

Mission and Strategy

Most of the sciences came into existence because of the needs of human life. The need to heal was felt, so a science was developed for this purpose: medicine. There is an aspiration to improve the well-being of individuals and communities, so economics was developed to fulfil this need. Sciences are invested with explicit and implicit missions. They accomplish them more or less efficiently depending on the resources as well as on the management of production, diffusion and implementation of knowledge. Even if the rationale of science is often implicit, its roots can also be found in its own definitions. Thus, the purpose of economics is to explain the mechanisms that allow the use of scarce resources for the most desired ends. This is one specification among others. We would gain in precision by refining the definitions and the mission.

However, around every science, there are always struggles to focus on its priorities. There is no doubt that if research and development resources were channelled mainly towards knowledge and technologies that protect ecosystems and promote more social equality and conflict management, we would have a very different planet. But our nation-world system is structured voluntarily or involuntarily to create contradictions between individual interests on the one hand, and ethics and high human ideals on the other. Harmony of interests is a short-term illusion in complete denial of the deep aspirations of the very long term. The euphony of the invisible hand is only justified by a severe myopia. We count on the chance of historical events to build technological and social coherences in order to prosper and to avoid the unspeakable pitfalls of the operating modes of nation-world systems. We believe deeply in social Darwinism. But the pattern of nations is profoundly distinct from natural arrangements even if the latter are also more complex than we think.

The mission of 'Global Science' would be to contribute to building models of nations and world-nations that respect its code of ethics and/or that allow these entities to design solutions to fatal multidisciplinary and planetary challenges.

Thus, improving well-being, making good use of scarce resources, fighting internal and inter-nation inequalities, helping to reduce conflicts, and especially preserving planetary ecosystems must be included in its ethics and goals. However, for most of our social sciences, we have been satisfied with technical specifications, outside of any ethics, which has inevitably contributed to the current situation.

Definition: 'Global Science' is a multidisciplinary approach that mobilises all human intelligence to jointly design, in a coordinated and organised way, types of social formations endowed with common universal values and with an enormous potential to overcome together perilous collective challenges of very large scale. Thus, according to this definition, if one would like to develop a social formation endowed with freedom, social justice (e.g., inequality ratio 1 to 10) and ethics, then one could design the educational, family and economic systems, the political mechanisms and the priorities of soft and hard sciences to do so. This would be a real revolution in social engineering. Organising such a process will be developed at length. Afterwards, many qualified specialists will improve, develop or adjust certain aspects. It could then also be used to tackle perilous problems such as global warming and recurring conflicts. There is already very useful content developed by our brilliant scientists that would form the basis of the Global Science contribution. But there are also ways to improve our knowledge in many areas in order to have more sophisticated tools, in hard, social and human sciences, to accomplish its primary mission.

There is a whole philosophy behind Global Science that would be distinctly different from historical materialism or unbridled liberalism (overrated laissez-faire). For the first case, there is no predetermined destiny for humanity as advocated by historical materialism. Its future will only be the result of what we accomplish today. As soon as we perpetuate our ideas and practices, we will inexorably be heading towards fatal perils. Historical determinism so much advocated by the Marxist analysis appears more and more as an insufficient reading of the gigantic social mutations which had accompanied the industrial revolution, namely: the weight of the government, inputs of the scientific elites and the end of the political monopoly on the societal decisions even if the weight of numerous lobbies remains preponderant. Even if the owners of capital held more power over economic and social decisions, the fear of the poor and middle classes was sufficient to balance (insufficiently) public priorities. While benefiting the owners of capital, it was in the interest of the politicians to also look after the needs of the less fortunate.

Massive disillusionment would provoke social upheavals (May 1968 in France) or multiform punishment votes. Thus, many 'laws' and social mechanisms have been invalidated. Not only economics dictates social change. Human aspirations for more freedom, participation and scientific developments have all contributed to shaping the form and content of modern social formations. Economic interests have led to the fragmentation of classes into communities of interest. Faced with the distrust of a single, inevitable destiny advocated by historical materialism, we have been treated to a completely opposite view: pure and hard liberalism. According to its proponents, a large-scale laissez-faire approach that would confine the state to its regalian missions would create fair, clean nations in harmony with their environment. All they have to do is apply the 'polluter pays' principle. For Keynes, we can add a regalian mission for the state: smoothing economic cycles through fiscal and monetary policies. While societies with socialist connotations were quick to show their shortcomings, the followers of laissez-faire were swift to conquer the empty lots since there was no alternative system until now, the only two alternatives we have been offered are a watered-down capitalism or a statist monopoly power. We don't know how to build anything else.

The first system has practically collapsed, and the second, a more resilient one, has every chance of collapsing too in the longer term. The causes and mechanisms of these collapses are poorly understood. However, both systems have a common foundation: the inexorability of a happy ending according to their designers. The advent of communism or of an abundant society for all will put a permanent end to historical human suffering for the Marxists. The laissez-faire approach will produce a society of abundance that will satisfy the needs of all of the extreme liberals. Except that the result on the horizon blithely contradicts both doctrines. The first system has virtually given up the ghost and the deleterious laissez-faire has somewhat improved the standard of living in the vast majority of countries but has created social formations and technologies that endanger the very foundations of life on Earth. Myopic human planning could not see the distant precipices.

The second system is therefore also fundamentally flawed. Both doctrines believe in an inexorable evolutionary dynamic of social formations, but towards different destinies: communism for the former and an abundant and free society for all for the latter. The class struggle presented as the driving force of history by the former and the harmony of class interests assumed by the latter have proved to be gross simplifications. The ultimate reality that emerges is much an antagonism between man and nature where one would fatally destroy the other. Human beings have identified a compromise: to get the most out of nature to sustain their consensus. This would be a postponement of the class struggle for the former and a win/win process for the latter. However, the catastrophic scenarios predicted by our eminent scientists are highly probable hypotheses and contradict both approaches. The so-called advent of communism will definitively liberate human beings from exploitation and misery. The dream of the end of history with a victory and irrevocable crowning of a unique type of social formation (capitalist model of neoclassical type) proves to be close to a delusion. For both schools, a happy ending awaits mankind. We could prevent the historical laws from coming into play in the medium term. But in the very long term, we can only reach the promised happy conclusions. It is not by chance that these two schools have led to conclusions that are too far from reality. Their basic assumptions about human and institutional behaviour are too crude and too basic. Instead of revising their premises and improving their theories and models, the admirers of both schools are quick to criticise the developments of reality that do not correspond to their predictions.

Marxists blame international mechanisms (colonisation, domination, and terms of trade) for having prevented the impoverishment of advanced countries. But, if these mechanisms are important, they should have been incorporated into the medium-term models. The proponents of liberalism have done the same. The departure of modern nations from the scheme of pure and perfect competition would have introduced many fatal distortions to the system: excessive unionism, oligopolies and excessive statism, intense lobbying would be the most fatal elements that have appeared. But the dominant thought pattern has not revised its fundamental conclusions according to the appearance of this little foreseen and little explained evolutions. We are living in a deep crisis of social and human sciences, whose consequences have a strong impact on real historical evolutions.

In fact, there would be several possible pathways depending on our current strategies and structuring. We do not have a single predetermined destiny but many possibilities (alternatives) depending on our current choices. The recommendations of Global Science are only one alternative that seems to be among the most salutary. We can take other directions and undergo other

131

experiences and end up in different situations that are often much less optimal. But the idea of a single path, even in the very long term, is a heresy. However, humanity is really at a real crossroads for one main reason: historically it has just created, during the century before last, the capacities of its own destruction. Are we going to develop forms of nations and world-nations systems capable of avoiding partial or total collective annihilation or are we going to continue to follow a path with a high suicidal likelihood? Will the human and social sciences develop to a point where they will allow us to achieve an acceptable level of control over future events or will we give up such an ambition? This brings us back to the mission that should never be overlooked in developing the strategic process.

The prelude to strategic thinking, in the context of Global Science, always begins with a rigorous diagnosis of the overall situation. Strategic analysis is very different from business strategy practices. Business strategy methodologies are somewhat distant from those of Global Science. We are only on the cusp of being able to create new social formations that respect the ethics of Global Science and that respond to human aspirations. On the other hand, we have enough tools and mechanisms that are not yet used to make serious corrections to the major world disorders that can endanger the planet, such as the destruction of the major equilibriums of ecosystems. Unfortunately, what is being implemented is very far from the recommendations of Global Science.

Diagnosis

Global Science (GS) diagnosis is essentially multidisciplinary. This remains a fundamental requirement of its precepts and method. A classical approach would lead to a focus on one discipline at the expense of others for historical and cultural reasons. Let us consider the problem of global warming. At first, one might think that the crisis would be mainly economic: the incentive to externalise extra costs and enjoy the effects of the 'free rider.' But a closer look at the issue would show that the difficulty is mostly political: private money financing campaigns greatly affect the quality of public policy decisions. Politics is more about serving the interests of campaign financiers than it is about serving the interests of average citizens. And political science is called upon more than anything else to spot and evaluate promising alternatives. This multidisciplinary approach may well yield a better potential for discerning between causes and symptoms.

The cause/symptom dichotomy has always been a problem for social scientists and especially for superficial analyses. When prices start to rise in a country (inflation begins), a host of analysts start blaming traders and companies for their so-called greed. They rarely ask themselves why two years ago these same actors were far from showing such greed or why the same actors in neighbouring countries are not. So, we have a manifestation of an evil, not its origin.

This is why benchmarking is the beginning of understanding a problem. Certainly, the popular saying goes that 'comparison is not truth' but the comparison is the beginning of truth. A number or a fact in itself has no substantial meaning. It is only in relation to a standard, a norm, a performance or an objective that it begins to better reveal its foundations. A 4% improvement in a company's results would be good news if the average competitor had improved by 1%, but a cruel fact if the competitor had increased its profits by 10%. It is time to better understand diagnostic methodologies. We have done a lot of work on this issue. The essentials are known but can still be improved. On the other hand, many practices become too often the recommended methodological standards.

The ultimate aim of a diagnosis must not be overlooked. Its complexity is matched only by the diversity of factual situations. An analysis of a region's mode of operation in order to coordinate its activities with the rest of the nation in order to review the education system to anchor more egalitarian demands is not at all the same type as a national audit to coordinate global activities to control global warming. Moreover, we cannot do without a source of inspiration for the elements of the diagnosis: theoretical schemes, historical experiences and available models will be called upon to structure the investigation. In the end, we return to our three famous questions: What is known, the experiences and the lessons learned? This will differ according to many factors: the hierarchical level of the problem, the status of knowledge, the assets and the difficulties that exist are fundamental elements.

The checklists for GS diagnostics will become more and more elaborate as our knowledge in this field evolves. Interconnection of many disciplines and the development of qualitative models as well as the management of complex global systems require simulation capabilities unknown so far. The tools at our disposal, revolutionary in their time, will seem rudimentary to concretise the new realities that humans intend to achieve. We cannot be sure that the gap between the development of the knowledge of the hard sciences and the human and social sciences will start to reduce. We must first construct more revealing indicators to manage this evolution. These increasingly conspicuous gaps have created in the past a great potential for improvement in all fields but a most problematic and risky nation-world system.

Conceptualisation of the Scheme

The philosophy of Global Science is to move to a qualitatively higher stage. Neither historical materialism nor the invisible hand satisfactorily explains the complex system of evolution of modern nations. Let alone a combination of the two! The state of the world is that the likelihood of suffering great disasters that could endanger life on earth is much higher than the likelihood of developing harmoniously to create an intergalactic civilisation. We have somewhat anticipated the problem of resource shortages but not the more important perils such as the rapid destruction of global ecosystems. Global Science is a combination of democratic social choices, ethics and science to build new social formations consistent with human expectations and contemporary challenges. To reach such a stage, we would need to broaden the fields of our knowledge and combine them wisely in order to conceive social and economic formations endowed with ethics and aimed at achieving deep human expectations with the help of wisely harmonised scientific mechanisms. It is this careful combination of ethics, science and efficiency that constitutes the essence of Global Science. There are clear differences between the evolution of modern societies by the existing tools and a transmutation through Global Science: the main differences would be:

1. Better mobilisation of collective intelligence when making important common choices (see section on decision-making).
2. A global coherence by a multidisciplinary evaluation using the most up-to-date human knowledge, often helped by powerful simulators.
3. Avoiding intuitive biases from entering the decision package, which can derail the system's coherence.
4. Introduce ethics and human values as the ultimate constraints to the conceptualisation of the modes of operation of social formations.

Today we are beginning, in terms of potential in conceptualisation, a dynamic that would enable us to conceive social formations that are more equitable, in harmony with the biosphere and the fragility of ecosystems, and conducive to more universal peace. But it is our current institutional arrangements and our national and international operating mechanisms that would prevent us from creating these accommodations. Many countries still live under dictatorships (China), 'alibi' democracies (Russia) or confiscated democracies (Europe, USA…). The forces pushing for these salutary changes - especially young people, scientists, committed citizens and artists- are not yet equipped with a doctrine, a strategy or a structure capable of tipping the equilibrium in their favour. Status quo forces are more organised and more determined and their strategies are more carefully elaborated to better resist fragmented and spontaneous efforts, no matter how sincere and magnanimous they are.

Structuring

It has been known for a long time that in organisation, as in many other managerial processes, we do not have a unique alternative. Whether we are talking about a company or a country, there are several possible organisational forms, some of which are adequate and others totally inappropriate. The main thing would be to choose an alternative that is very promising and that would allow to achieve the socio-economic and human ambitions of the nation or of a nation-world system. The search for the best possible way of structuring an entity is legitimate but futile since we will not know what the ultimate organisational form will be. Nevertheless, we can outline one option among the good ones and from which many variants can be derived.

The philosophy according to which a democratic nation, through approaches of coordination, institutional improvements and a minimum of public orientations, would lead to a social and economic optimum and a global equilibrium is an optical illusion. This equilibrium would allow for a long-term equivalence between the productive potential of the biosphere and the satisfaction of human needs arising from the anticipations created by the political-economic and social modes of operation. We now know with a high degree of certainty that this is not possible. To make a Mea-Culpa is not a sign of weakness but of strength of soul. Such a move would be able to revolutionise our knowledge and practices. But, to assume that we are facing a minor threat would lead us to tinker with our old good methods and practices to actually face new perils of a never-known scale. We have more or less correctly assessed the fragility of ecosystems only very recently, at most the last three decades. We assumed that the old structure of the nation-world system, with minor modifications, would be able to meet the new, immense and unprecedented challenges.

Whereas the simple indicators on which the vast majority of analysts base themselves (the anticipated rise in average temperature) show, with very little doubt, that we are at a dead end. We still firmly believe that a slight reorganisation of our historical record is a sound prospect. We believe that the same slightly altered parameters will induce immensely liberating consequences. But the first experiences have mostly given rise to disillusionment and the next ones will risk revealing more. If a complex system is not directed towards the desired directions, then we would have one or more simultaneous constraints on the level of the objectives, the method, and the structuring or operating mechanisms. In our case, it is the last three elements that jointly cause the current scheme to seize up.

We must therefore restructure ourselves differently, formulate innovative solutions and radically transform our methods and our organisation in at least three innovative directions. We reiterate that we must not forget that there are many alternatives available. Planning methods, scientific conceptualisations and structuring are the drivers of the new nation-world architecture.

Structuring: The ambitions of structuring the current nation-world system were mainly to preserve peace, anticipate conflicts, act to stop them and coordinate for a minimum of cooperation. It would be tedious to deconstruct in depth the structuring of the system, but it is clear that many contradictions undermine the coexistence and coherence of its objectives with its mode of operation. We must work in conversion mode to move it towards the development of strong partnerships likely to overcome the enormous common perils.

Planning: Planning has always been a set of techniques, methods, and tools for forecasting and mobilising human, material, and financial resources to achieve socio-economic goals set by decision-makers. Economics and quantitative methods dominate the process. Former socialist countries have had mixed experiences at best with a centralised system. Contrary to popular belief, the market economies planned much more than the former socialist countries. However, the main part of the planning process takes place within firms. The activity is rather decentralised. But planning was much more concerned with cost reduction, short-term profit increase and a strict minimum of social and environmental impact. However, the planning activity was mainly focused on the economic aspects. This is how states functioned in all continents: minimal centralised planning in market economies but a strong centralisation process in state economies. This process, which was somewhat acceptable during the period of euphoria, would be quite inadequate for the new stage which is characterised by much more complex issues. We need to move from classical planning to 'Global Science,' which is more multidisciplinary, more participatory and more systemic. It helps to identify and mobilise all the available human knowledge and to identify the minimum that remains to be controlled in order to rise to the challenges of the day. We get all the human and hard sciences to communicate and work together in order to create sustainable social formations that incorporate human ethics such as equity and the preservation of natural ecosystems.

Countries with advanced market economies could no longer afford to ignore the structuring required by Global Science as they have done for planning. At the local, regional and national levels, one could not afford to ignore setting up Global Science cells at all levels. At the local level, one person could be assigned to this function on a part-time or full-time basis. At the national or global level, it would be a team of several dozen people provided with considerable material resources such as large simulators whose output should be considered with extreme caution (see method). Statistical and mathematical modelling would certainly provide added value to our understanding and our forecasts, but it would also make a tremendous difference in this field. We all remember that very expensive econometric models failed to anticipate the subprime crisis. In my opinion, this is because human expectations are insufficiently incorporated in the models and because we have strongly excluded the first-degree psychological and political mechanisms.

The Method Again

All existing social sciences employ a variety of methods to the delight of researchers: mathematical optimisation, econometrics, comparison, opinion polls, direct observations, etc. Sometimes, for the same research question, methods are diversified to obtain more robust results. This will certainly be the case for Global Science. We do not know which method will emerge as dominant. Perhaps all of them will have almost similar proportions of use. We can add one that seems to us to fit complex multidisciplinary systems. The model of 'incremental arrangement' (see A Lamiri: *The Economics of the Future*) could enable us to make a quantum leap in terms of social science methodology. A happy conclusion of a human or social experiment would be to perfect and improve our knowledge and our capacity to act. A simple tool alone cannot substitute for the rich diversity of very useful methods available to us. However, until now we have lacked the unifying and integrating tools needed to make a huge leap forward in achieving our prioritised societal goals.

Ethics and socio-economic objectives are democratic issues on which Global Science specialists should not have any monopoly. They must be determined through a participatory, pluralistic process and after many transparent exchanges. The rules and mechanisms that will be put in place by Global Science experts should ensure that the democratic process is not confiscated by minorities. Communication monopolies and rules for financing parties, associations and elections will be reviewed in order to free the political process from negative lobbies. However, the methodological issues are scientific and are, of course, the responsibility of researchers. Incremental sequencing would allow us to:

1. Integrate more effectively the complex and varied parameters for understanding the history of the outcome of a social event. For example, what are the forces at play and their degree of combination that led to

the beginning of the reintroduction of social inequalities in the 1980s after they had been dormant for decades?

2. Better shape macroeconomic and sector policies in order to optimise the combinations of the different choices with the chosen ethics and objectives. This would be especially relevant for the electoral programs of various candidates, often in contradiction with the psychological and sociological variables of the country, while their action plan does not provide for any provision to change these variables. For example, supporting more growth with the preservation of ecosystems with a minimum of profound reforms.

3. Predict more accurately the consequences of different alternatives.

4. Establish much better coherence between ethical principles, social objectives and sector and local details (everything should match).

Decision-Making

Rigorous conceptualisation and methodologies are transformed into tangible realities through the decision-making process. Blatant deficiencies in choice processes can invalidate a well-constructed approach to modelling and planning. The history of business and country successes remains extraordinarily complex. However, we always try to detect the famous Key Success Factors (KSF). These would be the practices that would explain an important proportion of the mechanisms that led to the envied institutional achievements. A plethora of factors can be listed for any experience. Nevertheless, one process has become a recurring custom in efficient institutions and countries: managing human intelligence. The latter includes two distinct aspects: development and use. There is a lot of writing and praise for investing in the development of human intelligence. Rightly so! There is no more salutary alternative. However, the temptation is strong to mobilise enormous resources to induce a derisory quality in education. It is this mystification that has trapped many developing countries. Learning has been politicised instead of being effectively designed in two dimensions: to help build the personality of tomorrow's responsible citizens and to provide them with the tools for reflection in order to effectively contribute to shaping an innovative environment in harmony with ecosystems. Such objectives cannot be achieved by bureaucratising or politicising the education system. For this reason, Global Science makes this a key part of its contribution. The second dimension would be to provide human resources with the most advanced knowledge and the most stimulating environments to innovate. This brings us back to integrating the decision-making process to this end. It would be a shame to qualify people and not take advantage of their expanded potential. Much has been written about decision-making. Scientists have proposed different postures.

One of the main objectives of the Global Science decision-making process would be to reconcile massive participation in solving apparently complex problems and to integrate the relevant contributions into a coherent, rigorous and Cartesian process. To achieve this, the Global Science approach to decision-making involves at least the following steps:

1. Never lose sight of the overall objective and the sub-objectives. For example: the ultimate objective would be to gradually re-establish, with a precise timetable, the parameters that would lead to stabilisation for a beginning of reversibility of the climate biodegradation process. We will have to quantify all this and stick to it.

2. Identify the root causes and not the symptoms: To stipulate that the essential cause of the problem would be the emissions of greenhouse gases would be a process of identifying the symptoms. Notifying after a diagnosis that the origin of the problem goes back to the process of creating expectations of more and more resources for citizens and the structuring of the political system that facilitates negative lobbying would reveal the root causes of the problem.

3. Broaden the circle of decision-makers: Organising a panel of experts or a seminar to make decisions is always the end of the decision-making process, but mobilising millions of human brains upstream would be the most rigorous model to rationalise choices. The other steps will clarify the process.

4. Same level of information: It is necessary to ensure that both distinct groups of participants will be provided with information on the different aspects of the problem (legal, economic, scientific, etc.). Ordinary citizens would have simplified information accessible to the uninitiated. Experts would have access to the latest research and simulations on the phenomenon.

5. Conducting preliminary consultations at all levels. This implies that representatives of a country (e.g., Brazil) would come to the international conference after having analysed and summarised the suggestions of interested and informed citizens from local (schools, universities, administrations), regional and national institutions. Farmers, workers, engineers and others would participate. There would have been a massive mobilisation of interested and informed people. The intelligence of as many people as possible would have been mobilised. Each country would do the same. We would thus end up incorporating

the best global inspirations. Who knows, maybe a draft of an Indian farmer could solve 10% or more of the problems we are investigating.

6. Brainstorming techniques: Psychology specialists know how to provoke fruitful meetings (brainstorming) and summarise them in a productive and coherent way.

7. Maximum alternatives: The first objective of these meetings would be to generate a maximum number of alternative actions to be taken (if possible with costs and removal of constraints).

8. Classification of alternatives: The next step would be to classify the alternatives according to their potential and their difficulties. After having listed and, if possible, estimated the advantages and disadvantages of each option, we can proceed to their classification. Sometimes we cannot avoid the vote to achieve this.

9. The decision-maker decides and coordinates: In the end, once all the recommendations have been produced at all levels (local, regional, national and international), it would be up to the panel of experts (Global Science) to make strategic and operational plans with the input of millions of people. We would then have combined mobilisation of the intelligence of all with a methodology that would turn the scientific intelligence into a coordinated, coherent action plan that would respect the principles of hard and soft sciences. It is still necessary that politics submits to science, unlike what is happening now.

10. Implementation plans and control measures: Once the strategic plans and operational policies are determined, traditional implementation measures are carried out: costs, expected results, persons responsible, measurement of deviations, improvement decisions, etc.

Our various experts and institutions have developed rigorous methodologies that fit perfectly into this framework. The approaches of USAID, the European Union, the World Bank and others have designed processes that adequately complement and enrich the approach. The essence of the method consists in mobilising the maximum of human intelligence that we have at our disposal—a real precious asset in the process of fighting against modern perils—which we combine with the methodologies and scientific knowledge that we have to extract a Cartesian response that makes all our strengths and capacities prevail. On the other hand, mobilising the maximum number of citizens will also have a decisive impact on urging people to adopt a responsible, participatory and committed attitude towards the challenges of the day. Moreover, this decision-making process can be scaled to solve local or institutional (business or government) problems. Nothing would prevent it from functioning in smaller bodies.

The complex process of mobilising the intelligence of all is summarised below:

1. Identify the complexity of the problem.
2. Identify the state of knowledge on the subject (the three key questions).
3. Agree on what we can know in a timely manner (R&D).
4. Identify the decision-makers and the process.
5. Inform of the optimum potential.
6. Multiple brainstorming (homework).
7. Research of multitudes of micro and macro alternatives.
8. Comprehensive decision: brainstorming and alternatives.
9. Classification of alternatives ('qualitative' simulation and advantages and limitations).
10. Decisions (harmonisers, final scientists decide).

The Principles of Global Science (GS)

In this section, we present for discussions, enrichment and improvement tentative principles which we think are necessary to begin creating this discipline. They are mostly economic and managerial ones. We need more contributions especially from psychologists, sociologists, anthropologists and others to initiate a dynamic of creating the missing knowledge. We need all the help we can get especially from experts and researchers to contribute to the process of turning around this situation.

Educational Multiplier Principle

Social scientists refer to an age when most of the values and ethics of human beings are acquired. This would be between the ages of six to ten. We never stop acquiring new codes of behaviour, but we get less and less. But few nations have metric systems that allow them to manage a process as complex and as essential as the acquisition of values and ethics consistent with the envisaged nation and nation/world system. The education system is strongly involved because it has a multiplier effect on the rest of the social structure. Consider a nation system where 50% of its citizens have values consistent with a particular nation/world system structure. The new education system will produce a pool of parents who are in tune with the new values. The family will reinforce the system of values acquired from an early age and thus we will have 75% of citizens who adhere to it, later on, 95% and much more. In the long run, the education system will prevail over the societal culture. Moreover, when the political and social culture perfectly reflects the philosophy of the education system, inducing a high level of coherence, the system is supported without fail and without contradiction with the main facts.

We cannot leave future citizens to accomplish their historical mission while they are insufficiently prepared for future challenges. Faced with giant corporations with increasingly sophisticated means of communication, it is essential to provide them with life skills so that they can live up to their values. Education will not only be a preparation tool for the tasks of tomorrow. It could be a boost for the types of future nation systems. We expect education sciences and psychology to develop qualitative and quantitative methods to measure the degrees of coherence between the actors of the system (the gap between the values of the student population and the envisaged system). The more significant the gap, the more futile it would be to try to build a similar system.

Once again, our psychologists and education specialists do not have the luxury of preparing only future generations to face the complex challenges of the day. We 'must retrain' active citizens to take on their present role in order to avoid cataclysms. Not doing so is irresponsible. We can no longer afford the luxury of waiting for future generations to correct our mistakes. The situation is exceptional. We must work on the short, medium and long-term lines and on all active generations. At a time when it is necessary to mobilise to act quickly, we can see a worrying lethargy. A key point in the educational dimension remains the self-responsibility on the development of ethical principles and the need to inform, educate and master better and better the themes related to the consequences of its behaviours on life, the environment, and the entire nation-world system. Learning to learn and to be responsible would be one of the foundations of the future education system. However, for this to happen, the priorities would have to be reviewed. Not only do we need the new modern theories of self-learning and self-empowerment, but we also need to take advantage of the new information technologies and artificial intelligence. Some countries have already made significant progress in this area and others are still lagging behind. Yet even the most advanced ones need to do more in light of the enormous challenges ahead.

The essential basis for real change lies in designing an education system that is able to meet its responsibilities, to produce 'once again' accountable generations and particularly to train those who are already operational and who will be integrated into the process of major changes. Education sciences should start thinking about their missions. We will propose some ideas and some themes to consider, but they are not at all exhaustive. The essential is perhaps there but much research is still to be accomplished. Global Science would be the precursor of many revolutions in social sciences and even in the deepening of hard sciences. Priorities will no longer be the same. It would be a question of directing human brains towards what is constructive, restorative and mobilising. From there, it would be possible to build many variants of typologies of nations and world-nations more in line with human expectations. The disappointments of the past will only serve to reduce our ignorance of social and economic phenomena. As we methodically compile significant events, we will begin to build knowledge webs that can feed our models and simulators. The principle of a continuum of learning and empowerment would be an eminent part of the ethical codes of education and Global Science.

Principle of Life Design

An average, non-oriented person would easily get lost in the labyrinths of life. The education system, in addition to preparing him to accomplish a historical mission, would play the role of a channel chooser. Not content with revealing one's potential and all one's assets, it would be necessary within modern notions to bring out what role a person thinks of playing within a new nation. This should take place as soon as possible. Societal ethics and the overall architecture of the system would offer plenty of opportunities to be usefully integrated into the way it works. It is always a question of consistency and management of expectations. We need to avoid at all costs designing a Brownian entity where the actors' expectations have no extension within the societal sphere. It is no less important to bring out the positive values of humans, from a young age, to develop them, and value them in order to turn them into future attitudes. The future material reality of society will become the mode of preparation for the rising generations. We can only reap what we have sown. What is anchored in one's self becomes second nature.

Nowadays, psychology and education sciences are suffocated by the weight of the political sphere. Political parties have taken over the environment, the economy, education and all the spheres of modern life with little regard for the sciences. Consider the environment. Experts in the field agree that we need to act quickly. But the political class is doing very little too late. We need to put scientific knowledge at the service of ethics and social construction which we have done in an insufficient way. Modern nations have atrophied the scientific input in favour of the political one. Once politicians are elected, which obviously gives them legitimacy, legislative and judicial checks and equilibriums are of little use on complex issues when scientific input is insufficient. The role of 'Global Science' is to fill this gap. Of course, scientists may not always be in a consensual situation. However, when a danger is looming on the horizon and a warning is getting the maximum of agreement (like the current environmental situation), we should be able to put enough weight on the political class to stop the degradation. We should create a fourth power and no longer allow the political class alone to decide human destinies. But even more seriously, when democracy is 'confiscated,' it hardly justifies the exorbitant power held by the political class. A clear sign of slippage would be the 'immobilism' and the procrastination when facing multiple perilous challenges.

What is engraved in the essence of the soul eventually becomes a life goal. The noble mission of education sciences and psychology is to engrave positive values in the citizen's minds in modern nations. Nowadays, education is often torn between the political orientations of the leadership. When it is close to the extreme right, it advocates a barely disguised racial supremacy, another barely formed government will instil a selective internationalism, and a third would provide the values of mutual aid, equality and social coherence. At the end of the day, we will have a Brownian effect that is not compatible with any project of modern society. Modernising nations has not been accompanied by an architecture that makes the societal basis, the values and the vision coherent. The societal basis includes both productive and social capital as well as forms of human and institutional interdependence underpinned by individual and collective values. These modes of interaction, unlike traditional societies, are in permanent conflict with their desired futures. Nation systems desire more equality and stability for their citizens but secretly create more social inequity and fragility. The nation-world system desires more peace and environmental equilibrium but ends up accumulating more weapons of mass destruction, endless conflicts and destruction of ecosystems. The reasons for this are the ethics and values conveyed by the education system and the vision advocated by the system's designers. Secondly, there is a profound reason, which is the nature of the systemic mode of operation and the values themselves.

Messages and Values

The contradictions between the ethics advocated and the societal messages are striking in modern nations. While we want to promote mutual aid, more social equity, eco-friendly consumption, and citizen honesty, almost everything concurs in urging social irresponsibility. The headlines are constantly revealing financial scandals of politicians and business managers. In business management, promotions are synonymous with improved income. Social considerations are a function of the amount of resources available to individuals and institutions. The financial weight of the individual often allows him to escape the rules of justice through many subterfuges. Marketing, the force of companies, encourages unbridled consumption by individuals. Everything is done in such a way as to introduce confusion between the volume of resources available and the level of consumption as conditions of access to happiness, peace of mind and the purpose of life. The satisfaction derived from wonder, family, mutual aid and contribution to a common societal project is far away. Our scientists have a lot of work to do in order to achieve coherence between the values advocated and the societal messages. Everything is done in such a way as to value oneself by money and for money. A businessman can count his yacht and the billions that he is proud of but rarely the number of school children he finances or the number of hospital beds he contributes to create through his taxes. Moreover, we could create a menu of (symbolic) options for activities that taxpayers would like to finance through the payment of their taxes. It would have a symbolic purpose through the payment of their taxes, for example, it would finance research and development on cancer to the tune of X Euros, a municipal road, building a school, etc.

In modern societies, however, everything that is gathered can be enjoyed by one person, but the contributions that he or she makes, even if they are great, to the smooth running of society and its equilibrium, are concealed. An honest businessman will have the impression that he contributes to the financing of corruption, embezzlement and waste of all kinds. This is what is highlighted by national media. He will have the impression of being a source of squandering of resources. He cannot get any moral satisfaction from it. All of this contributes to the gap between citizen expectations and the way a societal system works. When modern nations adopt Global Science, there will be a lesser gap between the ethics and values created within the deep personalities of individuals and the macro-scale behaviour of a society. We would then have to confront all the contradictions to eliminate them one by one. Some of the principles formulated are likely to contribute to this. But the main point would be achieved elsewhere. Communication and designs of the institutional web, social engineering by excellence, should be able to make thousands of modern institutions function coherently. The necessary managerial innovations are largely available, but it is a matter of freeing them from applications limited to large international firms.

Education systems are put in the hands of minorities by all the institutions of the modern world. Sometimes they are supported mainly by religious practices that normally should advocate noble values. But the vast majority of institutions, the most powerful and those that have the greatest influence on the political-economic system promote values that are sometimes contrary to the general good. We have produced invisible governments within nations. The financial system is the most powerful one. It creates decisions for its own benefit and wraps them in considerations of general interest as if the two were exactly overlapping. Legislation is often passed for its benefit. Who does not remember the subprime crisis in 2007-2008? Hundreds of billions of citizens' money were used to save the banking system from the crisis it created. It was thought that the money would flow mainly to the real sector through credits. But the banks were to give bonuses to their executives for having failed and triggered a major crisis that brought down the world economy. In the end, the owners should have been changed. This is the rule in situations of bankruptcy and finally, so that future owners of capital do not reproduce the same behaviour.

What about the ethics developed in schools? It shatters when confronted with a harsh and reprehensible reality. The power of resistance of citizens in front of the magnitude of systemic contradictions is limited by nature and by the magnitude of injustices committed, imposed by public force and mostly embellished by the preteens of a normal and inevitable outcome of a democratic process. Citizens adopt a strategy of every man for himself, of reluctantly denying acquired values and running the tremendous risk of trying to beat the system. Some of them group themselves in 'opposition institutions' too lonely to make any difference. They would rather lose alone than win with a confederation that could impose a more optimal solution. The educational ethic would then be swallowed up in a labyrinth of human and institutional misdirection. Thus, modern nations have been trapped by a system that is not functioning properly. On the international level, it is even worse. It is enough for authoritarian nations to have resources (energy, uranium, gold…) for them to deny their fundamental principles. The democrats of these countries are handed over hand and foot tied to their executioners, and sacrificed on the altar of the greed of the so-called democratic countries. This is called 'La Real Politic,' but in fact, it's a real destruction of the world democracy.

Institutional Alignment Principle

The conceptualisation of nations would take a great leap forward when it integrates the contributions of human and social sciences to build harmonious systems instead of deploying multitudes of inconsistencies that undermine modern societies. We can draw a lot of inspiration from managerial innovations to achieve such complex socio-technical systems that humanity has never experienced before. But in management, we have sound and lousy managerial principles. We have to perform a serious screening. It is also a question of making a multitude of human and technical subsystems interact by drawing on knowledge from the hard and soft sciences (human and social sciences). Alignment, or coherence, is an intrinsic part of the methodology. It can be broken down as follows:

1. Ethics: These are the main moral principles that guide the main systemic designers. It is for example the tolerated level of inequalities. One could imagine a nation that would allow people to hold fifty times the minimum amount of capital (movable and immovable property and twenty times the minimum individual income). The question of tolerated inequalities is always problematic. Beyond these gains, a menu of national and international social projects is offered to actors for financing of their choice. A person can therefore account for their wealth and the wealth created for others;

2. Values: These are the beliefs to be held and acted upon in order to build modern nations according to the ethics and the great societal objectives of modern nations. These are the strong points of the ambient culture to be developed or created by education systems and all kinds of institutional communication: political, social, etc. We could anchor the ideas of moderation instead of the materialistic quests of contemporary consumers, to derive more satisfaction from the wonder of the beauty of

nature and from the mutual help for others rather than from the unbridled material consumption that tends to expand infinitely. The role of education and psychology is recognised in particular, but economics and sociology are not left out.

3. Societal typology: This is the broad orientation that characterises the types of nations desired. For example, a nation can establish only cooperative societies of limited or unlimited size and public enterprises but under a democratic process. Many technical details remain to be formalised. However, societal choices should be legal and therefore democratic. We cannot substitute the tyranny of science for the current democratic process whose main characteristic is that it is confiscated. Only scientific innovation is a limit to our creative process. Certainly, it is difficult to believe that the typologies of modern societies will emerge from the prototypes of computer simulations. But these would only be the results, validated by citizens and specialised scientists, in Global Science. And by all means, the validated input of millions of citizens would be the final product. Afterwards, it still goes through a democratic citizen validation.

We start from the existing history to answer a whole series of questions. For example, what prevailed during the experience of the former Yugoslavia with self-management: the democratic aspects, management of the operation or a certain number of political characteristics went wrong? For this, we can call upon our methodology. We must free ourselves from the sole yoke of a confiscated capitalism or totalitarian socialism. Now, the only two alternatives are presented to us as unavoidable. There is no escaping them. But scientists (Global Science) do not offer a revered and unassailable doctrine. They have a range of alternatives with their contributions and their limits. By transforming oneself, one broadens the horizon of institutional possibilities, and consequently of the nation systems to offer as possible alternatives.

Transformation and operation strategies: It is not easy to change a political, economic and social system into another. A whole sensible ordering in the short, medium and long term would have to be deployed in order to transform oneself and to mutate a whole complex social formation. There would be human resources to be recycled in order to accelerate this process of mutations which are possible in the short term then to gradually operate the complex transmutations in a coherent whole. Many parameters lend themselves easily to quantification while others can be quantified through proxies. The global system can therefore be simulated but would have to overcome extremely complex difficulties. It would probably be the most complex human system ever simulated. It will force our anticipations and quantitative scientists to make decisive innovations. Human reactions to changes in incentives and to the effectiveness, or inadequacy of value change programs will be unravelled and catalogued to enrich our knowledge of societal functioning. The methodology introduced would be an appropriate framework for drawing conclusions about the way nations and world systems function. And to build multidisciplinary learning that would free us from the only despotic socialism and the only confiscated democracy that we are currently living.

However, the choice cannot be merely the choice of scientists. It can only be legitimate when the process is democratic. But scientific contributions can enlighten public opinion through simulations of candidates' programs for elections. This would make it easier to detect programs that are populist, racist or contrary to the ethics and values of the social project. Although candidates will rarely try to question the foundations of a nation's system, they may claim to modify it. In doing so, they could profoundly alter it or improve its mode of operation. We will then know, much better than today, if they will degrade it or improve it. We will have an analytical framework, which, although it is always perfectible, gives us better information on the future consequences of present decisions.

Organisation: The organisation includes all the institutions, processes and formal and informal mechanisms governing them. The implementation of the structures' operating modes will induce great efficiency or a great paralysis of the whole complex system. The management of these operations borrows from various existing and yet-to-be-created practices. The intention to create new social forms should not obscure the need for unparalleled managerial rigour. We can draw inspiration from business management, NPA (new public administration), intercultural management and many other sub-disciplines. We are not starting from scratch but much remains to be done. Managerial practices are one of the most important resources for the success of social projects. Eastern countries have practically collapsed because of their managerial failures. Just as developing countries pay an exorbitant price in terms of wasted resources for having underestimated the importance of a good conceptualisation and implementation of a high-class managerial system. These are not the only factors of success or failure, but they probably played a determining role.

Management is the resource of resources; the one that transforms resources into sustainable wealth. It is a social technology that can boost social and institutional performance beyond human expectations. It would be a pity to leave it in the hands of the world's largest corporations to make record profits without sufficiently integrating social responsibilities into their models. We will need more managerial innovations to mobilise the maximum amount of citizen intelligence to overcome contemporary challenges. Old proven methods, with more efficient variants, such as management by objectives, organisation by responsibility centres and prioritisation of human development, are among many others, necessary tools, indispensable, but not sufficient. We need to go beyond our current possibilities to bring about managerial innovations that are up to our quantitative and qualitative challenges.

A mistake in the sequencing of foreseeable reforms is costly. Human skills should come first and organisational patterns second. We have erred so much at the level of macroeconomic development policies that we should have understood by now where the mistake lies. But the vast majority of countries have not yet grasped the problem of underdevelopment. Basically, we have managerial problems. The source may be political, but the managerial interface shows the degree of efficiency of a national system.

Underdeveloped countries are squandering huge resources trying to prosper with the help of alcoholic and drug-addicted institutions and companies. They should have been transformed into efficient entities first before abundant wealth was placed in their hands. Other mechanisms at play amplify these processes (national and international corruption, frequent and inconsistent institutional changes, and the weight of the political process).

We could catalogue an impressive number of organisational principles that we already have. Business management and NPA have produced certain conceptual schemes that, used wisely, could help play their part in optimising the way this complex web operates. But we need to innovate more than ever and boost social science knowledge and practices beyond what we have done so far. The need drives innovation. During World War II, operations research had made impressive leaps. Necessity pushes human beings to the edge and to improve the tools at their disposal. The challenges to boosting social sciences are simply extraordinary. Whether it is to evolve a nation's system or radically transform it, there is nothing more complex to manage. Missions of the past will seem starkly simple compared to the complex challenges of the future. A few principles will be mentioned here. The main responsibility lies with the specialists of the different disciplines in their quest to structure them in order to make them coherent with each other and reconcilable with Global Science.

The Principle of Protected Hyper-Transparency

The debate on the issue of data protection is raging around the world. First, we have the data collected on people. The vast majority of citizens proclaim that they should be vigorously protected. It makes sense! Everything must be done to strengthen their security and penalise those who use them illegally. However, there are sometimes situations that are difficult to understand. Citizens refuse to provide their DNA for a national database that could have prevented thousands if not millions of crimes, robberies, rapes and all sorts of misappropriations. Better data protection does not mean causing serious social dysfunctions. It means protecting access and abuse, not depriving ourselves of a tool that could have saved dozens of lives and colossal losses of resources. Most developed countries have experienced similar situations. Honest citizens refuse to provide their DNA. However, there are hundreds of ill-intentioned people among them. The former are often the intended victims of the latter. The debate on the methodology of access and data protection would be long and tedious.

At the institutional level, however, the situation is worse. Each institution tries to over-protect its information and practices under the pretext that other entities are not able to understand and participate in the management of their own institution. Thus, the legal system, police, medical profession, teachers and the rest will all claim that their work is incomprehensible to others and that making it socially transparent would be inappropriate. On the other hand, they would not be against making the practices of others hyper-transparent. On the contrary, they would benefit from it. A police investigation and a teachers' council should be documented (after the job done) and be able to be audited to improve processes. But it is the political power that prevents the most non-transparent operations. Dozens of agencies operate with a high degree of anonymity. Any operation would be a state secret. They are rarely controlled by elected officials, let alone by auditing structures. This makes their improvement problematic. In fact, modern societies have to face the fact that a protected hyper-transparency has to be structured. Data integrity and non-transmission, except to duly authorised persons, would be an absolute necessity.

The more hyper-transparent a nation becomes, the more it eliminates social ills such as corruption, racism, favouritism, and all institutional dysfunctions. There are many ways to better protect data such as putting it in computers not connected to the internet to make hacking more difficult. When we work together we always end up finding solutions to the most difficult problems. Instead of making the data inaccessible to outsiders, it is assumed that the information will be disclosed, regardless of the degree of control, and it is prevented from being made available. Thus, the political sphere and national security agencies act with impunity in committing serious illegal acts. The process of hyper-accountability is to establish provisions so that people can ex post verify that the legal provisions are respected. Some Scandinavian countries allow their citizens to monitor key institutions to make them hyper-transparent. Provided there is no rush, this would help to significantly reduce institutional dysfunctions. The citizens will be an integral part of a social system structured to accommodate them. They are both actors and observers. At the workplace, they make themselves available for transparent controls and they carry them out themselves. It is not a question of purely indicting controls to expose malpractices, although this mission includes them, but the inspection can lead to salutary reforms. A judicious structuring of the operations allows to expose the difficulties of the modes of functioning in various fields and to remedy them.

Hyper-Accountability Principle

All active individuals and institutions are linked in the same chain which contributes to the momentum of a global approach. The requirement of awareness and self-responsibility is the first step that would ensure that everyone assumes the consequences of their actions properly. The first control is therefore self-control. Humans will be prepared to give their best, to improve continuously, to share their experiences and those of others; in short, they become learning resources. It is the volume of knowledge put into practice and shared that will be the key success factors of tomorrow's modern nations. A system that cares for protects, and even nurtures the most vulnerable can only do so if it manages all of its active citizens in an entirely different way. We will need indicators for every job and every institution. Management learned early how to do this and developed practices to do so, as did the NPA. But, we will need to innovate because we want to integrate ethics and values in addition to the results objectives that are inescapable. Not to create requirements for each institution and each person would mean spreading an undeniable irresponsibility. Some transferable business management practices are very useful and can become best practices in the complex web of modern institutions. The same is true of the NPA. But, new innovations will mostly boost managerial practices and new forms of institutions.

Where economies of scale are not obvious, it would be useful to introduce a high degree of competition and even rank people and institutions in order of merit. For example, city councils could be ranked according to job creation, wealth output, and citizen appreciation for ecosystem advocacy. Current practices can already greatly help in setting up these systems. Only in this way, when a person is in need, will he receive all the help and support he needs to provide in such circumstances. Peace of mind for all is a matter of science and effort. As long as people are trained, immersed in professional principles and ethics and managed properly, they will, as a whole, make major contributions to the smooth functioning of the system.

The usefulness of managing resources by objectives is manifold. It allows focusing on results and not on a certain way of doing a task. This could lead to a significant improvement in performance. However, communication becomes easier within an institution. Objectives can include the values and ethics of the different entities. In the absence of management by objectives, the situation can be read in different ways. A human resources manager would be able to judge his subordinate's effectiveness by the decreasing absenteeism in their entities; while their supervisor can judge their performance by the increasing productivity of their staff. The two elements can only communicate properly when a results-based management process is put in place. However, there is no reason to consider objectives as an instrument of tyranny. It is not because a person misses a target that he is liable to be reprimanded and penalised. Rather, it is the other way around: full support from the institution, better qualifications, help from all sides that would be helpful and all kinds of kindness that will be reserved for him. Thus, this tool will become an element of empowerment and promotion of human potential and not a tyrannical management instrument that would oppress human exuberance. In most cases, a person who achieves unsatisfactory results will be given the opportunity to improve and will have the full support of the institution to make it up. He/she can change his/her job position if he/she has not been properly positioned. Following a promotion or a positioning of a person, it is too often the institution that should be blamed for a poor individual performance.

Intelligence Mobilisation Principle

There are multiple levers to act on human performance and satisfaction. Some are more appropriate than others. Among the most powerful tools is the mobilisation of intelligence and information management. The first mentioned would be by far the most suitable. The best institutions are those that transform the results of intelligence into better products and services for their customers. It is not necessarily commercial companies but all kinds of non-profit institutions that make use of it. When the institution is required to improve or finds itself in a perilous situation, a methodological approach to decision-making should be deployed. The practice is described above. Good institutions follow this methodically. Only a massive mobilisation of brains, especially where the problem lies, would be able to produce the desired effects. It is unfortunate that only large companies are close to the proposed model. They benefit mainly in terms of profits but very little in terms of services provided to the public.

We have devoted a considerable amount of time to the mobilisation of intelligence, whether it is for the proper functioning of an isolated institution or for a national system. The development and effective use of brainpower is one of the least protected and least imitated managerial secrets. It is one of the inexplicable oddities. Underdeveloped countries suffer from this phenomenon and the former Eastern European countries have simply collapsed—to a large extent—because their practices are incompatible with these facts. The 'democratic' centralism has been fatal for these nations. Certainly, there is a great deal of responsibility for the political process that was put in place. A single party can rarely bring welfare to the whole population. But it also freezes initiatives and introduces many distortions in the management process. The worm is in the fruit. Urging everyone to participate is also a process of empowerment and participation. All kinds of managerial benefits are being combined. A maximum of inclusion is devoted to it.

The process of generating the maximum number of ideas is hopeful. There would often be sensible ideas with a minimum of perverse effects that would be revealed. When a population is trained to work with a maximum of formulations of proposals, we would be secure about its future. A whole work is needed upstream and downstream. Preparing future resources to fulfil their historical missions and channelling resources to them would be an optimal use. We will have nation systems where problems are managed and solved at the grassroots level. No need to clutter up a centralised national system. A monitored and evaluated initiative is proposed at the most decentralised levels possible. Town halls, schools and counties are places where complicated situations are solved. Only in this way can good practices from the best institutions be spread.

The Leaders-Managers Principle

Managers of institutions are a body of servants of the nation's systems who have a clear impact on the way the whole works. Their job is to lead others. Their task would be greatly facilitated if they had leadership skills. This would make it much easier for them to pursue their mission as managers. Their qualifications would include management techniques and practices as well as leadership training. This means that they will need coaches specialised in leadership and specific NLP. Leading managers will bring out the best in their human resources. They will reveal their deepest humanities as well as their extraordinary skills. Tomorrow's institutions will experience a strong managerial revolution. They will be able to transform nation systems into a chain of invisible and united hands. Only when every person builds a common future will everyone be able to benefit in the long run. The problem of global warming and the destruction of ecosystems have put the philosophy of the invisible hand to the test. To continue to rely on its mechanisms to curb the environmental problem would mean exposing ourselves to the worst risks we have ever known. Humanity seems to be moving inevitably towards this alternative which follows directly from this philosophy. Institutions and people are not able to direct their energies towards the forces likely to put an end to these plagues. This is because they are structured to act according to the invisible hand philosophy.

Tomorrow's manager-leaders will have to transform institutions and people according to an entirely different philosophy. Managers alone, despite their technical skills, will have limited capacity to play this role. A manager has the right to give orders and be obeyed only by his formal position. His authority comes from his position alone. A leader is appreciated for his other qualities (skills, sensitivity, courage, adaptability etc.). These can sometimes be acquired through reliable coaching or naturally. The bottom line is that a person who has both attributes (manager plus leader) is able to radically transform human behaviour and the way institutions operate. We need to introduce a chain of individual and collective ruptures in order to contribute to the success of a historic mission, which is inevitable if we want to last and prosper. It is not a question of reproducing a web of human and organisational actions from the past, a previous culture that we must move beyond. We will strive to build institutional webs that will allow us to grow and achieve an unparalleled evolution.

At Country Level

Global Science is primarily a science of transformations of nation systems. At the moment there are mainly sciences and disciplines that can bring about desired changes in individuals and institutions. Psychology and management serve this purpose in particular. There are also many sub-themes that are dedicated to making changes, such as business turnarounds, quality systems, NLP and so on. Everything is aimed at changing the behaviour of individuals and organisations. By moving these entities towards desired types of behaviour we make the assumption that a nation's system would automatically improve itself, but we are beginning to understand that there is little correlation between the two aspects. Human beings have improved their productivity and most institutions are better managed than they were fifty years ago, but nation systems are not evolving towards desired trends. The effects will only be felt positively when there is full alignment between the key components of the model. First, we will discuss the problem of the relationship between the method and the driver of the objectives of the nation system. Secondly, we will discuss the complexity of the key components of the different elements.

Consistency Between Method and Objectives of Nations

We will summarise in a few lines the problematic of the method as well as the interaction between its key elements and the different possible trajectories of the whole society. We have a cumulative process of knowledge of which we have little organisation to take advantage. We are only beginning to see its potential for improvement. Nowadays, when we model social formations, we make generalisations that are very useful but sometimes harmful. We remain at the level of global generalisations that have allowed us to make significant economic progress, but too little for social objectives within different cultures and structures. We wanted to export the Washington consensus to developing countries where circumstances require very different policies. Economists have treated the problem of Greece like that of Germany, opting for the same therapeutic scheme. The reason is simple. We lack a methodology that could make useful distinctions between these two different situations. We have opted for a methodology that does not distinguish between the different social formations. In doing so, we have generalised the mode of operation of advanced social formations and tried to understand the mode of operations of developing or intermediate countries through a distorted prism. We need to incorporate into our overly restrictive models key variables that allow us to differentiate between analyses and formulate more appropriate therapeutic plans.

Moreover, we have also come to accept whatever it will be. This is one of the reasons why we have ended up burying active monetary policies. We do not differentiate between helicopter money and laser money. The former is distributed without differentiation of actors, and the latter devotes choices of sectors of business to be promoted and thus opts for promising and desirable growth areas. There would always be target businesses, socially desirable, which with fiscal support and credits could be transformed into useful growth sectors.

A minimum of inflation would follow and we would not have to suffer a significant impact. It would be much less than development inflation. And yet the central banks are sitting on their hands. Inflation control is even preferred to the risk of ruining life on our planet. We have come to make incomprehensible choices about the values that should guide our decisions.

We should understand that investment resources will eventually make choices based on many social parameters, including profitability and risk. But when parasitic businesses take place, they have a higher risk and profitability than many traditional businesses. They will eventually take over many investment resources. The gambling (betting) and alcohol businesses, more negative for the meagre social benefits they provide, (like drugs) have the most favourable risk/reward ratios. Unless public authorities get involved to change the system of incentives within economic and social activities.

The methodology presented will make more refined proposals. However, it would require statistical refinements that we may not have. But it is worth the effort. We have become accustomed to a diversity of methods in social sciences. No doubt we will continue to use a variety of approaches. We could mention among others:

- Modelling,
- Mathematical optimisation,
- Opinion polls,
- Comparisons,
- Statistical and econometric methods,
- Simulations (rare), and
- Others.

We will continue to use these methods when appropriate. We are just adding one more tool that could make a significant difference to our diagnosis systems and therapy plans. The method of significant increments would allow us to incorporate into the history of nations relevant variables that will in fact reintegrate the analysis and be considered an enrichment of our understanding of social phenomena.

Table 3 Model Transfer Hurdle

We are losing much of our historical developments in order to transpose simple model situations. Certainly, the case of simple models is advantageous. Wherever we can use it, it will be of immense help to us. However, we sometimes make mistakes in our analysis by being simplistic when we ignore important relevant variables. We will take two examples, one macroeconomic and the other microeconomic, which are the focus of our analysis. Avoiding the intersection of several variables and, especially, of related sociological or psychological themes would inevitably lead to interpretation errors. Let us consider the Keynesian doctrine once again. Many economists in developing countries have recommended it as a means of stimulating economic growth, almost exclusively through the construction of infrastructure. In doing so, they would be mimicking the Roosevelt-style New Deal that had pulled the US economy out of the Great Depression. But the degree of institutional efficiency (businesses, public organisations and NGOs) is incomparable. The US economy has regained its growth momentum through dynamic entrepreneurship and proven management methods. However, an underdeveloped country that stops its stimulus plans quickly returns to a situation of serious disequilibrium. Economic orientations have to be diametrically opposed. Our second example would be again microeconomic. When Peter F Drucker proposed a management-by-objectives approach in 1947 at General Electric, it became a historical fashion for many decades. Many companies took advantage of it by introducing many variations. The companies generally improved. However, when developing countries adopted it, there were more failures than positive advances (Brazil, Mexico). The model assumes that, in key business activities, the superiors become coaches for their subordinates. They guide, advice and evaluate them. This presupposes a properly structured skills pyramid. However, in many companies in developing countries, we find inverted pyramids (skills are at the bottom). So we can wonder how a superior who has lesser skill than his subordinates would improve them.

Many similar situations exist within all the humanities and social sciences. We need to combine, improve and make these disciplines and sciences work together. We need at least one methodological element that captures these relevant variables to allow us to differentiate among situations. We cannot

> allow ourselves to remain in abusive generalisations. We have made historical progress through the various methods employed but we must accomplish much more.

Today, however, it is a question of surpassing ourselves in order to put back on track nation systems and a world system that has organised itself more to self-destruct than to last and prosper. We will then be able to create nomenclatures of nations quite relevant to the themes covered by the various investigations. Indeed, when designing policies aimed at taking responsibility for the environment, we can make use of these. In the first place, a distinction is made between the parameters related to the problem and those as close as possible to the situation. We will need to parameterise the variables as well as measure them in the most appropriate way possible. Consider business management problems, for example. We have situation parameters that will require very different attitudes and decision-making with the same problem for instance how to improve the productivity and the morale of the company's members. Everything will depend on the parameters of the situation we will be confronted with. Although 'universal' situations exist and are the essence of social and human sciences, such different environments can mislead decision-makers or analysts who are not sufficiently prepared to deal with diverse cases.

Current neoclassical theories have difficulty in identifying the 'Chinese economic miracle.' The experience is outside their fundamental hypotheses of analysis. It is as poorly prepared to give the story of the experience as is Marxist analysis. Both foresee only one form of success. The first is situated in the context of the patterns of pure and perfect competition and the second is in line with the prism of historical materialism. The liberating pattern would be the one that admits a diversity of success and failure alternatives. Although one can argue immensely about definitions, is an economic success grafted onto an environmental disaster (the case of China and the USA) enviable? The situation gets worse when confronted with diversified economic environments. Running a business in Pakistan, Europe or Africa is somewhat confusing, considering a limited number of parameters for the purpose of our analysis. We draw on the work of authors who have explored in depth the cultural diversities of managers' environments (Hofstede, Franz Rieger (9) etc.)

An illustration has been provided in the table above. This illustration (and not a rigorous study) would benefit from thorough parameterisation of the variables, obtaining and confirming significant differences that might exist between nations by different methods of analysis and adding situation variables for more accuracy. The illustration is an example. We are close to a microeconomic experiment in order to differentiate and treat different situations of context when they are divergent. We could then temporarily manage different companies, the time to mutate the various cultures, according to the alternatives chosen. But it would rarely occur to a seasoned manager to deal with similar issues in the same way in diverse contexts.

Multinational companies have learned to manage this diversity better through human skills and experiences. Small and medium-sized businesses that are learning the hard way about diversity are doing what they can by analysing the best practices of entities with relevant experiences. However, the problem is still there when it comes to macroeconomic environments. Modern macroeconomics deals in its various chapters with universal situations that are sometimes relevant, but the differences that characterise them are often overlooked. As a result, students feel that they are being taught hard science courses and often trained as such and inexperienced people are suffering from standardisation. Many developing countries have followed demand-side policies rather than supply-side policies. Once again, the usefulness of these models is no longer in question, but their abuse is often fatal for many countries. Many international institutions have established the universal model culture.

Prioritisation Principle

The time is somewhat inconvenient to design future social formations that will prevent us from creating too much social inequality and too much destruction of the natural systems that sustain our lives. The damage done to the second dimension is impressive. The uncertainties that weigh on the future of humanity are confusing. We have questions that are most delicate to consider in this context. Should we consider building more ethical, more egalitarian nation-world systems that are more in line with the equilibrium of the biosphere, or should we prefer the option of urgent repair of damaged ecosystems? Logic would suggest that we can work towards both alternatives, especially since they are mutually reinforcing. However, the social requirements remain the same, namely to gain the upper hand over the forces of the status quo. The Gordian knot of the problem remains at this level. The proponents of an overhaul of the entire national and international systems should take into account the need to prioritise. In this context, urgent and corrective actions for the severely damaged biosphere would be the only way to protect national and international systems before the harm becomes irreversible.

These choices are necessary and cannot be made unconsciously. It is then better to make them explicit and to take decisions with more rationality. Not having a choice implies that one makes them anyway, but is more likely to prefer doubtful options. But if we consider them explicitly, taking into account the different relevant parameters, we would greatly improve the quality of the alternative chosen. The main lesson that we should learn from this mess is that natural resources are limited and that their substitution by technological processes is far from sufficient. Therefore, we have to make informed choices. But we have lacked insight in this area. We have granted a mandate to politicians by giving them the illusion of knowledge and without having them accompanied by specialists in a discipline such as Global Science to support them and to inform the citizens of the consequences of their decisions. The IPCC is a good start, but it should be strengthened in many directions. The socio-technical system of modern nations is fundamentally biased. It gives politicians and the economic elite absolute control over the proper functioning of the system. A government with a majority in parliament makes laws under the influence of the economic elite. This regulation severely limits the scope of action of the judicial system. It is true that in many countries it is stipulated that the justice system is independent. However, it works within the limits of the executive branch. It cannot go outside the framework that has been drawn up for it. The rules of the game are confusing. What is missing is a scientific and independent authority that would inform the public, contribute to its knowledge and explain the consequences of the current economic and political choices.

In addition to the failing organisation, responsible for the human chaos we have created, and which we will have to analyse in detail throughout these discussions, the prioritisation operation is necessary. We need to allocate significant resources to the most beneficial alternatives. First of all, the budgetary dimension comes to mind as a first validation of the options confirmed. The budgetary process sets up a chain of action that will point to selected alternatives. The preferred options will be revealed to the public and will have a different impact on the course of events. When the choice would be to prioritise populist changes, this would mean fewer resources for the education system, the appropriate training of young generations and fundamental research and development. But when we want to address the emergency it would be logical to foster the development of human resources already available and the development of applied research. It is all a question of degree. In my opinion, corrective and rapid actions should be prioritised first. But it is all a question of proportions. Every stride will act as a catalyst for change in terms of social transformations. We would become aware of the devastation we have caused through ignorance and greed.

However, the costs of repairing the damaged systems become more and more exorbitant as hesitation and procrastination go on. The latter is emerging as the most important characteristic of modern politics. A cost/benefit analysis would necessarily lead to the urgent repair of damaged natural systems. Budgetary provisions would immediately take over and would mainly indicate the financial resources to be mobilised. However, the scheduling of human time is a far more important consequence than financial resources. Research, development and the mobilisation of all human genius is a cause that transcends all other themes. But, implementing actions, scheduling of activities and details are also ultimately settled. The world will resume planning on a large scale as it has never done before. The various supply chain systems of the commercial operations of large companies will appear to be paltry compared to the repair requirements of natural systems. But we need to direct research and development quickly into the unknown and useful avenues that would allow us to harness technological innovations and bring them into line with the ethics and practices of model nations.

Part III: The Practice of Global Science

Global Science Manifesto

We are in the prehistory of history or on the eve of its end: the final collapse of history. The inglorious subject of the deception of the end of history (Fukushima)—the history of class struggles or of the competing economic models, that lasted for so long, has proven to be a gross exaggeration of analytical appreciation. And the control of events by the traditional levers of economic, political, environmental and social affairs is beginning to elude us. Risks are becoming more and more inevitable, inexorable and beyond human control. We have failed beyond belief. And the rare survival strategies are little contemplated, desired and barely considered. An immense collective paralysis has taken hold of us and the few spectacular but shallow actions to be of any use in the long term are intended to fuel a vain hope incapable of maintaining either its credibility or its duration. Summit meetings of the world's top leaders, against a backdrop of irreconcilable differences, always result in minimal agreements, but without any credible and lasting consensus. The planet Earth seems more and more structured to self-destruct. Unless! Real mutation force them change their strategy and philosophy of concrete actions.

We have bequeathed nations with their hands tied to politicians without putting in place real warning mechanisms or providing the tools and disciplines needed to effectively manage this complex web of institutions and expectations that are the root causes of this slippage. The independence of justice, myth or reality, is insufficiently effective since it functions with laws produced by political actors who have their own logic, their own mode of operations and their own mechanisms which, most of all, reinforce their interests to the detriment of those of nation systems.

But there is something worse! It is the strategy of the forces of change. A large number of associations, political parties, groups of passionate, often honest individuals, who make enormous psychological and material sacrifices, have a strange idea of concrete actions. They confuse objectives and ways of action. Too dispersed, too proud of their own programs and their operating modes, they let themselves be easily distanced by the political profession, well-seasoned by their experiences and their material endowments. They confuse the nobility of their actions, their civic-mindedness and their sacrifice with their potential for success.

The forces of change also remain structured to fail. Neither their strategy nor their day-to-day actions give cause for optimism. Despite their dedication and selflessness, the results cannot match their sacrifices or their hopes. Their strength is considerable but their weight is feather. Each one is happy to distinguish himself from others by differentiated measures that they cherish and that they rarely find in similar or rival bodies.

Action programs—established as sacred cows—become an 'all or nothing,' a sine qua non, indivisible condition and the cornerstone of any common program with external entities. It is the ultimate justification for turning away from an imperfect but likely-to-succeed common agenda. The forces of the status quo are correctly assessing the situation and knowingly deepening the differences among the forces of change. This is a fair game! For which the forces of change remain deeply unprepared and are poised for the ultimate defeat. Unless! The energy of despair is channelled diligently and quickly into one of the salutary alternatives.

We should remember one of the most emblematic lessons of the twentieth century. It is imposed on us by the typologies of organisations and numerous sector action plans. When designing an action plan, we often do not have the choice of an optimal solution. And if it does exist—which would be doubtful— it is hardly ever revealed in a methodical way to the most experienced analysts. So we would inevitably have a multitude of good solutions and others of less good characters. We always try to identify one of the alternatives that seem to us the most appropriate and therefore settle for an option that has the potential of success—through effort, resources and devotion—among the most appropriate. In absolute terms, the best action program does not exist. It is often not possible to distinguish between action plans on the basis of pure scientific knowledge.

This reinforces the convictions of parties, NGOs and other entities of the relevance of their own visions.

But the Gordian knot of the problem lies in the management of expectations (see A. Lamiri: *The Economics of the Future*). What kind of expectations have we allowed to seize the consciousness and unconsciousness of the masses to lead to political actions of such inconsistency? For a long time, social and human sciences have taught us a lot about expectations, but too little about how to act on them. We have learned how to reinforce the acts of ease, but very little to manage them in order to take beneficial detours. Expectation management is the poor condition of the human and social sciences. We do not know how to build citizen expectations in equilibrium with the potential of the biosphere and human ethics. We have started by establishing the general conditions for obtaining partial equilibriums in specific markets or sectors. The English economist Alfred Marshall carried out the most meticulous analyses in this field. It was necessary to locate the requirements of equilibrium exchanges within limited circles. Markets for cinema tickets and potatoes were worthy of these analytical efforts. However, the conditions of a general equilibrium of exchanges, dazzlingly formulated by Walras, were a piece of ontology, brilliantly mathematised, but of very limited usefulness (see A. Lamiri op cited). In this area, we would need, by mobilising the necessary human and material resources, to force innovations in two essential directions:

1. The formulation of a global, but not general, equilibrium, is synonymous with a match between the volume of goods and services generated by human anticipations and the economic apparatus on the one hand, and the potential for reproduction of the biosphere without altering its capacity to endure on the other.
2. Managing human anticipations: Our knowledge is so poor that our actions are likely to have no future. We know so little about how to manage human expectations that if rapid and significant progress is not made, there will be risks of dysfunctions in all sectors of economic life. This is where everything is at stake. The forces of the status quo have understood this. They continue to confuse the amount of resources available to an individual with their level of happiness and promise 'more for all' while mobilising maximum resources for the military industry and very little for environmental issues. We continue to

maintain a deadly contradiction between the level of expectations generated by political activity and the degree of reproduction of the biosphere's productive capacities. We are living on credit at the expense of future generations. Soon we will consume in three months what the planet Earth is capable of reproducing in one year. We will consume nine months out of twelve on credit at the expense of future generations. They will curse us for not having wanted to direct science and resources towards the production of human and social knowledge and the hard sciences in order to make significant advances and effectively address environmental issues.

A challenge for which humanity is not prepared has appeared too quickly and too abruptly for the awakening of consciences asleep by many decades of carelessness. The situation is so urgent that only a miracle can save us. And some people believe in it: contrary to many scientists, some analysts have made us believe in the possibility of a reversibility of processes. We then lost too much time and too many resources that could have dissipated these perils. The trap has closed on us and the vicious circle of anticipations contrary to environmental requirements seems unmanageable. So we have formulated an ingenious strategy: the ostrich strategy (see Aktouf (1)). We pretend that the problem does not exist and it will disappear by miracle. For the moment this is the only serious strategy we have. Apart from pretending and taking insignificant actions! Another mechanism seems to be working wonderfully: we are giving responsibility to a whole host of institutions for the cause: the IPCC, the UN, the G7, the G20, the European Union, China and the USA who are doing too little too late. Previously, we used to say of an insurmountable problem (war, famine, epidemic) 'but life will continue on Earth.' This time, it is different: it risks being completely annihilated from our blue planet. We have organised our sciences, our institutions, and the destinations of resources to guarantee our own annihilation. And the organisation of the forces of change is part of our self-destruction arsenal. We do not see how the process can be steered towards beneficial paths with the current methods and strategies.

The tools of social science on which we were banking most of our hopes— Marshall's partial and Walras's general equilibrium—are of little help to us in addressing our problem. A global equilibrium between, on the one hand, citizens' expectations and the adequacy of the economic apparatus and, on the other hand, a match between the production tool and the potential of the biosphere is only in its early stages. It would then be too late to work with this tool because the process enters a labyrinth of irreversibility. And we keep thinking about the ways designed in a context of abundance. They are of limited scope for the emergency and the contemporary cataclysms. We are far, far from having all the knowledge we need to manage. What little we do know is strongly misunderstood even in democratic countries. But it gets worse.

We continue to invest heavily in destructive industries instead of research and development oriented towards ecosystem restoration and biosphere rescue. Soon we will happily exceed $2,000 billion in military expenditures and we do not invest even a tenth in new energy research and development. Supersonic missiles receive unlimited resources compared to severely damaged ecosystems. Neither the social sciences nor the hard sciences have been brought up to the level of the demands of the current challenges. The forces of change are advancing in numbers while deteriorating in the quality of their strategies and organisation. They feel they are powerful but are unable to move the situation one iota. They believe that the nobility of their cause can compensate for their antiquated strategies, organisation and tools. Their sacrifices, dedication and willpower are matched only by the inconsistencies in their strategies and action plans. Many would be willing to die for their cause. Their complete dedication is not questioned. The movement is beginning to recruit from all walks of life, including social bosses, but mostly young people, scientists, artists, etc.

Modern societies are structured in such a way as to develop too much precedence of political authority over scientific power. However, advanced countries are beginning to achieve scientific feats that jeopardise their national security, either with respect to their direct enemies or through their environmental and health consequences. Once a party is in power, it will only listen to its scientists, who are often in its pay. There is no independent scientific authority that would audit the action programs and give them a discharge. The political authority does not want this. The political power had to appoint scientists, often on duty and give those missions. What is allowed for the courts of auditors of different nations is not allowed for a scientific authority (appointment according to peer review criteria for example). Of course, political power is elected in modern democracies. But where are the safeguards that protect societies from collapse in the long run? A political party can create jobs and prosperity in the short term with massive deforestation, and endanger the nation and the planet in the longer term. We protect ourselves by setting up independent courts of audit against the plunder of a few million public dollars and do much less for dangers of millions of times more. It is true that the courts of audit are not sufficiently free from political powers, although they should be, but scientific powers are even weaker in the most democratic countries, and they are the very poor relation, the most important flaw and therefore the Achilles heel of modern nations.

A key indicator in the forecast is the flow of research and development and entrepreneurship (companies created). These are worrying in our context. We are mainly developing our destructive and ICT capacities oriented to the modernisation of the already available processes. Certainly, some action programs are mentioned on solar energy, wind energy and marginal advances on the restoration of damaged ecosystems but nothing that can revolutionise our methods of management of environmental programs. Only the miracle of reversibility of natural processes can save us. But we do not understand very well the scientific mechanisms by which this can happen. So we are hoping for a real miracle, an unexplained phenomenon that can come to our rescue. Humanity is heading towards a wall with an increasingly accelerated speed and hopes in the end to avoid a lethal head-on collision. This is the stage we are in. The pessimistic but realistic diagnosis that we develop is unfortunately impartial.

Most of the elements of this diagnosis have been made by numerous scientific personalities and independent institutions. But, is there an action plan that can give us some chance of success? What can we do to avoid being among the celestial civilisations that self-destruct instead of prospering (serious theories of many scientists)? We must think according to an appropriate methodology that embraces the following values:

1. The problem is global and interconnected, the solution cannot be partial.
2. In parallel with a scientific revolution (social sciences and hard sciences), we will develop a plan of action and urgent measures to be introduced in order to slow down and then gradually repair the maximum damage caused.
3. The essential mechanism by which all the complex devices operate is indeed the process of formation of citizens' expectations. Their level would happily exceed both the potential of the present economic

apparatus and, in particular, the reproduction capacities of the biosphere (global equilibrium instead of Walras' general equilibrium).

4. Mobilisation of all available and committed human intelligence. No human brain, even if it is endowed with extraordinary intelligence, can develop all the necessary measures. Moreover, no institution can also do it, contrary to what some organisations announce. However, the involvement of millions of brains in an organised consultative process is likely to produce this breakthrough. In fact, some organisations have made a brilliant record in this area. But it is not enough. The purpose of this book is to provide appropriate methodologies for this aim.

5. Operational actions are important, and the expression 'the devil is in the details' takes on its full meaning in the operating mode that must be established. It is essential to equip oneself with the tools of management of mass movements before getting involved in leading them. Marxism has paid the price for underestimating this aspect. One of the essential reasons has been the belief that the movement is of natural obedience and that it is in perfect harmony with the course of history. Therefore, consequent deviations cannot occur. There would be risks of slippage, but no serious dysfunctions that could jeopardise the movement and its objectives. Or so thought the Marxists and today the environmentalists.

These themes are covered in a previous book (Lamiri, op cited) and also in this work.

The overall problem, overall solution: the priority axis of a rescue movement of such magnitude would be the search for multiple alliances within national and especially international confederations. It would be futile to form thousands of scattered and insignificant NGOs to face a challenge of such a magnitude. The forces of the status quo are likely to have a bright future ahead of them and problems to be solved with disconcerting ease when they have in front of them multiple, disparate movements and moreover indirect competition for leadership and method. It is better to have a unified and imperfect action plan than a thousand ideal and isolated programs. Only a few values are sufficient to be claimed: democracy, hyper-transparency, peaceful transformation and the use of scientific power alone to influence events. Between success together and failure alone, the choice of an intelligent person must be quickly made. Should we fail alone or succeed together? If the goal is to have the most perfect program and let the forces of the status quo rule the world with the current methods, many NGOs have long since succeeded in this.

In fact, the first strategy of an NGO that would like to seriously influence the global mode of functioning and thus have chances to deeply modify the choices of political leaders would be to look for national and especially international alliances around the following values: peaceful and democratic transformation, hyper-transparency, and transmutation by scientific mechanisms (Global Science). It would be tempting to want to suppress by any force governments that say they are elected and believe they are democratic, even if in fact democracy is a minimal sphere of these systems. What the people believe becomes a palpable reality. The mechanisms by which the political system operates should be analysed, explained, undone and redone and made explicit to the citizens with them and by them. We have an embryo of knowledge to accomplish this task, but we need to expand our knowledge horizons quickly. It is much easier to restore truths than to maintain lies. If this has not happened in the past it would be due to the weakness of the forces of change.

Change through violence will rightly be seen as inhumane and may lead to unparalleled scourges of hunger, suffering, and wastage of resources at a time when they need to be channelled to more beneficial destinations. The strategy of violence also risks being confused with that adopted by the communist movements. The latter has backfired. We should not forget that communism was rejected and fought against mainly by the workers for whom it was designed to take power and manage society. The path of brutality is contrary to the ethics of Global Science. It is sometimes understandable that individuals and associations are pushed to the limit by a system that assassinates humanity in small doses while pretending to act to protect it. But this energy of despair would be better channelled into winning options instead of looking for avenues that would cause calamities for all. The battle would be mostly in the area of mass communication, in persuasion, and it must be won. We have to equip ourselves with tools that are more powerful and persuasive than our opponents. The solution is scientific. Even if we do not have all the tools at present, we have to create them.

The size effect will work in favour of collaborating institutions. Corporate strategists are well aware of the advantages of company size when they know how to manage the organisational typologies that result from it. But the international dimension that a well-structured institution will take on is multiplied by compared to its limited scope. There is no point in creating even more entities that are a force for change if not to increase their quality. It is better to ally than to multiply. Two or three global institutions (it would be better to be federated into two) may be enough, but as many as possible should be included in larger and larger groups.

Secondly, these large groups—preferably grouped in two coordinated federations—will seek the maximum number of alliances within the most distant layers of this front. We will have three types of alliances:

a. Natural allies: These are forces directly concerned by the changes in the way society functions. Youth organisations, trade unions, scientific organisations, the art world, religious institutions (the latter would be in a better position by defending the principle of the continuity of life).

b. Neutral allies: These would be all the categories that can place their position in isolation from the issue. Many government officials, security agencies, etc., with adequate persuasion work, we can integrate them at least passively (especially for voting) to the cause;

c. The beneficiaries of the status quo either directly or indirectly. A majority of businessmen as well as the lobbyists' corporation, a large majority of the current political class have direct interests linked to the way current companies operate and would be favoured by the continuity process. Only a minority of them may be committed to the cause, but their number can be enlarged by rigorous communication during decisive actions (voting). No potential support should be overlooked. Minimalist support for the cause is sought (voting). The movement will grow through the federations that need to be initiated and the collaborations to the cause of more and more committed people. An unprecedented human tide will break over the last bastions of resistance. The human potential should then be transformed into a real force for revolutionary change.

Mobilisation from the top (federation) and collaboration from the bottom (social strata to be mobilised) will form the greatest coalescence in history for peaceful, democratic, transparent change, and will have as its source the mobilisation of our best multidisciplinary scientists and millions of human brains who will speak and choose among the best alternatives that human brainpower could have conceived. Our best specialists in innovation, organisation, intelligence management and other soft and hard sciences will know how to structure the movement and its mechanisms through this Global Science that will soon be created. But urgent actions for which we already have the know-how must start promptly.

The Need to Accelerate Scientific Innovations

We have allowed ourselves to jeopardise our only home through the weakness of our social innovations and the orientation of scarce resources mainly towards destructive industries and technologies harmful to the environment. We have some insufficient knowledge—human, social and hard—too unsatisfactory to have a salutary influence on the course of events. And we continue to direct resources in the same way with minor adjustments. Our nations need a budgetary re-engineering. During the 1980s and 1990s, many companies learned to re-engineer their processes. Some of them were able to better mobilise their human resources to take advantage of the situation and were able to improve their operations while saving on resources. After all, we need to better channel the flow of resources and re-prioritise according to the new strategic and operational directions. The operation consists in recreating more ethical nations, focused on essential needs and especially on repairing the damage inflicted. Process re-engineering is still in its infancy. Currently, the tools to take advantage of it at the macro level are not available, but our research and development teams will focus much more on developing life-saving tools rather than supersonic missiles. There can be no great changes in economic and social functioning without a revolution in the allocation of resources. Consider the budgets of even the most democratic governments. They have rarely evolved in the direction of urgency. Palace revolutions are not enough. Neither for the forces of the status quo nor for those of change. There are so many areas that need to be revolutionised in order for the strategy of change to work that a matrix of actions to be taken would be quickly obscured.

An emergency plan, however, cannot wait for a scientific revolution to be defined. Current knowledge can begin to rebuild the damage done. Of course, it may be insufficient, especially in terms of economic and social organisation, but an emergency plan is necessary. It would depend enormously on the process of the mobilisation of the scientific and citizen intelligence which will be discussed in our next section.

Mobilising Citizen's Intelligence

Federated NGOs would benefit from structuring themselves differently from current political parties and many independent institutions. They could take shape along the lines of Global Science and the principles of ethics, hyper-transparency, democracy, science and increased citizen participation. A key variant could take the form of an organisation built around a multidisciplinary scientific entity. The latter could take the form of specialised commissions headed by representatives who would be part of committees higher up in the hierarchical reality. Likert (24) has explained the process in detail. But a citizen participation committee is an integral part of mobilising and choosing citizen options that could be part of the chosen plan. As has been said, it is not impossible that an Indian farmer could graft a tree that would retain ten times more CO_2 and therefore the idea could become widespread. The opinions developed can also concern organisational typologies, expectation management and technological orientations. Suppose an NGO manages to mobilise 300 million people worldwide and 100 million participate each year. If one idea out of 100 were to be considered, we would have one million options to integrate and perhaps the scientific committee would use 1000 of them in its action plan. This would be a complete game-changer. It is not only senior scientists who can propose innovations, although the essential work would be based on their conceptualisation. The management of human intelligence is the number one key success factor for companies and countries. Those who can harmoniously mobilise millions of human brains will win the battle for political, social, economic and technological supremacy. It is impossible to gain a competitive advantage without using it.

The leadership of the democratically elected movement also participates in the process of elaborating scientific programs but without the power to impose its points of view. It is not a question of recreating modern societies in miniature, where political forces take precedence over scientific authority. Moreover, today, the financial establishment has too much power over the elections. Access criteria should be established for all positions in addition to democratic elections. The nobility of task and dedication cannot compensate for managerial shortcomings. Furthermore, the management of non-profit institutions must take on an unprecedented scope and increase the knowledge and know-how in this field. It is not easy to generate, select and decide among millions of proposals which ones will be part of the official agenda.

Probably intermediate selection commissions structured by geographical area and by discipline would be set up before being included in the lists of the final commissions for the choice of actions to be taken. Today most of the leaders of change movements consider that their program would transcend all others and that if and only if it was universally adopted we would then have the final solution. But no outcome is possible unless it involves compromises and is the result of a rigorously structured collective outcome. Moreover, the ideas of a small group of individuals cannot prevail over the rest of the forces of change. Only the mobilisation of millions of human brains structured by our best scientists using rigorous as well as democratic methods will have a chance to be accepted by the vast majority of the forces of change. Multidisciplinary and integrated Global Science dealing with the question of designing reliable economic and political systems can only propose principles to be respected and tools to help in the decision-making process. It cannot produce programs on behalf of millions of citizens. It provides them with the method and the working procedures, but it cannot carry out the tasks that should be undertaken by millions of human brains unless it has been done within the participation process.

Mobilising the maximum amount of human brainpower around the issues of the day is what non-profit organisations will be able to do in the future. No one would have the right to jeopardise a nation or the planet under the banner of entrepreneurial freedom. Tomorrow's technologies will be assessed primarily in light of their environmental and social impacts. A brilliantly supervised innovation, on the opposite, would leave indelible and eminently positive effects on society and the biosphere. Current patterns of gross irresponsibility of public authorities cannot be reproduced.

Expectation Management

Most of the programs of the forces of change minimise what is an essential mechanism of the entrenchment of the vicious circle that endangers us. It is about the formation of expectations and their impact on economic and political mechanisms. But there we have the Gordian knot, the essential mechanism by which the trap that is set for the whole of humanity operates. The peril has become inexorable only because it operates through us. We have become our own destroyers because of the social and especially political way of functioning. Everything is done in such a way that we confuse the volume of resources at our disposal with our own happiness. The school would be a social elevator especially to claim an appreciable level of resources, entrepreneurship would be a medium to accelerate the appropriation and the acts of innovation, image development and communication would be a medium to guarantee the maximum of resources. This could only lead us to a higher level of social satisfaction. The essential mission of political parties becomes to promise to put more resources at the disposal of the maximum number of citizens. The eve of the elections would be the right time to promise more to all. We have locked ourselves in this logic of equalising satisfaction and material resources from which we are not able to get out. We economists talk about utility, but we reduce it to its simplest material expression, whereas it can be psychological or disinterested. Even if the expression is general and can be translated in many ways, people would equal it, especially with the level of satisfaction that comes from the volume of resources available to us.

So, how do we get out of this death trap that works so well? In the distant future, if we could get out of it, we could hope to build nations with a strongly controlled level of equality, thanks to Global Science. The differential between the most deprived and the most endowed would be 1 to 10 or 20 or 50, a consideration controlled by the democratic process. The most productive people would then receive psychological or symbolic remunerations: choosing a symbolic activity financed by their tax surplus (for example, schooling X number of handicapped children), medals, diplomatic passports, being part of national personalities, etc. But while waiting to pretend to be able to create economic and social systems that work efficiently, with more social justice and respect for environmental rules, we must deal with the nagging question: What should we do now? In the future, we can hope that educational programs will be revised, parents will be better trained to play their roles, the political system will be cleaned up and freed from the power of money, hyper-transparency will be enshrined and a whole range of measures will be taken to strengthen economic, social and political ties. Technologies will be oriented to the maximum for the sustainability of the biosphere. But what should we do now?

It is not a question of recycling future generations but also of recycling the present, those who are operational, live, decide and are infused with the ambient culture of always more to live better and bask in absolute happiness. We would gain enormously by recycling the maximum number of people available according to various methods, hoping for a snowball effect, a sort of Ponzi scheme, but to achieve healthy consequences for the biosphere and the political and economic systems. It is in moments like these that the mobilisation of human intelligence takes on its full meaning. No one can produce an exhaustive program in this area, but mobilising millions of brains will surely lead to thousands or even millions of proposals, many of which will be included in the final action plan of the right institution. The time has passed when a human brain, however intelligent, could single-handedly direct all of humanity to appropriate destinations. Didn't Einstein, as brilliant as he was, get it wrong with quantum physics and his equations on the expansion of the universe? But the operation would be better supervised by our best scientists who will draw up the final plan. Selection committees will do the usual job of thanking for contributions and explaining options not taken into account. The Global Science decision-making methodology would be the source of operationalisation of the choices that would come from relevant institutions. We are not totally without tools, but we need many more to complete the array of instruments we will need.

But the matching of expectations with the possibilities of the economic apparatus and particularly with the reproductive potential of the biosphere remains the thorny issue on which all current change projects stumble. The question is quickly settled at the level of human intuition. Pro-growth advocates, who are often interested in the process, consider that all that is needed is to stimulate it with new, more environmentally friendly technologies, and the gamble would finally be won. Most of the pro-radical change proponents are thinking about a recession so deep that in the current context, we have neither the organisation nor the strategy nor the mechanisms to make it happen. And the mountain on which we are stumbling remains the citizens' expectations, which are too high and always pushed up by a class of politicians often not very responsible. Perhaps we need to operate a recession before its recovery when we will have these missing technologies and knowledge. But, we are now witnessing one of the most incongruous situations: directing very few research and development resources towards the development of a green industry and hoping that the disequilibrium created can be repaired as if by a miracle. We are mostly funding supersonic missiles while hoping to have positive spin-offs with the scant resources we invest in the green economy. We are not far from nonsense.

The diagnosis of the first stage of the process is likely to show whether the recovery mechanism would be compatible with low growth, decline or recession before initiating sustained growth later (see section on model building). Human intuition is the product of too much subjectivity to be considered as the source of our inspiration for rigorous program designs. Certainly, intuition can be salutary and should be encouraged in the search for options, but it would be validated when submitted to a rigorous analysis. The political parties are drowned in intuitive and often erroneous ideas, but they still keep using them. They often resort to secrecy, as when the radiation from Chornobyl affected part of Western Europe. Since the problem is global while they promise to solve everything within their limited territory, they are devoid of real solutions.

The question of citizens' expectations is central. In parallel to these actions, it is necessary to lead a citizen debate on the issue. This is where the size of the NGO, the quality of its organisation and its overall management will make all the difference. It is vital that a catalogue rich in options be evaluated by the scientific committee from which thousands of interesting proposals will emerge. There may be no idea that will save humanity from its peril, but there may be one or more combinations of thousands of options that could make up a bouquet of salutary actions to be undertaken. It would be useless to look for the magic hero that would save humanity. Thus, we would be truly entitled to say loud and clear: 'Only one hero: the people.'

Complementary Details

The real is more complex than the conceptual therefore perpetual adaptation is a permanent leitmotif. A frequent adjustment of the actions to specific situations that complex institutions would be confronted with requires consequent preparation. The relevant entities would need many more tools than the current organisations. We will need to perfect the management of non-profit organisations not only to partially integrate what businesses have developed that is useful and substantial but also to innovate in the sense of adapting as well as creating. Thus the notion of management by objectives would make sense in such institutions. We have seen that many communication problems and conflicts are mainly due to the lack of objectives. One manager complains about a team member who is not recruiting enough members, yet the team member boasts that he distributes more flyers than anyone else in the organisation. The number criterion would be recruitment for the former and the number of items distributed for the latter. Communication becomes impossible and the situation can only get worse without working by objectives. Also, a very flexible job description would be appropriate. Criteria for access to the different positions in addition to elections at all levels should be maintained. Specific training is required (often provided by the organisation itself) for key positions of responsibility. It is important that as many of the leadership positions as possible be held by people who have proven themselves at lower levels.

But these organisations should never be bureaucratised neither have long lines of authority. They need to be smooth, flexible, encourage opposing viewpoints, accommodate non-permanent staff, and develop an institutional culture consistent with the battles they want to win. A multitude of details (such as motivating one's staff) will need to be addressed through learning, science and adaptation. Of course, we cannot formulate in this context all the management aspects of such organisations, just a word about the role of leadership in question. Obviously, it is elective. Democracy is a sacrosanct principle of leadership.

Furthermore, it would have a great influence on the scientific committee. The leadership gives its opinion but the different leaders will mainly try to carry out the program of the scientific committee conceived with the participation of all members and allies. Mobilising human intelligence is a constitutional principle. The power of the leadership is mainly exercised to motivate the members, to recruit, to represent and to find financial resources (without questioning the independence of the scientific committees). If two or three world federations were to be formed—with coordination—the project could attract the attention of the masses. It is not certain that one organisation can do a better job: some form of competition is necessary. Monopoly always gives birth to forms of drift and precedence over the essential objective of organisations.

Karl Marx, in spite of the immense theoretical revolution introduced, often constituting major advances and sometimes failures, was a victim of the idealism of uniqueness. He believed that a communist party with absolute monopoly power—based only on so-called class consciousness—over the army, politics and society as a whole would direct the economic system for the good of all the people. The subsequent failures that occurred belied this assertion wherever the experiment was carried out.

Structuring and Probability of Success

We should not delude ourselves. Professional management of complex organisations is indispensable. Dedication, sacrifices and human suffering cannot compensate for strategic and operational mistakes. We need to structure organisations around scientific but democratic projects. Multidisciplinary commissions can even concoct two or three action plans: the timing and the allocation of resources can differ but the purpose is the same: to achieve objectives but with different timings and more or less important sacrifices to endure. Today it is the political world that formulates proposals, based on scientists—often on duty or they will be marginalised—chosen for their docility or for the most part by ignoring their most rigorous recommendations. The alliance between the world of finance, a part of the communication sector, and some zealous employers is in a powerful position. Only due to the weakness of the opponents! The followers of change are not able to reverse the situation by their courage, sacrifices, willingness and suffering. Too scattered and often divided, they are easy prey for the forces of the status quo that are well-structured, resourced and equipped with the most modern means of communication. They have as their best soldiers some of the programs in the economics and business administration departments.

The neoclassical school and the finance departments confuse the elegance of mathematical equations with the way the real world works. There are no modules that integrate the many disciplines that make up the social sciences and humanities, and even fewer those that harmonise them with hard sciences. Formatting of minds is a valuable mechanism to guide the thinking and actions of the future world's leaders. Certainly, one cannot lump together the teachings of cultural management, human resources, and financial models of options and the creation of financial securities, although even the former contain questionable developments. We must realise that this is how the system is perpetuated. It regenerates itself by creating innovations to make profits for some and perils for all. Only the branch of insurance would have an interest in promoting global equilibrium. But the forces of change did not create the necessary partnership to integrate them into the battle. There is no such a strategic approach.

The problem of growth is somewhat misstated. The role of Global Science is also to assess the content of growth. It is recognised that growth that damages the environment does more harm than good, especially in the long run. But there are segments of growth that create little or no wealth for a country. An investor who sells a package of shares creates value and taxes (transfer of purchasing power to the treasury) in an accounting way, but what resources are created for the nation? Alcohol and gambling industries should be taxed more severely in favour of green industries and promising research and development. We often mix the types of activities and talk about growth. Positive growth should be developed and encouraged and negative growth should be reduced as much as possible. We should not forget that we need to revolutionise the flow of resources if we are to continue to make a difference. Wealth distribution cannot be left to the market alone. The capital we need to survive must be democratically chosen to achieve rescue. The market cannot override the democratic process, although its proponents believe that market mechanisms are the best democratic process available. However, when the issue becomes one of survival, this changes everything. Resources are requisitioned during wars. But, this situation is akin to a conflict that does not declare its name. A minimum or a maximum of means would be mobilised for positive activities depending on the assessment of the situation.

Communication is the Keystone of the Project

The leadership of change organisations will be primarily concerned with fundraising (without pressure on the action programs) and communication. They are strong believers and wherever possible rely on public funds as well as on membership fees, which at the start form the bulk of the organisation's budget. In addition, business activities can be incorporated into complex NGOs. Moreover, the organisation of these entities can reveal a functional organisation chart around key activities: communication, financing, training, research and development etc. An ethics committee could improve the transparency of funding methods. It is mostly well-endowed and under-resourced citizens (volunteers) who believe in a structured rescue that can make a difference. Dedicated people offer their time and resources to accomplish one of the missions that deserve to be dedicated. For this to happen, the communication process must rise to the level of the challenges we face.

Currently, the forces of the status quo have the upper hand and control the process through sophisticated communication: major investment in the mass media, intensive lobbying of the political class and security agencies, and an education system that manages the consciousness and unconsciousness of the rising generations. This leaves only 'marginal' spheres for the forces of change. Yet, these targets are strategic because they represent the class that votes or should vote. These are the millions of people who need to be persuaded to vote not only for the volume of resources expected to be delivered by politicians but also to participate in a rescue effort of unparalleled magnitude. Making them part of the proposed solutions will certainly help to integrate more people (neighbourhood representatives who come together to find common solutions as advocated by the intelligence mobilisation process). The more people are involved in finding solutions, the more they will be part of the larger movement for change. Currently, we are witnessing a limited awareness that does not translate into strong support for profound social change. Given the enormous weaknesses in the communication process, the vast majority of citizens have a heart for the environment and a vote for the forces of the status quo. It is a matter of being able to match feelings with actions. Professional communication can make a difference. Of course, one should not ignore the human resources that can be converted, especially among the young people who are being trained in social sciences and those among the political class who are becoming aware of the magnitude of the disaster that is looming on the horizon. But the focus is indeed on the massive segment of citizens who advocate for the environment and vote for its destroyers.

The emergence of a handful of international confederations coordinated among themselves could be sufficient to reverse the present process of environmental lamentations and the channelling of resources to activities harmful to the biosphere. Furthermore, they can facilitate the development of peace in the world, the reunification of countries and the strengthening of democratic and ethical principles. What is needed, however, is the recovery of ecosystems and the rescue of the biosphere. Professional communication on the possible need to temporarily reduce the standard of living, but in a fairer way (societies with a maximum inequality gap of 10 or 50 or other) should be launched. A whole bunch of measures to make life more enjoyable without mobilising a maximum of resources would be implemented. This is where the mobilisation of collective intelligence takes on its full meaning. The experiment led by Kurt Lewing (30) on the consumption of offal during the Second World War could be significant in illuminating the way forward. Citizen participation committees changed their behaviour (consumption of more offal and less meat) than those who had listened to expert speeches on the need for change. It is up to communication professionals to suggest solutions, but always in a process of collective intelligence management.

One must respond intelligently to adversaries (not enemies). An average citizen in place of the political class, lobbyists, financial executives, security services would probably have reacted in the same way. We should avoid the expressions 'these selfish people,' 'these vampires who destroy life,' 'these ignorant of realities.' These are life paths that have led them to confuse their interests with the paradox of the current situation. It is necessary to help them to become aware of future challenges and to develop a whole arsenal of specific communication tools in their direction. Interest dictates class consciousness, as Karl Marx would say. But who made Frederick Engels side with the proletarians? By studying the cases of thousands of examples that support causes contrary to their interests, we will eventually find the determinants of these changes. One cannot change people whom one hates. We take them for what they are. They are victims of trials and trails of life that provide them with the psychological material to form a conscience. Very little is known about what might contribute to shaping the conscience of a Mother Teresa or that of a Nazi. This is one of the greatest worksites of Global Science to create nations (or one nation only) that are ethical, democratic, civic, more egalitarian and more respectful of ecosystems. So, the objective is neither to hate nor to make people feel guilty but only to make them more sensitive to the question of life on Earth and to make them at least sympathisers while trying to reintegrate them into the movement.

Moreover, natural allies that are available, organised, and can drain hundreds of millions of individuals to the cause are the religions (see specific section on religions). If they have not been integrated, it is because no integration strategy exists. Of course, there is a minority of religious people who are paedophiles, corrupt and linked to the interests of the existing political system. Normally they are natural allies because they would defend most of the same objectives: life, social justice and nature. The process of communication would make them a top priority target. Communication is the process that would win or lose the battle for change. It is at this level that everything risks being played out, while the forces of change believe that through violence or through the nobility of their task there would inevitably be a trigger that can restore the priority of their cause. The forces of the status quo welcome these choices, options chosen on the basis of intuition. Most movements become radicalised and prepare for hopeless battles. The followers advocate the destruction of the system but to replace it with what? Communists have tried to build a completely different system. They have failed in all fields, including the one in which struggles are taking place: the environment. And there are as many choices of alternative systems as there are speakers. It is not easy to move from one social, economic, political and technological system to another, especially in such a short and perilous period of time. We need all the multidisciplinary scientific intelligence and all the citizen's brainpower to hope for a rescue.

It is easy to fall into a disconcerting ease. Many activists would say that if citizens, governments and authorities think like them, the problem will be solved instantly, but consciences are the fruits of lived experiences. And the paths of life have taken us to different places, which would have left indelible traces in our ways of thinking and setting priorities. Most of the forces of change, with pro-status quo citizen's paths, would most likely have made the same choices as them. So, there is no point in condemning, stigmatising or even abusing these people, especially if the central objective is to make them allies. It is not by unnecessarily multiplying the groups of opponents that the movement will gain in size and quality. The forces of the status quo are so powerful, so organised, and have a firm grip on the situation. We would have to dig deep into the depths of these forces, to wring the intelligence of the maximum number of citizens and our best scientists to overcome them. They indirectly control the formation of the citizens' consciousness. They have at their disposal millions of poor citizens that compose their security forces. Most of them will die if conflicts appear. Most of the rich are sheltered. The masses may cry for the biosphere, but they end up voting for the political class. One always hopes that those who have failed will eventually solve the problems they have created. Even though this class has shown itself to be very adept at the game of 'procrastination,' the same citizens still hope for a happy outcome to their dilemma.

But it is mainly the promises of more and for all that is enticing and that allows the political class to control the consciences and unconsciousness of the masses. Communication and efforts can only be effective if they aim at unifying the masses while creating different types of consciousness through collaboration. We are too focused on the very short term. Things will be different if we think about how the future generations will live. They will curse us. We are leaving them unmanageable chaos. This is where the focus should be because no ethical nation should destroy the future of its children. Certainly, we have public authorities who believe that they can do no more, considering the circumstances. They may have a good conscience about wasting a decade of last chance. They are not able to achieve more, considering the budgetary resources. But, have we made a budgetary re-engineering effort for a situation more urgent than war? Global Science has some chance of contributing to the final solution, but we have run out of time or when we can recover with only slight consequences. We will pay a high price and probably get away with significant consequences for many decades to come. Otherwise, we will inflict the final solution on ourselves, which is to self-destruct and deal with the massive damages that await us.

About Religions

We will mainly expose some facets that concern the problem we are dealing with. The subject of religion is probably one of the most complex and delicate to elaborate on. There are so many sensitivities around the question, so many controversies and divergences that we will refrain from commenting on anything outside our concern. First of all, an observation is necessary: the whole of the 'scientific' schemes that wanted to exclude religions from their conceptual field and especially bet on a negative role that they would play in the future have failed miserably. Marxism considers religion as part of the superstructure that would evolve according to the real economic base to accommodate the new modes of production that would replace the old ones. Therefore, the communist stage, the last stage of human evolution, would not need it. We confuse the tool with the use that is made of it. An aeroplane can be used to transport people, goods or sick people or to drop atomic bombs. Powerful people sometimes control its use, but the tool remains neutral.

Communism paid a heavy price for having disqualified religions. The latter are vital human needs so necessary that they must be included in the physiological needs in Maslow's pyramid. Freud's schemes also make religion a complex human construct and would be a social phenomenon designed by us humans. Departments of psychoanalysis are losing grounds one after another in the world's major universities. In its heyday, the discipline of psychoanalysis fascinated, inspired respect, and had many admirers. Today its decline is matched only by the vanishing of communism. Nowadays there is another theory that is at its peak but has begun its decline: Darwinism. The vast majority of modern conclusions try to accredit Darwin for limited changes (change of colours, length of legs, beaks of birds etc.) but disprove his conclusions for changes of great magnitude (change from a fish to a human being, for instance). The decline is inexorable and we would appreciate better his scientific contributions to their right scope. But we were too quick to bury religions on the basis of Darwinism.

Pure and hard materialism is cracking in many ways. New publications as well as recent scientific conclusions are beginning to discredit it (see Stephen Mayer: *the Return of the God Hypothesis* (44). First, materialism states that the universe has always existed and that therefore there is no need for a hypothesis of its creation. But the Big Bang Theory is being verified every day in cosmology. It is widely accepted by modern astronomy. Secondly, the parameters necessary for the appearance of life on Earth are numerous, finely tuned and require such precision that the probability of their appearance by chance is near impossible. Thirdly, the discovery of an astronomical amount of information in living organisms (DNA of the cell) which is used to function properly and to divide poses a real problem to materialism. Information can only come from intelligence and super intelligent information from a supreme intelligence. Where does the information in the cell come from? No materialist can answer this question in spite of thousands of desperate attempts such as Dawkins's, which states that life on Earth was probably seeded on our planet by extra-terrestrials. The only thing left for the materialist is a flight to the multiverse. The possibility of the existence of an astronomical number of universes is debated by modern physics. Materialists have not failed to use this possibility. To them, our universe would be a special place that would accommodate life while many would not have the characteristics to do so. We are just lucky to have been chosen (by chance) to exist in a universe suitable for life. It would take too long to continue the controversy (it is not our problem) but the argument would be weak according to the knowledge of current sciences.

Finally, a new phenomenon would upset the conceptual scheme of pure and hard materialism: the near-death experiences which are becoming widespread because of modern medicine which has made immense progress in terms of resuscitation. The people who have experienced these events have been the subject of rigorous and very thorough studies. There is no explanation for the phenomena of people who are blind from birth and who see for the first time, as well as those who do not leave a hospital bed but visit their homes and tell scientifically verified facts (See the tremendous work of Dr Mario Beauregard at the University of Arizona). A triple-blind scientific methodology states that real psychics (as there are many more charlatans) are able to communicate with the deceased, disturbing conclusions with very rigorous methodologies (See the 20 years of research of Gary Schwartz at the University of Arizona). We are witnessing the beginning of a revolution in science.

The post-materialist sciences project has been launched. One would then accommodate the idea that religions hold a part of the truth. Not that materialist science has died a death, but it would coexist better with some rare phenomena that we observe and that point to an omniscient creator. The Seattle Institute, which has advanced research on Darwin's theory, is at the centre of this scientific revolution. Moreover, it has been known since the beginning of the twenty-first century that quantum physics defies human rationality. Yet it has contributed to the major innovations of the last hundred years. Particles in atoms can be in several places at the same time; they behave as waves when not observed and as solid particles when they are. Quantum entanglement adds to the mystery when two particles become entangled and the position of one can be known by the position of the other, regardless of the distance. Physicists are not completely surprised: subatomic particles pass through solid masses (walls for example). The M theory, a version of the string theory, states that the universe contains 11 dimensions, including the four that we observe and in which we live.

We should stop stigmatising religions when, by their missions and their nature, they try to make comprehensible phenomena which escape our understanding. This does not imply that we should stop materialistic investigations, but make them coexist with religions. If science would tend to identify supreme intelligence as the cause of all creation, then what is the problem? It turns out that the omniscient being has given us scientific phenomena and mechanisms, which can be explained, predicted and verified. A scientific approach can be reconciled with an attitude of post-materialist thinking. Researchers in quantum physics have invented the formula 'shut up and calculate.' They have been able to derive a whole range of innovations from it, such as lasers, microprocessors, microwaves, etc., so post-materialist science already knows how to deal with incomprehensible phenomena. But this hardly implies that we should give up trying to find explanations. Quantum physics has been able to cope with a century of quantum incomprehension. Some social scientists reject the religious phenomenon on the basis of the behaviour of its extremist members, while the vast majority of followers are convinced that they convey a message of love, peace, mutual aid, social justice and protection of life. So a major challenge awaits them. They can only join the forces of change and not the forces of the status quo. To do otherwise would be to abandon their noble mission of protecting life and would be contrary to their principles, missions and ethics.

We cannot ignore that religions recruit billions of members. They are potential allies to mobilise the maximum of resources, intelligence and energy to advance the cause: to create societies with economic, social and political systems that are fairer, more peaceful and more respectful of ecosystems, because today we are unable to do so.

Box 4: Will the Multiverse Save Materialism?

Materialism has reached a dead end. Everything overwhelms it. The universe has a beginning (Big Bang); the parameters of life, the physical constants, are impossible to be formed by the simple fact of chance and the information contained in the living (DNA) whose quality and astronomical number can only come from a supreme intelligence have sown the doubt then the incomprehension of the materialist theses. Many other phenomena such as NDEs point in the same direction. There is one last hope: the multiverse—basically the existence of an infinite number of universes, debated by modern physics. Our universe would be one of the lucky ones which would have by chance (always) the necessary conditions to accommodate life. In the beginning, materialists suggested that life was brought to Earth by an extra-terrestrial civilisation. Given the age of the universe (13.7 billion years), the latter did not have time to produce human beings according to our model in order to be able to bring us life. In all likelihood, these extra-terrestrial sowers would have come from another universe. Some have calculated that a simple cell would require more than 10 to the power of two billion years to be constituted by the Darwinian process. But let us suppose that the multiverse would be a reality and that our universe would harbour life by pure chance. After.

Let's suppose that we would find within a sampling of universes that we would have had to observe that 10% or 20% or 1/X universes would possess life forms. We are talking about a sampling of a limited number of universes that intelligent beings could observe while the number would be infinite. Then we will have our X which would exceed 10 to the power of billions of billions of billions of billions etc., since nobody has calculated the probability that all the parameters of life (biological, physical…) are met. It is not enough that our universe has a form of life within the multiverse to postulate with certainty

---

that pure chance has made us win the lottery. We need to have the following conditions:

$1/Y > 1/X$ (greater or equal) or $1/Y = 1/X$

$1/Y$ is the proportion of universes that contain a life form

$1/X$ is the probability that the parameters of life appeared by chance. This would be the famous X which would be equal to 10 power of billions of billions.

For the time being, there is no indication that they can show that this is the case, but they will probably argue that a tiny part of infinity would be infinity. The debate with the materialists would be somehow infinite no matter what form of evidence was brought forward. According to their arguments even if 99% of the known finite universes contain life and the remaining 1% do not would be enough to justify the appearance by chance alone. The mere existence of the multiverse is far, too far, from rescuing the materialist cause. In fact, the controversy between impiety and religion is deeper. If an omnipotent and omniscient being is not behind this universe or multiverse, we would have one of two situations: an absolute vacuum (no matter) or a multitude of inert matter components; but instead, we have a multitude of matter elements (atoms, quarks, neutrons, electrons perhaps strings and smaller constituents) that are cleverly arranged to produce coherence, a harmony and to bring a sense to the great masses that compose them to produce a coherent whole predictable for them in order to secrete life or not but ultimately to build a grandiose work that would not have been possible without their precise and determined behaviour. Thus each particle, however small, acts as if it foresees the behaviour of all the others and adjusts its attitudes to enable them to contribute to the work for which they exist. If we refute the god hypothesis, then we would have all the elements of the multiverse (infinite) acting on their own and by themselves according to the infinity of coherences and harmonies by chance. Thus each element of nature would be a god because it foresees the consequences of its actions, predicts and acts to produce a sense for the whole. Today, a multiverse or not, this is what we have. The materialistic philosophy that believes to have finished with God finds itself with an infinity of gods. But, fortunately, the celestial religions do not carry this contradiction. Most of them believe in an omniscient and omnipotent God who distils his programs of behaviour to the smallest as well as to the biggest elements of the matter in order to produce rational behaviours of matters and energy comprehensible for human brains. Chance cannot equal infinity. It is better to bet on post-materialist science that works both with rigour and openness.

Contribution of Other Sciences

It is not easy to think about building other social, economic and political systems at a precise moment of our historical evolution when we are facing perils that risk annihilating our civilisations. But we have no choice. We have to face both challenges simultaneously: building methods to do so and undertaking rapid actions to save or limit the risks involved. All the evidence suggests that we are currently unable to design social, economic and political systems that produce societies of peace, social justice and ecosystem protection. Historical hope came from the historical materialism of Karl Marx. But, Marx, who explained reasonably well the historical course of nations before the socialist revolutions, was unable to predict future developments. In other words, he analysed the past so well but unfortunately did not correctly predict the future. The explanation lies in the fact that from the beginning of the twentieth century institutions, people and science were going to have a greater influence on the evolution of nations, but within narrow constraints defined by the guardians of the temple (the political class).

Historical materialism was appropriate for a period in which social, economic and political developments were independent of human consciousness. When societies became more democratically organised, they were able to take advantage of some outstanding institutions and personalities that helped to make the system more cooperative and conciliatory, without, however, solving the basic problems. The social organisation was much more accommodating to the conscious efforts of the citizens to better reconcile it. Marx contributed to this unknowingly. The spectre of communism allowed the introduction of profound reforms in the Austro-Hungarian Empire. Fearing socialist revolutions, the decision-makers had produced social measures that would spread throughout Europe. Keynesian-style full-employment policies were to put a brake on the rise of unemployment (the industrial reserve army). Overall, the system, due to internal mutations (democracy) and the fear of communism, was going to reform itself in depth and break the momentum of historical materialism. Thousands of reforms contributed to distancing historical materialism from reality. It is true that it operated during the previous centuries only because human brains could not contribute to changing reality. As soon as the opportunity presented itself to the mutations induced by the concepts and the human brains, it did not delay to see the consequences on the ground. But the other side of the coin is that we do not have a methodology to mutate complex societies towards healthy situations. Thus, the thousands of contributions from citizens and especially from analysts were often ad-hoc practices that superficially seemed logical but that would cause perilous consequences for humanity.

When plastic bags were introduced, it was thought that they would solve the logistical problems of households. We did not foresee that later on there would be more plastic bags than fish in the oceans. We had no science, no method and even less a model of socio-technical interactions to integrate the different elements of the process of change. However, when it was necessary to do so urgently, we imposed on ourselves the heavy tasks of minimising the consequences of our ill-prepared and too-risky actions. We believed that the generalisation of the Western-style consumption model in such a short time would bring happiness and comfort to all in a sustainable way. But barely two generations after the Second World War, the after-effects of this appeared as a surprise to many. Certainly, the report of the Club of Rome had drawn the attention of those in charge to the impossibility of generalising the Western way of life without running the risk of unpleasant consequences. However, it clearly underestimated the effects of the degradation of ecosystems and the chains that risk creating multiple vicious circles on the way the biosphere functions. We need to change our methods and tools in order to meet the contemporary challenges. The key piece of the device is yet to be created: Global Science. We will then have the necessary multidisciplinary schemes to direct our actions in beneficial ways. We need to combine our knowledge into a coherent system in order to diagnose in depth the way modern nations function and to target the knowledge to be developed and the actions to be taken in order to hope for recovery with the minimum of harmful consequences.

In this part of the document, we will explain some of the contributions that need to be made by the different sciences or disciplines in order to achieve significant advances in the development of Global Science. We will mention what we consider urgent and essential. It is not a question of being exhaustive in this field, nor can it be. Moreover, we are not starting from scratch. A lot of research has been done in these different fields of science and some conclusions have been drawn. We need to know more or better operationalise the approaches. We note, for example, that most citizens are beginning to see an affinity with ecosystem issues and are trying to take them into account (insufficiently) in their product or service choice process, but most are ignoring them in their political choices. We need in-depth work in psychology or other fields to determine the causes and to better specify how to remedy them. We have many issues related to all sciences and disciplines taught.

Certainly, the methodology of Global Science is always multidisciplinary. It is no longer a question of trying to elucidate a research question by one discipline in isolation. But, there must be a leader in any research and development project. The team contains most of the main partners who will have a say in the matter. It is rare these days that when a prototype of a new vehicle is developed, a sociologist or political scientist is involved. Few companies do. When real change occurs and when the forces of change are in control of the decision-making process, a real revolution will take place in two complementary directions:

1. Research and development flows will be massively directed towards urgent actions to restore ecosystems and to correct all kinds of abuses that we have committed at the political, social and especially ecological levels.
2. The mobilisation of human intelligence and energies to confront the perils that are imposed upon us. The decision-making process of Global Science can handle this dimension. We will only see improvements in these three dimensions—social, environmental and political—through gigantic efforts and colossal attempts. No human brain can save us, but if we mobilise tens of millions with an efficient structure and vision—that of Global Science—we will have a chance to ensure the continuity of life on Earth with a minimum of unfortunate consequences.

We will outline the essential and urgent investigative questions. They will be under the umbrella of the disciplines mentioned but only before setting up a coordination methodology. We have seen that teams organised according to the perfected Likert method (24) could lead to efficient coordination of dozens of multiple and complex committees and subjects. Thus, the scientific panels of Global Science cannot afford the luxury of waiting until the end of investigations to start acting. First, we put out the fire and then we start investigations on the causes. An emergency plan would already be in the process of stopping the mechanisms of ecosystem destruction, social injustice, and impediments to peace while refining our knowledge of what we need to build nations in a nation-world system that would accommodate human ethics. Research and development efforts would aim to expand knowledge and know-how to refine amend and perfect action plans while they are already in operation. These roadmaps will be the summary of the ideas of our best scientists and a process of mobilising the intelligence of the vast majority of our citizens. It is a massive task, and cannot be otherwise. We aspire to take up a challenge of extreme complexity and in record time. We can select a first sample of the themes of investigations to be carried out by multidisciplinary teams but under the leadership of a particular science. Each discipline or science would work on the most urgent questions. We can mention as an illustration different urgent themes in a few concerned disciplines:

A. Psychology

1. How can a human being derive more pleasure, happiness and meaning in life from participating in a noble project (humanitarian, environmental, social etc.) rather than just accumulating more resources?

2. How can we better get massive and structured participation in the brainstorming sessions from which the proposals of the involved citizens emerge?

3. How can we raise awareness that the lives of future generations are as important as those of the present?

4. How can we better counteract the forces of the status quo?

5. How can we better influence the political class to adhere effectively to the plans of the forces of change?

6. What control mechanisms should be used to ensure that political plans are consistent with scientific plans (Global Science)?

7. How can we better manage citizens' expectations so as to make them consistent with the potential of the biosphere?

8. Summarise the knowledge acquired in psychology by classifying them according to their degree of accuracy (e.g., sure, very likely, moderately likely, and unlikely) by harmonising them with the methodology of Global Science);

9. How can the forces of change be made aware that they must unite to better face modern challenges?

10. What are the cultural factors to be taken into consideration when managing international confederations of forces of change? Etc.

B. Communication

1. How should we communicate to influence the forces of the status quo to better influence their positions?

2. What types of communication to deploy for average citizens who are environmentally sensitive but vote for traditional politicians?

3. What communications should be used to recruit status quo forces?

4. How to make the forces of change aware that they have two and only two 'alternatives: Unite or die?'

5. How do we get the maximum number of citizen proposals to enrich the action plans for change?

6. How to avoid wasting citizens' time in brainstorming meetings?

7. How to conduct effective meetings? Etc.

C. Education Sciences

1. How can we create ethical consciousness in the new generations and life goals other than making money?

2. What tools can be used to retrain the present operational generations to join the projects of the forces of change?

3. Better adapt school and university curricula with respect to knowledge of how the biosphere's ecosystems function.

4. Understand better the responsibility of citizens' actions in the degradation processes of natural ecosystems. Etc.

D. Sociology

1. How to create elite pressure groups (without violence) that would influence the rest of the citizens to support change through their behaviour?
2. What strategies to adopt to influence opinion leaders to support the recovery plans of the pro-mutations community?
3. The process of recruiting and mobilising as many dedicated members as possible to the cause of radical and peaceful transformation;
4. How to gain the respect of members for the strict respect discipline and authority necessary to achieve the goals of the movement?
5. How to unite disparate and culturally diverse groups under the same banner and for the same cause?

E. Hard Sciences (physics, biology, etc.)

1. What are the priorities for funding research and development to optimise the use of resources and restore a maximum of environmental imbalances in a short period of time?
2. How to delay the reversibility of degradation processes in order to address them more effectively?
3. How to create environmental indicators (metrics) within the different ecosystems forming the biosphere?
4. What metrics should be included in the different action plans to correct sector imbalances?
5. What types of growth should be encouraged to restore imbalances more quickly?
6. What types of knowledge are we lacking to quickly restore imbalances in the biosphere?
7. What investments in research and development should be prioritised?
8. What actions can be taken quickly with the knowledge we have to reduce the consequences of global imbalances?

9. How can we better communicate the equations of the hard sciences with those of the human and social sciences in order to improve our simulations and our action plans? Etc.

F. Management

   1. How to better and more professionally manage non-profit institutions that have to deal with survival emergencies?
   2. What managerial leadership is appropriate for global confederations of change forces?
   3. What strategies, types of organisations, human resource management and control processes are best suited to local, regional, national and international institutions of the forces of change?
   4. What managerial principles are already available to enhance the institutions of the forces of change?
   5. What knowledge needs to be developed to enhance the performance of institutions that advocate for change?
   6. How can the performance of international non-profit projects be improved in the context of the current biosphere issues?
   7. How to align thousands of projects with the ethics and requirements of the change movement?
   8. How to manage the process of generating millions of ideas with a minimum of time and resources?
   9. What types of management training are best suited to the different jobs of permanent and volunteer staff in non-profit institutions?
   10. How to set goals for oneself and for others?
   11. How to measure one's own and group's performance and improve it? Etc.

G. Global Science

   1. How to design economic, political and social systems based on the ethics of Global Science: Peace, more social equality, respect for environmental norms and freedom?
   2. How to rapidly evolve our capacities to create social formations relevant to our human values?

3. How to make our knowledge in human and social sciences evolve rapidly in order to reduce the gap with the hard sciences and to allow us to control their consequences?

4. Develop metrics for difficult-to-measure humanities and social sciences parameters;

5. Create more sophisticated simulation systems where the humanities and social sciences can better communicate with hard sciences and make better predictions;

6. Design evolutionary plans: with knowledge already available, then revise programs as knowledge evolves;

7. Achieving simulations of society projects on the basis of new knowledge;

8. Show the most beneficial alternatives to citizens and politicians to improve their programs;

9. Simulate the political programs of the different parties and inform citizens of the results of simulations;

10. How to evaluate the impacts of an important decision on a vector of strategic variables of the nation or nation-world system? Etc.

The list of themes is presented for illustrative purposes only. It is neither exhaustive nor immutable, but it does include certain themes that deserve further study. Later on, necessity dictates that the designers of Global Science and the specialists of the different sciences or disciplines will appreciate the need to develop something else. Practice makes perfect. In facing the difficulties on the ground, we will be urgently called upon to use knowledge that the designers never imagined. The two activities complement each other. We will necessarily have to develop other themes and we will have to deal with other priorities to which Global Science should adapt.

Lessons from Experiences

Humanity has produced many experiments including those in the real world and through multiple scientific experiments. Vital lessons have remained unheard. One of the most likely reasons is that we do not codify these findings properly. We need a different methodological approach. The one proposed in the context of Global Science would be a huge step forward in leveraging these findings. It is not only about representing life lessons or scientific experiments but also about properly coding the context variables that are as important as the facts themselves. In fact, the interpretation of events results from the analytical goals that have been set. For the purposes of our problem, four particularly interesting experiments offer perspectives for the application of Global Science. We have many others. These experiments are not unanimous but have been the subject of much controversy. It is not possible to focus on the many details that are relevant to these developments but rather to take their conclusions with caution and discernment. We are not going to extrapolate the results to the extreme but rather to consider the turns that events can take with the quintessence of these experiences in mind. We will consider them in turn.

The first experiment that is revealed is the one known as 'Blue Eyes Brown Eyes' by Jane Elliott (6). Despite ethical and technical reservations about the conduct of the experiment, it is to be credited with allowing us to understand the mechanisms of racism and its ramifications. Not all the consequences of the experiment were drawn. The educator divided the class into two groups: blue eyes and brown eyes. She had the first group believe that those with blue eyes were inferior in most areas (intellectual, emotional) to the other group. She had planned different treatments for the two groups (the first group had to drink in paper glasses and so on). The second group became arrogant. They improved their work and their grades improved, while the first group became more and more discreet, less and less hardworking and their performance deteriorated. Later she did the opposite: the first group became more successful, more arrogant and started to gain the upper hand. Once again, the experiment was not carried out by professionals who would have taken many precautions, especially considering the age of the participants. But it was not carried out as it should have been in order to rigorously reconstitute the causes and the mechanisms to better understand the origin and the workings of racism. It is interesting to note that perception affects performance and sensitivity. Moreover, Global Science would have much to contribute to our understanding of a phenomenon that leads to dividing entire nations and ruining the chances of entire continents to come together because of racism.

The second lesson comes from an experiment described by Milgram (34). Just like the first experiment, it is presented as an indication and not as a definite fact. It concerns human behaviour when confronted with the distress of others. People are placed in the position of referees. They are called upon, each time an individual gives a false answer to a question put to them, to progressively increase the doses of electrocution intended for them. Fortunately, the individual is an actor and the doses are fictitious. But, many people continued to give doses that made the actor writhe in pain while the torturer thought he was actually hurting him. Some refused, but this was a smaller percentage than the people who acted like real torturers. This experiment, carried out by professionals, is more rigorous but can be improved. The main lesson that can be drawn from it with caution is that even the most evolved democracies function with citizens who are not very sensitive to the distress of others. This has made the task of dictators of all stripes much easier, but we continue to 'create' citizens with little concern for others. As long as it is not me! Seems to be the dominant saying in even the most democratic nations. This may explain our lack of sensitivity to the fate of future generations. A person we see writhing in pain leaves people unmoved, but what about an unknown person in a distant situation? We need to focus more on the humans we are if we are to make a difference in the future.

The third experiment is the one conducted by Kurt Lewing on the consumption of meat during the Second World War in the USA. The American consumer was reluctant to consume offal even though it had certain advantages. The idea was that offal would replace meat and that the US troops would be better supplied with proteins. Two types of methods will be tested. One would be that experts would provide information on how to best utilise the offal for consumption purposes. The second would be that a simple facilitator would organise debates for the generation of ideas and recommendations by citizens.

The second group had a much higher rate (almost twice) of behaviour change than the first one with the expert.

Type four experiences are related to the behaviour of actors in the real world, and we have accumulated an impressive volume of practice from them. History is full of events that could have better informed us about how we shaped ourselves and what kinds of social formations would be compatible with the kind of humans we modelled. In fact, we do not have a rigorous methodology for doing so. The one proposed by Global Science is only an attempt to channel and perfect our knowledge in this field. In reality, we hardly know anything about what contributes to a human being becoming a Nazi or a Mother Teresa. We need larger and more inclusive research teams than in the past to uncover the mechanisms that deeply govern our behaviour.

We have an extraordinarily rich pool of experimental practices that can already allow us to draw several valuable conclusions about the human condition. We know, for example, from life-size experiments that the uniqueness of decision-making power causes more harm than it provides privileges of better functioning. Socialist countries quickly realised that the fable of class consciousness would hardly be credible. A social formation with a single power can function well for a period of time, of an enlightened leader or of extremely favourable external conditions, but it cannot meet the test of longevity in which several leaders succeed one another. These are 'visible' episodes, very perceptible and even quantifiable with statistical improvements in terms of proxies (variables as close as possible to a quantitative estimate of a phenomenon, such as the managerial efficiency of a country's administration), but many vitally important episodes are passed over in silence by our 'social sciences,' or they have been given a derisory interest in relation to the potential contributions they conceal.

We can mention the case of the Russian, Vasili Arkhipov, who narrowly avoided a third nuclear world war through his cautious personality. During the Cuban Missile Crisis, his nuclear submarine was equipped with a nuclear torpedo and was cut off from all communication with Moscow. The situation of the submarine was catastrophic (temperature, ventilation etc.). The crew thought that the third world war had started. A trio of three decision-makers had to decide whether the submarine should go into action, especially since the US aircraft carrier Randolph was at a distance that could worry the submarine. Two of the decision-makers were in favour of a nuclear attack. But Vassili refused until communication with his country's authorities was restored. He had practically avoided a nuclear attack, which would have had disastrous consequences for the entire humanity. But, this incredibly rich human experience shows, beyond a reasonable doubt, that we are taking ill-considered, ill-judged, and ill-managed risks. Bombers fly over continents while carrying nuclear weapons with safety protocols disproportionate to the risks they pose to all humanity. The recent war between Ukraine and Russia puts humanity at risk of a nuclear blast today. Russian leaders say they are considering this alternative. Mankind is waiting with dread for the unfolding of a process that depends on a handful of men (sometimes only one) and that has devastating potential. The whole planet is trapped in extremely complex mechanisms linked to power games.

Few people know that a nuclear conflict was narrowly averted by a single man unknown to the general public: Vasili Arkhipov, a senior officer of the former USSR on board the B-59 submarine with a nuclear torpedo at the time when tensions were rising between his country and the United States during the Cuban Missile Crisis. Undermined by technical problems and unable to reach their country as they were targeted by US grenades to surface and get away, the officers believed they were the target of a war that had already started. To use the nuclear torpedo required a unanimous vote of three of the submarine's most senior officers. Two of them were in favour of launching a nuclear attack on the aircraft carrier USS Randolph, but only Vasili Arkhipov refused to use it as long as he did not receive official information about the beginning of the conflict. Thus, the future of mankind would have been played around the voice of a single man. Other incidents took place (with Boris Yeltsin, Jimmy Carter and others), fortunately without consequences for humanity. How long will we continue to hold our breath and pray that a serious incident does not occur to threaten life on Earth? This cause alone deserves a human mobilisation that transcends race, religion, gender and any other divisive tool.

The primary cause that follows these observations is the fact that the political function transcends the rest of the human activities. The rationale is that the democratic process enshrines the will and choices of the majority of citizens. It is assumed that the democratic process functions without friction, and therefore reflects the deep aspirations of people. But, we have seen that even in the most democratic nations the process has been emptied of its quintessence and remains only an opaque form of a hollowed-out process. We have seen that the democratic process has been subtly hijacked by narrow interests and that all that remains is a sketch of mechanisms that would reflect a confiscation of real power. This is when social formations are created where the political function transcends everything else. The activities of education, communication, science and law are de facto attached to it. When pressure groups gain possession of the executive and the legislative, they would pass any desired legislation and consequently neutralise the legal power. As for the scientific power, it would be the weak link of these unbridled social formations.

Our nations and international relations are much more shaped by political systems than by anything else. As for totalitarian nations or those with a sham democracy, the situation would be worse. The input of scientific power is limited, reduced and determined by the priorities of the political system. The current situation of social sciences is proof of this, with contradictory patterns between different nations. The volume and destinations of research and development are done to the detriment of more efficient, more fairer social formations, and more in harmony with the way the biosphere functions and the respect of global balances of the different ecosystems. The supremacy of the political function over scientific activity always leads to a democratic confiscation and to national and international institutions functioning according to narrow interests. It is no accident that we are too far from a reasonably acceptable approach that would guarantee a minimum of results and allow the continuity of life on Earth. Our institutions are designed to operate in a distinctly sub-optimal mode in terms of ethical, social justice and ecosystem preservation deliverables. The worm is in the fruit.

We need to consecrate the pre-eminence of several functions that would result in neutralising the harmful mechanisms of the political system. We should consider Global Science as a filter for social formations. It is by mobilising the bulk of acquired knowledge, by harmonising it, by mobilising the vast majority of the human brainpower and by directing the research and development of hard and soft sciences towards useful alternatives that we will have a chance of getting out of the collateral damages that we have committed. Then we will have a different understanding of the human experiences we already have at hand. We will have better microscope lenses to interpret these actions. For example, consider the first 'brown eyes and blue eyes' experiment. It has been commented that by claiming the superiority of one group over the other, the children believed in this fable (reinforced by discriminatory practices) and contributed by their actions to reinforce this line of thought. It is normal to be interested in these practices in order to reveal the mechanisms that contribute to the emergence and entrenchment of racist thinking. However, far less research has been done on the consequences of the performance of both groups. When one group is given more value and respect than the other, its intellectual performance improves and the other group's performance deteriorates. Consequently, the disadvantaged groups lose confidence in themselves and the prophecy becomes self-fulfilling. Exploring this possibility should have given us a better understanding of the relationship between the stigmatised groups of individuals and the impacts on their performance. It would then have better helped to correctly evaluate the relationship between racist practices and the performance of stigmatised people. This would have had a much more comprehensible impact on those groups that would have been discriminated against because of their performance. However, it is never too late to do the right thing.

Experiments could then be carried out on different socio-professional categories to evaluate and better quantify the relationship between discrimination and real performance. We would then have improved the performance of the most disadvantaged groups for the good of the entire population. For the experiment of electric discharges, we can affirm beyond a reasonable doubt that we cannot build types of social formations more ethical, fairer, and more respectful of the ecosystems with the types of citizens we are contributing to create. Psychology, education sciences and a variety of disciplines would be questioned by the conclusion, and most importantly to answer the following question: What do we need to do differently to make ourselves intrinsically responsible for the future social formations we want to build?

The second lesson from Kurt Lewing's experience is that mobilising citizen intelligence is not contradictory to expert assessments. The two reinforce each other and contribute to producing better deliverables. But, there must be ample room for citizen participation in the debates and the decision processes. Vasili's decision calls out to us for two complementary dimensions: first, what in his personal experience contributed to shaping his personality and psyche (he was exposed to intense radiation during his life) and second, the insufficiency of precautions that would have led to a lethal risk for all humankind.

Most of the experiments remain insufficiently interpreted and their findings are clearly not disseminated across the soft sciences to allow for their transformation into social and environmental policies. We have accepted to live with a too big gap between the performances of social and human sciences and those of hard sciences. We can only end up in a situation where the latter's put us in too risky positions. The fusion of the atom, nanotechnologies, robotics, and poorly analysed human intelligence is sliding the human species towards a multitude of uncontrolled risks. The transcendence of the political function over the rest of social and human activities is especially opposed responsible. The latter would be too intuitive, too subjective, endowed with few rigorous methods that it could be too permissive with the type of events that are looming on the horizon. So, we cannot allow ourselves the luxury of not transforming the experiences into useful but partial principles of Global Science.

For example, if we simulate the methodological tables of Global Science we could come up with beneficial principles for understanding and action on many levels. As for the first experiment, one of the useful principles would be: 'If a society can afford to stigmatise (on the bases of race, gender, religion, etc.) citizens, they will increasingly see their actions and performance conform to the predictions of the racists.' Moreover, a second principle drawn from the second experiment would be: 'The socio-educational and other systems of modern nations contribute to the formation of citizens who are not generally very sensitive to the harm done to others, as long as they are able to exonerate themselves from the intention of personally doing harm.' This would be insufficient to build ethical, fairer, more responsible and more respectful types of nations for the fragile ecosystems we have. For the third experiment, we can reasonably conclude that: 'collective participatory empowerment (in addition to expert facilitators) would better mobilise the intelligence of all and contribute to a better awareness and particularly achieve better results in terms of behavioural changes.' Above all, we may find that for most experiences related to treating humans: 'the values of participation, accountability (goals), group work and efficient leadership are valuable assets to mobilise human intelligence and move together with goals and ethics to achieve.'

Of course, this would depend mainly on situational and contextual variables. When we learn to manipulate these parameters we can better elucidate and benefit from the different human experiences. But for the moment only a few very general principles are being rigorously applied in companies and non-profit institutions. With Global Science, we will capture a maximum of principles from our rich human experiences. We have materials and principles hidden within our rich history by a glaring methodological inadequacy and often buried by a misunderstanding of their values. There is no room for procrastination. We need to recover our historical heritage and interpret it better with more elaborate methodologies. We can then better model human behaviour. We will assign probabilities to each case with its parameters of situations and context. This will allow us to make great strides in terms of modelling.

Simulations and Trends

We already have a long history with simulations whose processes can serve as a basis for designing better economic, social and environmental policies. However, substantial improvements in these modelling processes are needed. But let us first appreciate what already exists and then consider introducing useful and beneficial advances. Econometric simulators have experienced a galloping inflation without substantially improving our forecasting capabilities. They have been criticised, and rightly so, for not having been able to warn us about the 1987 crisis and especially the subprime crisis (2007-2008). Even the largest simulators with hundreds of equations had made mistakes in prediction, especially when they were most needed. Simulations of climate phenomena are often more accurate. This is because they contain mostly quantifiable variables. The confidence of investors and buyers is difficult to identify in economic estimation work, but the average temperature of a given geographical area is more easily estimated.

However, apart from econometric simulators, which have their own concerns, the most sophisticated models at the moment do not correctly interconnect the hard sciences with the humanities and social sciences. This is why they produce scenarios that are hardly credible, considering the way current social formations operate. Thus, the model that has been much talked about is the one proposed by the Club of Rome (8). It is true that it has made gigantic leaps forward for humanity. It highlighted the problems that our world would face in terms of access to non-renewable resources if we continued on the path of the sixties in terms of growth of the world population and economic activity. The broad categories of parameters reflect five main areas of focus:

- Population;
- Agricultural production;

- The status of non-renewable resources;
- Industrial production; and
- The pollution generated.

The Club of Rome had the merit of drawing attention to the problems of the environment and access to non-renewable resources when they were marginal intuitions at the time. The average citizen who heard about it cheered and then went on to his usual business of accumulating more resources. Professionals admired it but are much more fascinated by the scenario of ever more sustained growth, even if they do not fail to make a furtive reference to the problems of stress on resources. If the initiative was about improving our ability to model our problems, to sound the alarm and to highlight the critical issues facing humanity, the mission would have been greatly accomplished. But if the objective was to shift economic policies in such a way as to have a significant impact on the trajectories of the major parameters of humanity -growth, pollution, population-then it could be said to have been very limited in scope. The same is true for the IPCC's work. If the objective was to draw conclusions on the evolution of the biosphere and ecosystems, we could be satisfied. It has also awakened the sleeping consciousness of many citizens. There is also an increase in the power of ecological movements, but if we were to evaluate the impact on economic, social and environmental policies, there are reasons to be disappointed.

We continue to consider small commitments and almost always too late whereas ecosystems do not accept mini solutions. However, one could retort that the responsibility of models is to explain and to foresee and in this sense they have done their duty. Keynes managed to get the political class to test and then enshrine the budgetary and monetary policies he had advocated, but this was because he presented solutions that were pleasant to implement and at the same time could contribute to the re-election of politicians in power ('Political and economic cycles'). Many candidates for political office could manipulate macroeconomic policies to get re-elected (inflating spending in the run-up to elections). But forecasting models had bad news for politicians. De-growth cannot be achieved without political risks. Besides, they do not know how to manage it. Only Karl Marx was able to raise a whole historical movement with his science. He had a multidisciplinary perspective. Everything is interwoven in his work: history, economics, sociology, psychology, etc. The only thing missing from his work was the knowledge of modern management. Otherwise he would have known that a communist party with extraordinary power over the army and the whole society could only use its power to structure the whole society according to its interests: to last in power and to direct more resources to itself and its supporters. Class consciousness never played a role. And this is known through modern social and human sciences. For a class consciousness to take root, to last and to become the cultural basis of a social formation it should be precisely structured. And the uniqueness of political power is and will never be a solution. Global Science cannot commit such a crime.

Modern simulations have allowed humanity to make gigantic progress, but we will never stop improving them. The destiny of humans is to innovate and constantly innovate. It is the heavy toll of contemporary Sisyphus to carry this overwhelming but sometimes beneficial burden. We need to diagnose these simulators in depth to allow them to positively influence economic and social policies. The theories of human and social sciences, from the classics to the most modern, are not sufficiently harmonised, integrated or very operational. They all have their parts of truth, but none of them can alone complete the incomplete picture of the schemes we should use. Yet economics, which sits atop the social sciences and humanities, claims to fill in the rest of our ignorance. Modern simulations would benefit from being improved in several directions, namely:

1. A regulatory entity;
2. Citizen anticipations;
3. A political market;
4. Greater multidisciplinary paradigms;
5. A reference scheme inspired by a global equilibrium rather than a simple Walras equilibrium; and
6. Logic of allocation of resources to R&D.

The different models can be simulated from the changes in some selected variables. For example, from the number of tons of CO_2 emitted, we will have different average temperatures with appropriate delays. In this sense, they can support certain trajectories of changes in economic, social and environmental policies but not others. But for the most part, these public decisions are made exogenous. We do not know why or how the regulators choose one decision over another. This is partly due to our ignorance of the mechanisms underlying these choices. Only partly! But as soon as we become more ambitious in terms of scientific knowledge and simulation potential, we will gain a lot by making the regulation process as endogenous as possible.

We already know enough to integrate it into the model in a more appropriate way. We also measure the efforts that need to be made to better understand its operating mechanisms. We will then have better impacts on the decision-making process. Global Science will help us to better understand the fog that surrounds policy choices, and we will better influence public decisions. Of course, we have some clues, some intuitions and even some very serious hypotheses about the mechanisms of public decisions. However, it would be beneficial to make their principles, elements that are part of the nomenclature of cases specific to our methodology. We would then be able to better influence political decisions. We would then avoid the present situation of understanding what we should do instead of what we are doing and not being able to change much. We would be one step ahead of the roots of the problems. We will see more in-depth the deep nature of the mechanisms that can prevent us from being inert when facing fatal dangers. We will at least be able to know under which conditions we could be able to rise to the level of the national and planetary challenges that risk annihilating us. Or would we be condemned by our own traps, by the structuring of the social formations that we ourselves have created? At least we will know a little more about our fate.

So now we must understand that we do not have sufficient tools to act. We lack the knowledge and most of all the institutional structures to claim to have a greater influence on public decisions. We have the impression that we will always continue to do very little too late until the fateful dates when the costs will be out of our reach. Certainly, we are at the threshold of understanding the phenomena. We know that we must reduce pollution, be more egalitarian, better protect the various ecosystems, better control population growth and perhaps stop growth while encouraging the channelling of resources to sectors that restore the biosphere's mode of functioning, etc. However, the choices of regulators can be treated as working hypotheses. One only has to figure out the decision and simulate it. But it would be better to make regulation endogenous so as to force researchers to better understand it and to enrich the theories that support it in order to eventually better guide the recommendations that are mainly aimed at operational actions. What actions should be prioritised for normal citizens, committed NGOs, researchers, etc.? This has become a nagging question.

The expectations of citizens are also a fundamental issue that should be given top priority. It is through the manipulation of this variable that some political groups manage to control the system and avoid large-scale actions. Citizens, conditioned since birth by the attitude of 'more and more' and by the confusion between happiness and the amount of resources at their disposal, view with suspicion anything that might hinder their march towards greater material prosperity. Political parties that promise to satisfy their demands for more and more material possessions take precedence over everything else. Most citizens have a heart for the environment and a hand to vote for its enemies. Parties and NGOs that advocate either de-growth or moderation in citizens' behaviours start with a big disadvantage. Economic agents shaped by family, school and the whole of their life environment are programmed to exchange their work or ideas for a material remuneration that would allow them to consume more and more. And there is no limit to their demands. They will hardly make any effort to consume products that degrade the ecosystems less. At the moment, experts in these social formations do not know how to completely deprogram these behaviours. We need to better understand how these expectations are formed, how they take root, and how they impact human behaviour and its political, economic, and social consequences.

Internalising a political market is the best way to get to the heart of the decision-making process. Of course, behavioural variables are more complicated to quantify. The work becomes more complicated, sometimes gigantic, but the output would really be of greater value. We would necessarily come back to the need to invest more time and resources in what we lack in human and social sciences. Global Science would be necessary to make our different knowledge coherent. It may be that it would sometimes be recommended to decrease economic activity. Firstly, we do not know how to manage this process. Secondly, just as we can slow down, freeze or reduce undesirable activities (polluting sectors), we would benefit from boosting the repairing activities of ecosystems. Overall, it is not easy to quantify the impacts on global growth. Only a methodical simulation could tell us the extent of the phenomenon. Moreover, it is often advocated to abandon the capitalist system and not only to reform it. And here we do not know how to create other systems in the absence of Global Science.

Marx had sold us the idea that socialism and its ultimate phase communism were not only better than capitalism but that it were an inevitable outcome of history. They would be independent of human consciousness. Their occurrence could be slowed down but nothing and no one could deprive humanity of their emergence. These results were largely extrapolated from historical materialism, a scheme that served as the basis for analysing the evolution of economic and social formations. We explained which environmental mutations had rendered the mechanisms and projections of historical materialism obsolete. It was impossible for humanity to conceive another system other than a hybrid one. China has almost retained the political process as a derivative of the socialist experiment while proceeding to greatly liberalise (market economy). But the result is that China is with 29% of greenhouse gas emissions remains the largest polluter on the planet, followed by the USA (19%) in 2020.

The fact is that we do not know how to create new economic and social formations. Certainly, they cannot be compared to technological products (vehicles, aeroplanes, etc.) where computer-aided design (CAD) greatly facilitates the work of engineers. The design of new social, political and economic forms is highly complex. We are just beginning to glimpse the principles, mechanisms and primary methods of designing new economic and social forms. By comparison, we are not even at the same stage of aircraft design as when the Wright brothers created their first prototype aeroplane. This will be the ultimate goal of Global Science. But for the moment those who advocate changing the economic and social system may underestimate the task. It is simply colossal. We do not even know where to start. With the current methods or their derivatives, we are condemned to trial and error and to mainly use intuition, since we are venturing into unknown territory. For this reason, the internalisation of a political market within a large contemporary model will allow us to make enormous progresses.

The political market is a central part of the movement of socio-economic evolutions. Making it more endogenous will allow for serious leaps forward; first, in terms of a better understanding and second, in terms of a better contribution to addressing the challenges of contemporary nations. International relations will then be an integral part of these models. The interrelations between nations contribute to improving or degrading the world system. However, future models will be extraordinarily accurate because they will take into account a large number of endogenous variables, better integrated multidisciplinary models with more precision in the quantification of proxies. Nevertheless, simple models can coexist with large complex ones. One could therefore examine one part of reality and link it to others for a better understanding. Just as in economics, we would distinguish between microeconomic, sector analysis, macroeconomic and international analyses, the same configurations would be found in simulation and in Global Science. However, the models should be better guided with a more balanced philosophy. Semantic logic has as much room as mathematical input.

The decision-making processes at the research and development level should also be subject to a measure of internalisation within the central global models. They should fit the global recovery paths chosen. Science is not neutral. It is oriented by political (even dictatorships have small political markets), economic and social markets. The structuring of nations and their interrelationships steers science towards destructive or beneficial processes. It so happens that we earthlings have chosen above all to favour the development of goods and services that destroy ecosystems, potentially annihilating ourselves, while directing a minimum of resources towards beneficial market and non-market goods. The mechanisms of mobilisation and choice of destinations for research and development resources must be better explained and revealed. If we advocate more ethical and egalitarian nations, it is mainly through these means (R&D) that we could bring about substantial improvements.

To change a nation or the world would be to change the nature of its research and development. We can ask ourselves what human logic has prevailed during the structuring of nation and nation-world systems to come to a situation where we are developing supersonic missiles while the biosphere and ecosystems are facing deadly challenges. Just as making political markets endogenous will require more efforts and investigations on the part of model designers to better explain the mechanisms of choice in order to act effectively. The interaction of political markets and research and development management is obvious but would be better highlighted by more investigations. A nation is above all the fruit of its research and development and its future is shaped by it. The world as we know it will therefore be the scaffolding of our R&D choices. We cannot continue to finance indefinitely the armament, fossil energies and polluting products and services and pretend to restore the major balances of ecosystems. Most of the degradation mechanisms are not even understood, and if they were, we rarely have sufficiently controlled processes to remedy them.

The future models, simple or complex, will be derived from a particular philosophy. They will be more multidisciplinary, more methodologically rigorous and reflect the Global Science decision-making system. Researchers will integrate their science and citizen's intelligence every time they can. They will do so, but only after exhausting the rich potential for inputs from the grassroots. The first key factor of success would be to mobilise the collective intelligence, first, and then operate a better synthesis by our best scientists. Today's world is shaped by politicians. It is time to recreate it through the collective intelligence of our citizens and our scientific elites. This would be the goal of Global Science.

Finally, we will raise a last point without exhausting the theme of models of the future and simulations of the upcoming. We cannot fail to emphasise the role of their basic philosophy. From now on, we will think, in the central context of the methodology, in terms of global equilibrium and not of any partial or general equilibrium. The partial equilibrium brought to its peak by Alfred Marshal had inspired whole generations of economists wishing to deal with specific markets of goods or services. Walras's general equilibrium, more sophisticated but less operational, had amazed by its mathematical rigour and the splendour of the work had aroused the admiration of a large proportion of economists. Some principles could be drawn from it (general equilibrium automatically implied the Pareto optimum, if N-1 markets are in equilibrium the ninth market is automatically in equilibrium). But consciously or unconsciously, the neoclassical theory was underpinned by the abstract idea that the more markets were liberated, the closer we would get to this general equilibrium. Keynesian theory considered that this equilibrium could be sub-optimal and that one of the most important markets, that of employment, could experience long-term imbalances. But eventually, from the 1980s onwards, the neoclassical school dominated the economic campuses, especially after the fall of the Berlin Wall. So we only had this general equilibrium microscope to analyse economic issues. It simply became a must for markets. But for Global Science we could not accept the domination of a single discipline over the dynamics of economic and social formations.

For precision and repetition, global equilibrium is a stable relationship between two levels: the first is related to human expectations. These should be compatible with the current productive potential. The output would be sufficient to meet human needs and reach a high level of satisfaction. The second level concerns the potential of the biosphere. Renewable resources would be sufficient to achieve this production, which would satisfy human expectations and allow the renewal of natural resources (without pollution or alteration of available ecosystems). We can act on the expectations (by human actions), on the volume of the output (by scientific innovations) and on the renewal potential of the resources (also by scientific processes). The general equilibrium is what most inspires simulation models nowadays. We work very little or even very rarely with very large interactions between social and human sciences and hard sciences. However, it is by digging deeper, by perfecting this kind of work that we may one day see high-level simulators. We aspire to a greater multidisciplinary scheme that would free us from the yoke of one or two disciplines that monopolise simulators. And it is only at this cost that we will improve our understanding of the phenomena that surround us and that we will be able to act better on them. We will then get out of the unconvincing slogans of 'destroying capitalism,' creating a new world or any other cry of human distress.

Yes, we need to get out of the types of social formation that have inflicted on us challenges of atrocious ferocity. But, in order to replace them with what? Especially, since humanity has just come out of a most awful communist experience. We do not know how to manage expectations neither a long decline nor even less large-scale economic and social transformations such as changing a whole system. The task seems simple only to those who do not deepen their experience and knowledge of the dynamics of civilisations. The difficulty also comes from the fact that we need to revolutionise our economic, social and political modes of operations in order to achieve more social and political justice and at the same time repair the severely damaged ecosystems. We need to manage, among other things:

1. A global societal engineering of a complexity never contemplated before;
2. Specify the envisaged societal ethics;
3. Organise mass communications (mobilise all the citizen's intelligence);
4. Create multidisciplinary scientific teams;
5. Specify the target scheme towards which we are heading;
6. Carry out a decrease in certain sectors and growth in others;
7. Determine the level of inequality tolerated;
8. Qualify the human resources to operate these tasks and change their behaviours;

9. Decide on the speed and types of coherence in the sector reforms to be carried out;
10. Make controls and corrections to improve the different programs;
11. Decide to undertake major overhauls when the situation deteriorates severely; and
12. Set up the necessary incentive systems to accomplish these transformations; Etc.

Unless reforms are carried out through a lot of trials and errors like those of the communist parties in the twentieth century, you will be led to meticulously plan this global engineering which comparatively will make the creation of a prototype of a new rocket a child's play. Most of us would agree that we are obliged or even forced by the many contemporary challenges to create new social formations, but we should seriously prepare to do so instead of launching slogans. What if by changing social formations we would do worse than the communist movements?

Certainly, we have to take this risk because the existing systems can only lead to the destruction of everything we hold dear. Whoever hopes for minor changes and major results will go from disappointment to disappointment. Moreover, the longer we wait, the bigger the bill we will have to pay. We need to mobilise all our scientific knowledge, all our resources, all our collective intelligence and all our means, organise them, channel them and optimise them with the help of scientific methodologies structured by our best experts and scholars. This is a colossal task and up to now we mainly entrusted to our political parties. We ask them to lift mountains, but they will avoid conceding that they have been given an impossible mission. They are only prepared to talk about the difficulty of the mission but conclude that they will succeed. Today, the average citizen demands more and more purchasing power, confuses happiness with material resources and hopes that the political class, because it is elected, will be able to carry out these tasks while repairing the damages caused to the biosphere and the ecosystems.

Interconnection between the hard sciences and the humanities and social sciences would be mainly through the management of expectations. An average citizen, living in a liberal country, makes the assumption that the democratic system would function according to the ethics, the priorities and the needs of the vast majority of the population. Indeed, this is what would happen if we did not live in systems of confiscated democracies. We have managed to structure nations and the planet according to the needs of a minority. This is achieved through the management of expectations. So, we should internalise this black box that controls everything else and which the most complicated models most often treat as an exogenous variable.

Cycles of Civilizations

There are countless studies on the cycles of civilisations and the causes and mechanisms of the foundations and collapses of the great powers that had spread throughout the world. The complexity of issues related to this theme requires numerous investigations as the degree of difficulty to grasp is very high. We need to better synthesise the different contributions and make them explicit according to a rigorous methodology, of which the one proposed by Global Science is only the beginning of improving investigation tools. Ibn Khaldun, Rand and Cohen, Tainter, Luke Kamp and Toynbee were among the pioneers, to name but a few, who had to innovate to describe phenomena of legendary complexities. Their contributions have been invaluable to us and each one has contributed to clarifying this complex picture. However, no theory in this complex phenomenology can claim to apprehend all the interacting variables and patterns.

Major Theories

Many courageous pioneer works have been undertaken by many world-class researchers. It would be impossible to cite even most of them. We only touch on the themes close to our preoccupations. According to Oswald Spengler (27) civilisations would go through the stages of birth (genesis), growth, maturity and decline. Of course, the length of these phases may differ, but the chronology would be the same. The work was the subject of much controversy but was widely commented on and sometimes acclaimed.

David Rand and Jonathan Cohen consider the rationality or irrationality of the decision-making process as a starting point. There would be two main categories. The first would be spontaneous but not very flexible. It would be close to the intuitive type that we discussed. The second would be close to the analytical mode, more flexible, more methodical and more rigorous. It is the first one that would explain the absence of a vigorous response to the problems of the moment. We have not been able to raise ourselves with an adequate decision-making mode to a level where we can successfully face contemporary challenges. The cost of not adapting is high. As the problems become more complex, we are sliding more and more towards an intuitive mode. The world's leading economic power, the USA, withdrew from the Paris COP 21 without measuring the potential consequences of this option (Joe Biden had reinstated the country to the group).

Tainter (48) goes further. He qualifies human decisions as containing more irrationalities than the other way around. He considers that technological innovation has a declining return on investment and therefore it could not by itself solve contemporary problems.

Arnold Toynbee (3), author of a colossal work (12 volumes), has made considerable progress in the field of historical studies of civilisations. He ends up himself partially rather opposed to the historical determinism of Oswald by proposing stages that certain civilisations would follow. They would be: genesis, growth, beginning of imbalances and universal situation followed by disintegration. According to him, 'Civilisations die by suicide and not by murder' as internal factors are dominant compared to external causes.

The author Jared Diamond tried to support his observations with real-life examples, including the remote corners of the United States and different places in the world that have suffered or are in the process of falling victim to the beginning of the collapse process. This allowed him to identify the most important factors responsible for the chaos of certain nations, namely:

1. Irrational exploitation of the biosphere's resources by using more than their regeneration.
2. Climate change.
3. Hostile neighbour.
4. Degradation of commercial activities with the rest of the world.
5. Refusal to change: Keeping the old paradigm while a new one is needed to claim to rectify the mistakes of the past. This will be accompanied by policies of small steps (doing little and too late) when only huge changes can save us.

We can learn a lot from this colossal work. No single work can claim to clarify the collapse process alone. However, the work allows us to focus on the essential even if it underestimates other deeper factors such as the formation of expectations as a decisive factor in this decision-making process. It also has the merit of being able to explain largely the situation of the current world where we have inflicted on ourselves challenges of a potentially fatal collapse.

The most incriminating factors in most studies are:

-   Natural disasters (pandemics, drought, global warming, famines, floods, earthquakes, volcanoes etc.);
-   Environmental degradation: deforestation, inappropriate farming
-   Excessive use of resources;
-   Population: excessive increase (Malthus) or low reproduction;
-   immigration;
-   Wars and invasions;
-   Internal violence;
-   Too much internal inequality;

- Loss of social cohesion;
- Drastic drop in economic activities (reduction of trade, excessive taxation);
- Political decision-making process is too intuitive;
- Weak process of adaptation to new challenges: the unwillingness of the elites to change the governance paradigm; and
- Sometimes even luck would play a role.

All these factors would be interrelated with mechanisms so delicate that even specialists in complex systems have difficulty interpreting them. The different theories do not do justice to all cases but to only a few specific situations. Many civilisations do not collapse and even become a second or third category of power (contemporary history of Great Britain). Some nations will only dilute into other more powerful or weaker ones. The concept of collapse only really applies to the future potential of modern nations.

There would be two questions that interest us in this context:

1. What can we learn from these multitudes of investigations to act on contemporary challenges more effectively?
2. What do we need to do differently to get out of the deadlock and the self-inflicted challenges?

It should be specified that the concept of collapse is relative to a given historical period. Karl Marx's historical materialism does not account for the collapse of civilisations. The modes of production described by Marx are long periods, sometimes several thousand years, within which civilisations die, are dispersed into others or reintegrate into social formations that are insignificant for world history. Karl Marx's aim was to understand longer phases and to give a better account of human history. He was especially interested in how each mode of production evolved into another. For example, for capitalism he sought to grasp its essence, the foundations and the quintessence of capitalism and the mechanisms of its evolution and its transition to the socialist mode of production with the help of the reproduction schemes. A mode of production includes dominant civilisations, nations of medium influence considering the historical contexts of the moment and countries or entities of low scale and sometimes chaotic.

There is, however, a major difference between the historical context of present situations and the history of the collapse of civilisations. The latter are generally conquered by others, destroyed, or spread among smaller nations. When we speak of collapse nowadays, we are talking about a progressive mass extinction, about the survival of humanity and the risks that we are running for the ecosystems and for all forms of life. The risk is multiplied. Before that, civilisation collapse benefits some nations and others will have a chance to recover. These were not definitive experiences, but ours is likely to be. Humanity is unlikely to recover from a nuclear winter or from an 8 to 10-degree average temperature rise. There would be factors at play in both situations to varying degrees. In our opinion, however, the two parameters that would stand out as major causes would be:

1. The refusal of the elites to change their mode of governance;
2. The decision-making process that is increasingly becoming intuitive in relation to the threats facing citizens.

The governing elites do not abdicate actions or openly decide not to act. They may even claim to be staunch defenders of the environment. They even ally themselves with pro-environment politicians. But, their results and actions show that they do too little and too late. The political class is tied up, hands and feet, by interest groups that are too powerful for them. They act mainly through the management of citizens' expectations. Of course, the financing of political campaigns makes their task easier, but they would not have been able to greatly influence the political market if citizens did not adhere to the 'Always More' doctrine. Citizens love the environment but vote against it. There would be a great responsibility of the environmental movements themselves. They are the very architects of their defeats. Their strategies, their structures and the rest of their mode of governance could not allow them to weigh heavily in the balance. Some of them will even adopt strategies of violence for the greater good of the interests of the status quo.

The Red Brigades could not avoid the defeat of a certain concept of Marxism in Italy. Those in favour of continuity are already talking about 'ecological terrorism.' Violence breeds hatred and marginalisation. The forces of the status quo would like ecologists or just the defenders of future generations and of the continuity of life on earth to resort to these procedures. It will make their job easier. Huge resources will be wasted by a society that will inevitably mourn for lives and resources wasted. The objective of politicians would be to restore peace instead of making complex and useful decisions instead of correcting the biosphere damages. Then, violence will accelerate the divisions within the forces of change. Fractures between different factions will be exacerbated. They will be further fractured. Then we will have the real ecologists who have understood the manoeuvre will have as a slogan 'union or death.' The divisions will multiply the strategies of different groups. Very few would focus on the number one key success factor in the fight against the status quo: citizen expectations. While they are at the heart of the problem, those who think right receive marginal attention. Violence will permanently widen the gap between the vast majority of citizens and the forces of change. They will then vote more in favour of the right-wing and further prevent change from taking place. The 'revolution can wait.' There is a mortal danger to the proponents of rigorous economic and social policy transformations: more splintering of the change movements and rejection by citizens. The cause for which one has sacrificed oneself is ultimately destroyed. The goal of beneficial changes will be secondary to the citizens and the governments rather than a pacification of the situation. We will waste much more time in bringing political and social peace than in fighting the real perils that threaten everyone. But, the rebellion will have a good conscience. It is confident in the rightness of its cause, but fighting for a noble alternative does not guarantee the success of the mission. Modern conflicts are managed by appropriate communications, strategies and operational actions. The shift to violent action is the most destructive strategy for a change movement. There are many historical examples that prove this.

A second factor blocking change is the adoption of an intuitive mode of governance by the highest authorities. Intuitive reasoning leads immediately to the easy way out, to giving priority to one's own interests beyond what is reasonable, to giving priority to the short term and to questioning with disconcerting ease what science has or is proving every day. Researchers have established that entire civilisations have withered away because of governing elites who have practised intuitive governance instead of more efficient practices. Entire nations are caught in vicious circles of underdevelopment because of intuitive governance methods that condemn entire countries to misery and the ravages of social and international injustice.

The problem of contemporary challenges is global. It can only be understood in its entirety. It would be astonishing if a group of nations with different interests could adopt strategies to fight against the global scourges that weigh on humanity. They will cooperate but not beyond a certain threshold. But, time is the most implacable enemy of procrastination. Every day that passes will leave a mark and a more dangerous world. We can learn from civilisations that have procrastinated too much only to realise later that the price is x times higher than in the lull. There can only be hope in the forces of change. But, with the right strategy and the right management style! If they cannot unite themselves around a common program of struggle to change citizens' expectations, they will find it even more difficult to unite politicians with divergent interests. The mere fact of uniting would give the citizens extraordinary motivations to follow them, to support them, and ultimately to resort to acts consistent with a beginning of recovery. The probability of radical change is high with unity but nil with violence.

The intuitive mode of governance has spread through the most subtle communication to citizens who seek solutions to complex problems without restricting their unaccountable actions. Right-wing governments are being elected everywhere in the belief that the solution will be easy. If violence takes root among the followers of revolutions then this will benefit the hidden blocking forces. There will be a total reshaping of the political landscape in many democratic countries and a deepening of tyranny in non-democratic nations. International collaboration will be strengthened but at the expense of a real willingness to change. Thus the supporters of violence will realise that they have triggered mechanisms that work against their own causes and will irreversibly derail their own hopes. They would have forgotten that the force of ideas is more powerful than any other force and that when citizens embrace the options of progress the locks of procrastination can only be broken.

The Economics of Global Science

Most sciences should make themselves fit into Global Science by developing themes and methods for this purpose. Economics should play a prominent role by creating a specific branch dedicated to this purpose. Preliminary work has already been done to that end (see Lamiri, op cited). But most remain to be spelt out. We just had a drop in the desert. A gigantic task remains to be undertaken. This theoretical conceptualisation will have tremendous consequences on fiscal, monetary, international trade investment, consumption and other economic topics. And we need to adapt what we already know to make them fit within the methodology and the practice of Global Science. It would be the case for fiscal policies that might know re-engineering processes never done before. Monetary policies will undergo similar revolutions. It needs to review its optimum monetary rule and will develop money laser practices to channel more resources to useful sectors that will re-establish environmental equilibrium. Consumption and investment policies will have the heavy burden of dealing with the management of expectations. We are just on the eve of undertaking such a modernisation of our knowledge and practices. Compared to the automobile industry we are just at the Ford Model T prototype compared to the products of a thousand years from now (if we are still here). The situation requires us to foster new themes and ask new research questions such as:

1. How can biosphere protection metrics be better integrated into project assessments?
2. What steps should be taken to place the safeguarding of the biosphere before profits?
3. How can market mechanisms be reconciled with the continuity of life on Earth?
4. Innovate in order to complete the carbon tax and pollution rights schemes to constitute a real sub-discipline of environmental economics.

5. What are the new conceptualisations to be introduced in order to participate in the 'Multidisciplinary' required by Global Science (see A Beginning of Answer A. Lamiri: *The Economics of the Future*)?
6. How to better integrate environmental concerns into the teaching of economics?
7. How monetary and fiscal policies can facilitate the fight against modern threats?
8. Renew the theories of trade in a context of uncertainty about the future of nations.
9. What economies of scale can be derived from a global confederation of economic policies?
10. Costs and benefits of pooling resources on a global scale to face modern challenges, etc.

We have just a sample of themes to develop. We can only measure the immensity of the tasks that await us. But we understand we are just beginning to appreciate the costs and benefits of such an approach.

The 'Unite or Die Principle': A Choice Between a Galactic Civilisation or Annihilation

We have already insisted on the historical need to unite the forces of change. This is the only way they can accomplish their historical mission. Remaining divided would be the equivalent of committing suicide. Yet this is what is happening under our eyes. The situation is complicated by the multiplicity of countries that cooperate too little to overcome such immense threats our world is facing. We have three alternatives we can contemplate:

The first and ideal one is to transform our world into a federation of democratic and decentralised states. The management of the lethal risks would be in the hands of the federal state. But this option would be made impossible by the present politicians unless the forces of change conquer most of the countries that count. This ideal situation is a nice dream that unfortunately would not be realised under the present circumstances. This would facilitate our world to reach the status of a galactic civilisation by focusing on what matters: science, global equilibrium, more equality, environmental questions and peace. But most politicians who do not think they have a future in that configuration will invent thousands of false excuses to reject this opportunity. And they will win at the end. They prefer to die with a slight hope of being elected than to survive within a hopeful world with little perspective for them.

The second would be more efficiently cooperating blocs. Nowadays we have competing blocs who do not collaborate sufficiently to overcome the recently created perils. The strategies on which they are built do not sufficiently accommodate the degree of teamwork required to disable de modern hazards. For this to happen the different blocs should reconsider their strategies to focus more on the world perils and less on creating more prosperity for the member countries. One must say they can do both. It is a question of extent. They need

246

to act rapidly on common projects, on channelling more resources to salutary aims and on prioritising their action. But they are geared rather to compete for more material goods than cooperate to save the world and themselves. Here also the forces of change cannot watch and hope for a miracle. They need to count only on themselves. Their unity can make a difference, but they are far behind in achieving it.

The third option is the traditional business as usual. Nowadays everyone knows that it is futile to hope something useful would come out of it. It has been sufficiently developed in this book that we understand by now that this alternative would make the perils more certain than ever.

Once again the forces of change have no alternative than unite and hope to weigh heavily on the course of events. Otherwise, they should blame themselves as well as others to be part of the destruction mechanisms. When we analyse the conundrum from all angles we reach a bizarre conclusion: either humanity will rise to a galactic civilisation or be annihilated. For the first option to happen, we need to review our priorities, our channelling of resources, our sciences and most of all our missions, strategies and structuring. Global Science is a drop in the ocean compared to what awaits us. And we are barely contemplating the first option. For the moment we are rather swaying in the logic of annihilation.

Summary

This final chapter is devoted to summarising the main conceptualisation developed in this work. We focus on the central themes that appear in this book. It is an express reminder of the main mechanisms, theories and models presented that could be referred to in a quick and precise way. It is not a substitute for reading the book. But it is very useful if you have already read the book in detail. The latter is a continuation of a previous work (A. Lamiri: *The Economics of the Future*).

We do not know how to design nations endowed with the ethics of social justice, peace, mutual aid, and most of all respect for the biosphere and fragile ecosystems. At a time when we are just beginning to reflect on the design of nations and world systems in accordance with human values, we are faced with deadly self-inflicted challenges: the risk of the disappearance of life on Earth in the long term;

- One of the worst dangers facing humanity would be a purely intuitive decision-making process. The USA, the world's leading economic power, has withdrawn from the COP21 (the Paris Agreement) against the vast majority of scientific recommendations. However, the country reversed its position. Faced with a major problem, it is necessary to answer these three questions before making a choice: What does science know about the subject? What can we learn from the experiences? What lessons can we draw from them? Sometimes we do not have decisive answers but at least we can assess the situation by a rough probabilistic approach. Underdeveloped countries are the biggest victims of the purely intuitive approach;
- Science takes its revenge in the sense that if we do not respect what it reveals, we risk severe sanctions. An example of this is self-medication.

But we are making a slight assessment of the damage done by not respecting human and social sciences;

- The social science models that can be appreciated are very often transferable within diverse and varied contexts. However, when assumptions are valid only in a particular environment, they must be made explicit rather than forcing a model on a particular nation. For example, the Washington consensus forced on countries did damage during the Asian crisis when it was imposed on countries in industrial policy mode.
- It is complex to venture to explain the origins of economic ideas outside one's own civilisation. Thus, it can be shown that Ibn Khaldun was at the origin of the theory of surplus value, of supply-side policy, of the damage caused by tax increases, etc.;
- The challenges of humanity have never been so perilous. There is simply a risk (not a certainty) that life on Earth will disappear. But as we face these challenges of unparalleled magnitude, we are armed with old tools of social structuring and technology that are barely geared to respond to these risks but rather reinforce the uncertainty of humanity's survival. We are compelled to accelerate our knowledge and practices in 'societal engineering' and in useful technologies. Without this, we may be condemned to a fatal self-destruction;

We are on the eve of an end of history, but not in apotheosis (not Fukuyama's) but rather probably a lethal setback. We are left with a small probability of being on the eve of a prehistory of history: saving humanity and rising to the rank of a galactic civilisation. But, for now, the reflexes and societal mechanisms and conceptualisation that we have predestine us to the first alternative;

Human beings create institutions to fulfil their ethics, values and reasons for living. But often misguidedly, they establish institutions that enslave them and divert them from their noble goals by building entities that divide, propagate greed, confuse purpose (between material goods and happiness) and in the long run prove to be destructive parasites of their benefactors;

- The central thesis of this book is that we do not have a satisfactory conceptual scheme that allows us to comprehend the dynamics of the evolution of nations and civilisations. In fact, nations went through three historically distinct phases of evolution:

1. The classical period;
2. The partially incremental phase;
3. And the present one of a crossroads of a choice between continuity and mutations by 'Global Science.'

The first option could be called partially oriented transmutation. It is simply the scenario of continuity. Politics allows elites and scientists to partially orient economic and social formations as long as their interests are not threatened. These entities are transformed too little too late to face contemporary threats. The perils are accumulating and the way they are treated is superficial. We are going straight to the wall while pretending to do the best we can.

The second and more advantageous scenario is based on the recommendations of Global Science. Economic and social formations will be endowed with scientific authorities that will mobilise all the intelligence of citizens and intellectual and scientific elites in a methodical and rigorous way. Research and development will be focused on technologies that will create growth for green industries and repair the biosphere and the ecosystems and decrease the polluting and socially dangerous sectors. We will then be able to master the 'societal engineering' that will allow us to repair the environmental, economic and social damages caused (more social equality);

We need to develop a doctrine of Global Science to better deepen its theoretical underpinnings, ethics, principles and priorities for actions. The goals would be to make large-scale corrections to nation and nation-world systems and to design new ones more in line with the values and goals of citizens. The methods used are those that today make up the set of methodologies of the social sciences in addition to the Global Science's scheme. The latter consists of creating historical monographs (variables of situations and contexts) through the historical cases that have occurred in the rich history of our nations. We could then identify the key variables that have contributed to shaping the nation's systems. At that point, we would be able to adapt economic, social and environmental policies to the different cultural matrices and levels of development of countries through the distinctive characteristics of different countries. It would then be easier for us to identify the types of economic, social and environmental policies to pursue in a particular context. This would prevent us from thinking and acting with the abusive generalisations that we currently tend to make. We presented in this work tentative themes of Global Science: The ethics, the strategy, the main principles, the method and the practice of Global Science to a general debate first within the scientific community and second to citizens interested in acting to change the status quo;

The nation and world-nation systems will be conceived through the ethics, objectives, missions and values defined jointly by a methodical citizen mobilisation of the intelligence of the vast majority of them that Global Science would allow mobilising and carrying out actions. Thereafter, the same operational modalities will clarify the strategies, types of structuring, processes of control and especially the human resources suitable for the modes of functioning of the systems that will be required to be built. Managing expectations and human qualifications would be at the centre of the processes. At that moment, nations would experience an unparalleled 'societal engineering.' Revolutions would be introduced in our budgetary, monetary and institutional processes in order to make all the elements of the system coherent.

We are on the verge of consolidating our knowledge and developing much more to weigh heavily in the process of social transformations. No human being and no institution could accomplish this task. We must transform ourselves before we can claim to transform our societies. We need to align all the components of the system (ethics, strategy, values, etc.) if we do not want to fall back into a Brownian process that would annihilate the entire system. For that to happen, we need forces of change united in two or three entities and coordinated between them.

The democratic process is a must. We need to channel valuable resources towards this mission. We are undergoing the 'Boiling Frog Effect,' an adaptation until the death of our economic and social systems. Radical change advocates seem to remain in the posture of dying divided rather than succeeding united. Yet they already have a tool: the Global Science version of decision-making described above. But, the leadership inspired by the surrounding political cultures is taking one step forward and two steps back in the unification process. We already have a beginning of preliminary principles that are advanced to start the process, but they need to be completed. The road is long. We are only at the first stone of the building. It will revolutionise our sciences and our lives. New statistical methods, simulation equations, advances in qualitative and quantitative analysis will allow us to make an appreciable leap in the science of transformations of economic and social formations of nations.

Current and re-invented communication methods will provide the essential instruments for the transformation of institutions and human resources. We need to accelerate these processes of change. Things are moving positively in this direction and much more is being accomplished faster with NLP and modern psychology tools.

However, all sciences will be called upon to contribute. For this, each one should identify the relevant available knowledge and the avenues for improvement that will be necessary for the complex engineering of nations. A first work already done for economics is already available (A. Lamiri op cited). But this work is a drop in the bucket and much remains to be done.

The potential contribution of religions to the preservation of life and social justice should not be underestimated. They are natural allies in the cause of social transformations. The works on the collapse of civilisations, on complex systems are precious and already constitute a significant basis on which to build useful knowledge.

Conclusion

We are probably—to be optimistic—living in the last few decades of the last chance. The hard sciences, too far ahead of the human and social sciences, have created potential perils that are difficult for the latter to manage. We do not know how to create economic and social formations other than capitalism with confiscated democracy, totalitarian socialism or a combination of both. We can hardly get out of it, and under drastic conditions. The first would be to create the models, the concepts and the tools that we lack, thus a completely new discipline or science: Global Science. The second would be to unite the forces of change into two or three large international movements that would carry more weight than the traditional political parties that have always done and will always continue to do too little too late. The third would be to mobilise all available citizen intelligence and our best scientists and provide the process with democratic accountability to design and manage a recovery plan for nation and nation-world systems. We need to think and act on the basis of global, not general, equilibrium. The former is a two-dimensional balance. First, it serves to harmonise citizens' expectations and the volume of goods and services produced by a system. Secondly, it allows us to make the production(s) coherent with the biosphere's renewal capacities.

The victory of the forces of change will allow them to channel the resources needed for this great work of recovery. However, they must know that they will eventually unite and succeed or divide and die. We earthlings are up against the wall. We must pull ourselves together and evolve into a galactic civilisation or perish. Economics has to enlarge its scope of knowledge in order to integrate itself within Global Science and play accomplishes its share of the burden of facing the lethal challenges we face. In order to do so much should be accomplished. We have to make the central piece of the economic architecture the global equilibrium instead of the general equilibrium. The conduct of monetary and fiscal policies would go through a radical revolution.

Fiscal policy should be conceived under the seal of the re-engineering process. Monetary policy should be profoundly revised in two directions. First, we need to analyse its present foundations in light of its integration into Global Science. The optimum monetary rule has to be reviewed to accommodate social designs: more equality, less stressful economic life (buying the unemployed hours of work) and efficient sector policies. The second direction has to do with channelling resources. We need to consider the money laser scheme instead of the money helicopter model. Investment and consumption and international trade policies have to undergo abysmal theoretical and practical mutations so as to conform to the need to fit within the Global Science scheme. The underdeveloped countries cannot remain outside the process of these sweeping transformations. Remember we need to become a galactic civilisation or be annihilated. We cannot afford to leave more than half of the human beings in a situation of distress. We would rather better develop schemes based on the economic pyramid model which has the potential of changing the paradigm on which underdevelopment theories were based.

Most of these themes were developed in a previous work (see Lamiri op cited). But this is just a beginning, a starting point whereas much more is needed. Every discipline or science is called upon to develop contributions by which it would fit into Global Science. A few immediate contributions needed are presented above. But much more work remains to be identified, planned, financed, finalised and acted upon. We may be living in the decennial of the last chance. And Global Science might well be our last option before the collapse. Today we have most of the technologies and the hard science knowledge we need to act on the perils we created, but we have neither the will nor the social sciences we need to get a grip on those dangers. We are structured to fail and to be subject to the frog effect. We are running out of time. The time to act is now and fast as many scientists warned. But as for now the comfort of inertia has been more appealing. We can call upon the millions of human brains in our earthly home to save it and to preserve ourselves. But most of us prefer avoiding their responsibilities by asserting 'if only they would listen to me' instead of mobilising all our brains by a rigorous methodology.

Bibliography

1. Abdelhak, Lamiri (1992

    a. ' *Théories Economiques et Crises contemporaines* ', OPU, Alger.

    b. *La Décennie de la Dernière Chance, Emergence ou Déchéance de l'Economie Algérienne*, Chiheb Editions, Alger.

    c.   (2022-24) *The Economics of the Future*, Fulton Books.

2.   Aktouf Omar (2005) *La Stratégie de l'Autruche. Post-mondialisation, management et rationalité économique*, Ecosociété.

3.   Arnold Toynbe (1934) *A Study of History*, Oxford University Press.

4.   Arrow J.K. et G.Debreu 'Existence of an equilibrium for a competitive economy,' *Econometrica*, **22**, N°3, 1954, P 265-290 ;

5.   Baker Gary 'Crime and punishment: An Economic Approach,' *The Journal of Political Economy*, **76** : 169-217 ;

6.   Bloom Stephan G (2021) *Blue Eyes Brown Eyes, A Cautionary Tale of Race and Brutality*, University of California Press.

7.   Debreu G (1996) Théorie de la Valeur, Dunod, Paris.

8.   Cline Eric (2014) *1177 BC, The Year the Civilisation Collapsed*, Oxford University Press.

9.   Denis Meadows, Donelle Meadows, Jorgen Randers, William W. Behrens (2012) *les limites à la croissance* ; *ed Rue de l'échiquier*, Paris.

10. Durhane Wong-Rieger (Supervision Frantz Rierger) : International management research : Looking to the Future, Walter de Gruter, 1993

11. Drucker, Peter F. (1978) *The Age of Discontinuity*, Harper and Row, New York.

12. Fayol, Henri (1917) *Administration Industrielle et Générale*, Dunod et Pinat, Paris.

13. Friedman, Milton *A Theory of a Consumption Function*, Courier Dover Publications.

a. 'The Role of Monetary Policy,' *American Economic Review*, **58**, pp 451-72

b. Capitalism and Freedom, University of Chicago Press, 1962

c. Free to Choose, Harcourt, 1980.

d. Inflation et Systèmes Monétaires, Agora/Calman Levy, Paris, 1969

14. Fukuyama, Francis (1992) *The End of History and the Last Man*, Free Press.

15. Jaurion, Paul (2016) *Le Dernier qui s'en va Eteint la Lumière*, Fayard, Paris.

16. Hafsi, Tayeb et Toulouse Jean-Marie (1999) *La Stratégie des Organisation, une Synthèse*, Transcontinental, Montréal.

17. Hayek, Frederick

a. The Road to Serfdom, University of Chicago Press, 1944

b. The Pure Theory of Capital University of Chicago Press, 1941

18. Harris, John R and Thodaro, Michael P, The American Economic Review, vol.60, N°1, 1970, PP 126-142

19. Ibn Khaldoun, Ab dar-rahman, El Muqaddima, Prolégoménes d'Ibn Khaldoun, dar el Kotob al Ilmya, 2007

20. Jared Diamond (2009) Effondrement, *Comment les Société Décident de leurs disparitions ou leurs Survies*, ed Gallimard.

21. Kempf Hervé (2001) *Comment les Riches Détruisent la Planète, Editions du seuil*, Paris.

22. Perroux François 'Le Multiplicateur d'Investissement dans les pays sous-développés,' *Revue du Tiers Monde*, **7**, juillet – septembre, 1966 P 511-532.

Likert R. and Likert, JG (1976) *New ways of managing conflicts*, Mc Graw Hill, New York.

23. Theory of management : Implications for Organizational Behaviour, Mc Graw Hill, New York, 1975.

24. Karl Marx

   a.   Contribution à la critique de l'Economie Politique, Paris Editions Sociales, P4, 1957

   b.   Le Capital, Editions Sociales, Paris, 1950

   c.   Critique du programme de Gotha, Les Editions Sociales, Coll. GEME, 2008

25. Muth F. John (1961) 'Rational Expectations and the Price Movements,' *Econometrica*, **29**, pp 315-333.

26. Nurskse, Ragnar (1953) *Problems of Capital Formation in Underdeveloped Countries*, Oxford.

27. Oswald Spengler (1931 et 1933) *le Déclin de l'Occident*, Gallimard, Paris.

28. Popper Karl (1973) *La Logique de la Découverte Scientifique*, Payot.

29. Keynes, John Meynard (1969) *Théorie Générale de l'Emploi, de l'intérêt et de la monnaie*, Paris, Payot. ;

30. Lewin Kurt, Lippit, K, White R. (1939) 'Pattern of Aggressive Behaviour in experimentally Created Social Climate,' *Journal of Social Psychology*, N°10, PP 271-299.

31. Lewin K. Group Decision and Social Change, in Newcomb T.M. ; Harltley E.I. Readings in Social Psychology, Holt Rienehart and Winston, 1947 PP 269-288.

32. Lewin Arthur W. (2013) *The Theory of Economic Growth*, Routledge Libray Edition.

33. Marshall Alfred (1971) *Principes d'Economie Politique*, Gordon and Breach.

34. Milgram S. (1974) *La Soumission à l'Autorité*, Calman Levy, Paris.

35. Minsky P. Hyman *Stabilising an Unstable Economy*, Yale University.

36. Piketty Thomas (2013) *Le Capital au XXI siècle*, le Seuil, Paris.

37. Proudhon, Pierre-Joseph (2015) *Philosophie de la Misère*, CreateSpace Independent Publishing Platform.

38. Rostow, W.W. (1960) *The Stages of Economic Growth : A non-Communist Manifesto*, Cambridge University Press.

39. Samuelson P. (1975) *L'économique*, A. Colin, Paris.

40. Sen Amartha (2000) *Un Nouveau Modèle Economique*, Edition Odile Jacob.

41. Sidelsky Robert Keynes (2010) *The Return of the Master*, Public Affairs.

42. Schumpeter, Joseph A.

a. Business cycles : Business Cycles : a Theoretical, historical, and statistical analysis of the Capitalist Process, Martino Pub, Connecticut ;

b. Capitalism, Socialism and Democracy, (2 and Edition), Impact books, Virginia,

43. Stephen G. Bloom (2001) *Bleu Eyes, Brown Eyes, a Cautionary Tale, of Race and Brutality*, University of California Press.

44. Stephen Meyers (2021) *The Return of the God hypothesis*, Harper One.

45. Stiglitz Joseph (2002) *la Grande désillusion*, Paris, Fayard.

46. Samir, Amine (2015) *Le Développement Inégal*, Œuvre completes.

47. Taylor Frederick W, La Direction Scientifique du travail, Dunod, Paris, 1967

48. Tainter, Joseph (1988) *The Collapse of Complex Societies*, Cambridge University Press.

49. Zak, Paul J. (2021) *Trust Factor, The Moral Molecule, The New Science of What makes us Good or Evil*, Kindle Edition.

50. Veblen Thorstein (1970) *Théorie de la classe loisir*, Gallimard, Paris.

51. Vigne Eric, Stakhanov, ce Hero Normatif, vingtième siècle. Revue d'Histoire, Vol 1., N1, 1984, P 23-30.

52. Wackernagel M. et Rees W. (1999) *Notre Empreinte Ecologique*, Ecosociété, Montréal.

53. Wackernagel M., Monfreda C., Moran D., Wermer P., Goldfinger M. (2005) *National Footprint and Biocapacity Accounts 2005 : The Underlying Calculation Method,* Global Footprint Network, Oakland.

54. Walras Leon, *Eléments d'Economie Politique Pure ou Théorie de la Richesse Sociale*, Guillaumin et crie,

55. Willett, Thomas D. (1977) *Floating Exchange Rates and International Monetary Reform*, American Entreprise Institute for Public Policy Research.